P9-CMV-370

CLASSIC WALKS IN
The Alps
Edited by Kev Reynolds

The Oxford Illustrated Press

© 1991 Kev Reynolds, Martin Collins, Cecil Davies, Brian Evans and Andrew Harper as credited

ISBN 1–85509–205–0

Published by:
The Oxford Illustrated Press,
Haynes Publishing Group, Sparkford,
Nr Yeovil, Somerset BA22 7JJ, England

Printed in England by:
J.H. Haynes & Co Limited,
Sparkford, Nr Yeovil, Somerset

British Library Cataloguing in Publication Data:
A catalogue record for this book is available from the British Library.

Library of Congress Catalog Card Number:
91 – 72669

All rights reserved. No part of this book may be reproduced or transmitted in any form or by any means, electronic or mechanical, including photocopying, recording or by any other information storage retrieval system, without the permission of the publisher.

Acknowledgements

A number of people have helped in the production of this book, either by offering information or advice, or by contributing a chapter or two. Others have made days in the Alps extra special by their company on some of the walks. To them all I convey my deep gratitude:

Martin Collins, Cecil Davies, Aileen and Brian Evans, Nigel Fry, Andrew Harper, Roland Hiss, Bart Jordans, Alan Payne, Jim Reville of Sherpa Expeditions, Claudia, Ilsa and Linda Reynolds, Derek Roberts, Anne and John Shipley, and the staff of the Swiss National Tourist Office.

My thanks to them all.

* * *

This book is dedicated to Claudia and Ilsa Reynolds who visited the Alps before they could walk, and who have grown to love them too.

Contents

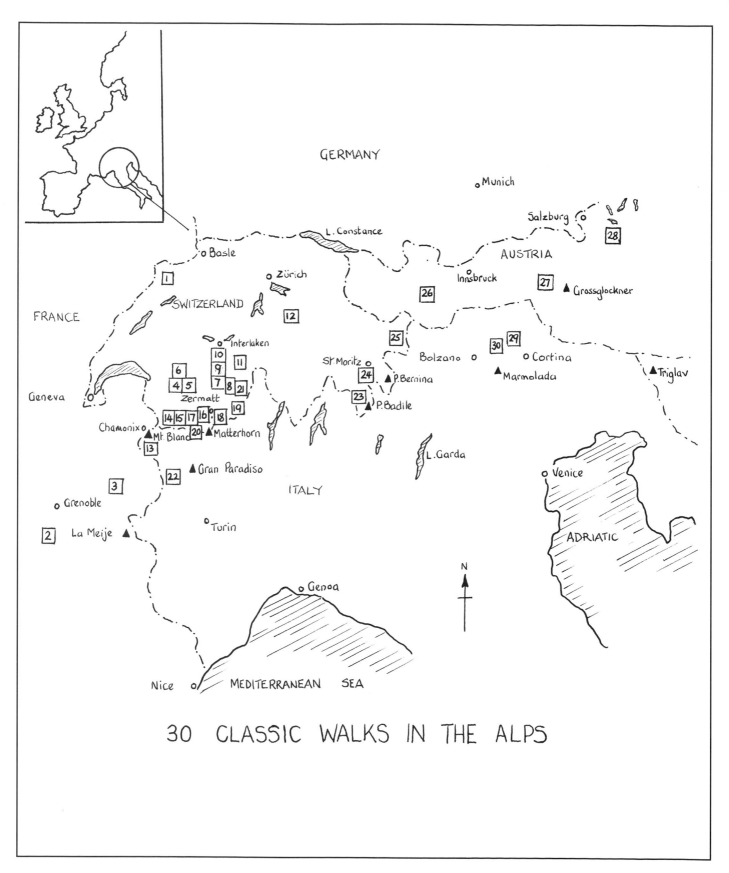

30 CLASSIC WALKS IN THE ALPS

Introduction

One summer, many years ago now, I bivouacked with two friends on the summit of a rather modest Alpine peak in Austria simply to capture the magic of daybreak. Throughout the night we were cold and uncomfortable on that rocky crown, but at last the stars were extinguished one by one, and at around 4 o'clock that morning the sun burst out of a hidden valley and flooded the world with its glory, painting summit snows and staining misted hillsides with its promise.

Revelling in the scene we descended over snow slopes, clambered down rocky patches and onto the first grass. Then we came to an isolated farm perched on a grassy lip with forest below and the sun climbing steadily above. The farmer's wife was standing on her balcony drawing strength from the sun; her face beamed and reflected its warmth. "Where have you been?" she asked. I told her. "It was good?" "Beautiful."

She invited us to breakfast and together we carried a small table outside in order that we might eat in the sunshine. Her husband came back from milking the cows to join us.

Feeding on home-made bread spread with home-made butter and home-made jam, and drinking coffee that was thick and creamy with fresh milk, we shared the wonder of morning with a stupendous panorama of mountains all around.

"Isn't this a bit early to be up and working?" I asked.

"We have no clock," said the lady. "When the sun shines through the window to warm our bed, we get up."

* * *

Wandering in the mountains gives an opportunity to put life into perspective. Our travels become ordered by the sun's progress across the sky, by the march of clouds and by the demands of the winding trail; less so by the clock. And even in these days of super-sophistication in the Alps, where some of the major resorts reflect the very latest technological developments, there are lives being lived that have changed little over the centuries. This is not a 'backward peasantry' unable to grasp the mettle of change, but a positive acknowledgement by educated men and women that some values are worth holding onto. Those of us who have the good fortune to stride the same hillsides as these farmers can learn much from them, from their steady, unhurried pace and their deep love for the mountains they call home.

I've been lucky enough not only to spend countless holidays walking and climbing in the Alps, but also to live and work there for a while—in Switzerland and in Austria—amid some of the loveliest scenery in the world. I've sat of an evening in some of these remote farms and chatted with the families who lived there, drawing warmth from their friendship and learning by their example of contentment. I've led walking groups across the green ridges and rocky crests, skied glaciers and empty valleys and wandered literally thousands of kilometres of Alpine footpath across the mountains of France, Switzerland, Austria, Germany and Italy over the past quarter century and more. And the love has not even begun to grow dim.

This book contains a selection of some of the best walks to be had there. A collection of classic outings of varying lengths and degrees of seriousness that should give many fine walking holidays in the years ahead. It's a tease, really, for a choice of just thirty walks among the many hundreds available has to be the result of a very selective, personal whittling-down process. I decided to strike a balance between well-known and lesser-known walks; between long, multi-day treks that traverse whole regions of the Alps, and day-long outings using a single valley base. In this I have been helped by friends and colleagues who share my passion and whose experience also covers a vast amount of Alpine territory. I value their advice and ready willingness to participate in this book, but accept full responsibility for the final selection of routes that are included.

Martin Collins was invited to contribute for I very much admire his work and recognise his authority. He has a great appetite for mountain walking, as well as considerable skill in drawing out the essential qualities of the landscapes about which he writes. He has produced several guidebooks to walks in the Alpine regions and elsewhere, and here he tells of the great traverse of the French Alps, the GR5, and of two exhilarating *vie ferrate* in the Dolomites.

Cecil Davies has known the Austrian Alps since 1964 and is the author of an authoritative guidebook to those lovely mountains. He was an obvious choice as the man to decide which are the classic routes of that country, and he describes here three multi-day walks using mountain huts.

Brian Evans and I had already collaborated on a book about the Jura and walked the Alpine Pass Route together. He's a true enthusiast who makes a first-class companion in the hills. There can be few active walkers, climbers or skiers with a greater love of the mountains than Brian, and his experience in these three wide-ranging disciplines spans several decades. When I asked his opinion about Alpine classics he surprised me by suggesting at once the traverse of the Vercors plateau. In winter. "But they're the pre-Alps," I said, and he chided me for splitting hairs. And of course, he's right. The traverse is a magnificent outing winter or summer. Try it for yourself.

The Tour of Mont Blanc is not only an Alpine classic, but it ranks as one of the finest walks anywhere. It has already been described in Walt Unsworth's *Classic Walks of the World* (Oxford Illustrated Press, 1985) but of course it simply had to be included here too. Andrew Harper has completed the route many times and is the author of the definitive guidebook to the TMB. He has also explored other Alpine regions over a number of years, and here he writes of the Chamonix to Zermatt walker's haute route and a tour he made in the shadow of the Gran Paradiso in Italy, as well as contributing the chapter devoted to the TMB.

* * *

The Alps stretch in a great arc for more than a thousand kilometres from the Mediterranean coast near Nice to the back-country of Vienna in Austria. They include, then, mountains of France, Switzerland, Liechtenstein, Austria, Germany, Italy and Yugoslavia; mountains of unbelievable grandeur, valleys of utter splendour. From huge snow-and ice-capped giants to modest green hills, from granite domes to dolomitic spires. And everywhere, scenes of glory.

5

Is it possible, I wonder, to know the Alps and not be inspired by their essential loveliness? Travellers, mountaineers and walkers have been doing just that for a couple of centuries and more. Being inspired; having their souls lifted by vistas of enchantment.

Switzerland, of course, was a prime ingredient in the 'Grand Tour', that cultural journey round the sites of Europe that was considered to be almost obligatory for the complete education of the aristocracy, and for those who aspired to it. It was mountaineers from Britain who first sparked, then fanned the flames for a love of mountain exploration, and who were so abundantly active in claiming summits during the so-called 'Golden Age of Mountaineering'. But always, always it seems, it has been the footpaths that have drawn men and women with their promise of fulfilment. Footpaths that were made by peasant farmers taking part in the transhumance—that annual migration from valley habitation to Alpine pasture that still goes on today in some regions. Footpaths that had been made by chamois hunters, or traders crossing from one valley system to another with their laden mules. Mule tracks, hunters' paths, farmers' highways, each have now been adapted and adopted by recreational walkers to create a network of trails that are among the finest in the world.

Understandably, the Alps have practically no real wilderness areas left. Every mountain, every valley has been mapped and photographed until there are few secrets or mysteries remaining. But none of this matters. Walking in the Alps—whether for the first time or the fifty-first—will always reveal some new discovery, some fresh panorama that will instantly repay any effort involved in finding it. (Writing these words I have a flood of images dancing before me, a sequence of memories that fill me with joy—and a great rush of eagerness to return for further discoveries in a few weeks time!)

Most of the walks described within these pages are on paths that are clearly defined and waymarked. Many will have signposts at strategic intervals and at the junction of trails. Some will be punctuated with places of refreshment. All will lead through landscapes of great variety and immense charm.

Some, however, will require navigational skills should visibility be poor, and some will definitely need a head for heights. Only one traverses the length of a glacier (the Petersgrat Crossing) when ice-axe and crampons will be required, while those in the Dolomites have some sections that make use of ladders and fixed cables to secure the safety of wanderers. Details of any particular difficulty will be given in the text, or in the fact sheet that accompanies each chapter.

* * *

First-time visitors to the Alps may be a little wary of the scale of these mountains, concerned perhaps about pacing themselves, or of getting lost. Worried, maybe, about the weather. Really, all that is needed is common sense and an eye for the country. But if re-assurance is still required I would suggest walkers consider joining an organised party. Having accompanied several trekking groups on journalistic assignments over a number of years, I am convinced that they represent value for money and create a welcome degree of assurance, as well as providing the company of like-minded people to walk with. Of the routes included in this book, the Tour of Mont Blanc, Alpine Pass Route and the Chamonix to Zermatt walk are all adopted by commercial trekking companies from Britain. Sherpa Expeditions and Exodus are just two that tackle these particular routes and advertise regularly in the outdoor press.

There is one immediate advantage to group travel: you pay an overall fee prior to departure and all arrangements are made on your behalf—travel, accommodation, route-finding, etc. All that is required of the individual participant is a degree of fitness, the provision of personal equipment and the capacity to mix readily with others.

* * *

As far as accommodation is concerned, every Alpine region has an adequate number of hotels, guest houses or camp sites. There are Youth Hostels in many areas, gîtes in some and Alpine Club huts (refuges) in the high mountains. Routes described in the various chapters will make the most of every type where available. Little needs to be said about hotels or guest houses, but perhaps a word or two about other types of accommodation will not go amiss.

Gîtes are rather like private Youth Hostels and are to be found in certain parts of the French Alps. Some of these are adaptations of separate buildings attached to a farm or private dwelling; others are part of a main house. What will be provided will usually be dormitory-style bedrooms, simple washing and toilet facilities and often a self-catering kitchen. In some gîtes meals may be offered by the proprietor. Matratzenlagers have similar facilities and will be found in various regions of Switzerland. There are many such establish

ments along the Jura High Route.

Youth Hostels are to be found in each of the Alpine countries, with specific national associations being incorporated into the International Youth Hostel Federation. Membership of YHA (England and Wales) and other British hostelling associations is recognised on the continent, and membership cards are readily accepted. It should be noted that it is cheaper to join the hostelling organisation of your home country than one abroad.

Mountain huts are invariably situated in remote high country. Although originally built by Alpine Clubs as a base for mountaineers, they are open to all comers and some of the walks described here lead to them, either as a destination for a day's outing, or as a place to stay on a longer tour. Again, dormitory accommodation is the norm, without segregation of the sexes, and in particularly busy huts the amount of space available on the communal sleeping platforms may be rather less than you would prefer. Stories of overcrowded huts abound in the Alps, but if you are fortunate enough to arrive when the refuge of your choice is fairly quiet its setting and atmosphere will make for a memorable stay.

Meals are generally provided in huts, and where one is visited on the course of a walk, refreshments are often available, provided by the guardian and his staff. It ought to be said that in some particularly high refuges, water is in short supply, and washing facilities will reflect this shortage.

As for camping, an admirable number of villages and towns set in good walking country have organised camp sites provided. Some of these will be simple meadows with rather basic toilet and washroom facilities, while others will be equipped with hot showers, washing machines and drying rooms. One should not assume that the classier resorts have the best camp sites, as often the contrary will be true.

Wild camping in the Alps should be carried out by backpackers with an understanding of, and appreciation for, the value of meadowland for hay crops. Practically all grassland in Switzerland will be of value to hill farmers, either as grazing or for making hay, and the thoughtless siting of a tent can have a serious effect on it. However, remote corners of the high mountains between the treeline and snowline will often have an ideal spot where a small tent may be pitched for a short stay. In such cases please be discreet, take care not to foul water supplies and pack all litter away with you.

* * *

Of your equipment required for a walking

The Alps in bloom: flower meadows in early summer add a vibrancy to walking in the mountains. (Kev Reynolds)

holiday in the Alps, the most important item will be boots. Lightweight, comfortable boots will give protection and ankle support, and you will be content to wear them for several hours at a time. Don't be fooled into thinking you will need really sturdy, heavy footwear. Comfort is all-important to ensure that the holiday is a pleasure rather than a drudge. So make sure your boots fit properly and are worn-in before you go.

On summer walks you can experience bright warm sunshine one day, and cold winds and snowfall the next. Or both on the same day and within an hour! Be prepared for the worst and hope for the best. Windproofs and waterproofs are essential. So are gloves and a thick pullover for those times when the weather changes some hours before you can get back to a valley base. Some form of head protection will be required against too much sun, and sunglasses for when the dazzle of sun on snow is rather too painful.

Breeches are more comfortable to wear than loose-fitting long trousers that can snag on rocks. Often you will find that shorts will be perfectly adequate. Take plenty of sun cream and spread it liberally on your nose and ears, for these are particularly vulnerable to the effects of high altitude sun.

* * *

Flowers will be a feature of practically every walk in the Alps, but one need not be a trained botanist to enjoy them. Alpine meadows are noted for their great variety of wild flowers and shrubs, but wayside crags and even otherwise drab glacial moraines will bear their own specific flora so that as you go from valley bed to upper hillside, so the walk leads from one vegetation zone to another. There will be varieties as easily recognised as the gentian in numerous forms and colours, the grey-white fuzzy stars of edelweiss, and the dainty bell-heads of campanulas. Soldanellas almost burn their way through the last snows in spring, while alpenroses—those beautiful dwarf rhododendrons—spread in low-growing blankets of pink or scarlet in July.

There will be cushions of androsace; tiger lilies and Martagon lilies and garlands of primulas strung over boulder and meadowland alike. And many, many more whose names may be learnt from study of any one of a number of handbooks available. Of particular value in this respect I have found *Mountain Flower Holidays in Europe* by Lionel Bacon (published by the Alpine Garden Society, 1979).

Romping among the boulder-fields and in rough upper meadows you will often catch sight of marmots. These hare-sized creatures have an appearance a little like that of a beaver. Brown coated, they live in burrows beneath the meadows and hibernate there throughout the long winter months. In springtime they emerge, feed ravenously on the lush grasses, and then mate. Their young are born during the summer, and I have often sat quietly by and watched these comical creatures playing beside a pathway, unaware of my presence. Adult marmots seem to have sentries posted near their burrows. At first sight of an approaching walker, or a predatory eagle, a shrill warning whistle will be heard, and this is followed by the colony dashing for cover.

Both red and roe deer may be seen in lower woods and forests, while chamois graze much higher and are sometimes to be seen crossing snow patches or scree slopes well away from habitation. Ibex, with their huge scimitar-shaped horns (also known as steinbock or bouquetin) are the more elusive of Alpine mammals. They occupy remote mountainsides in small herds, living off scanty lichens but descending in the early hours of morning to more habitable pastures before returning to the heights again. Some of the huts visited on walks in this book have herds nearby, and you may be fortunate enough to catch sight of them on your visit.

In common with other books in the Classic Walks series each chapter here is designed to draw out the essential qualities of the particular walk under review. It is not possible to give a step by step description of the routes, but sufficient details are supplied to enable you to choose where to walk, how far and how long and which guidebooks and maps will be needed. Accompanying fact sheets will also supply other essential information to enable you to make the most of your holiday.

This then is a celebration in words and photographs. It has been written with an enthusiasm that is difficult to keep in check. An enthusiasm born of a love for the mountains and valleys, and a result of untold hours of pleasure spent among them. Others might choose different routes to write about, and as your own experience grows you too may well stray to areas outside the realms of this particular volume. I hope you do. This is merely a beginning. An encouragement to all who enjoy fine scenery and exercise.

One plea rings through the pages of this book, and it comes from the heart. Love and respect all you find among the wild places of the Alps. Absorb all they have to offer and you will grow rich. But be determined too, that when you leave, the wild places are still wild and beautiful and unsullied for future generations. Let no-one curse your passage among them.

May this book be your passport to many hours, days and weeks of pleasure, and a waymark to some of the *Classic Walks in the Alps*.

Wild camping in the Alps: a small tent like this Phoenix Phalcon can be pitched in a discreet corner for a night. (Kev Reynolds)

Walk 1: *The Jura High Route by Kev Reynolds*

Location: Western Switzerland; Dielsdorf (Zürich) to Borex (Geneva).
How to get there: By air or train to Zürich, then train to Dielsdorf via Oberglatt (the Schaffhausen line). At the southern end there is an infrequent bus service from Borex to Nyon, which has main-line rail connections with Geneva.
Distance: 299 kilometres (186 miles).
Time required: 14 days.
Start: Dielsdorf.
Finish: Borex.
Type of walk: Long and varied, but on

mostly good paths. Waymarking is first-rate. For a comparatively 'low' walk there are some very steep ascents and descents. Being on limestone the route tends to be dry, but there are refreshment stops along the way.
Maps: Landeskarte der Schweiz 1:50,000 series Nos 5005 *Seetal-Brugg,* 5019 *Weissenstein-Oberaargau,* 5016 *Bern-Fribourg,* 241 *Val de Travers,* 242 *Avenches,* 5020 *Yverdon les Bains-Lausanne,* 260 *St. Cergue.*

Kümmerley + Frey also produce a series

of special *Wanderkarten* based on the L.S. 1:50,000 sheets with the JHR overprinted in red. 1 *Aargau, Lägeren-Bözberg,* 2 *Basel, Baselland-Olten,* 3 *Solothurn, Delsberg-Pruntrut,* 4 *Neuchâtel, Chasseral-Biel/Bienne,* 5 *Yverdon, Ste Croix-Val de Travers,* 6 *Lausanne-La Côte, St Cergue-Vallée de Joux.*
Guidebook: The Jura by Kev Reynolds and R B Evans (Cicerone Press) (also includes winter ski traverses in both the Swiss and French Jura).

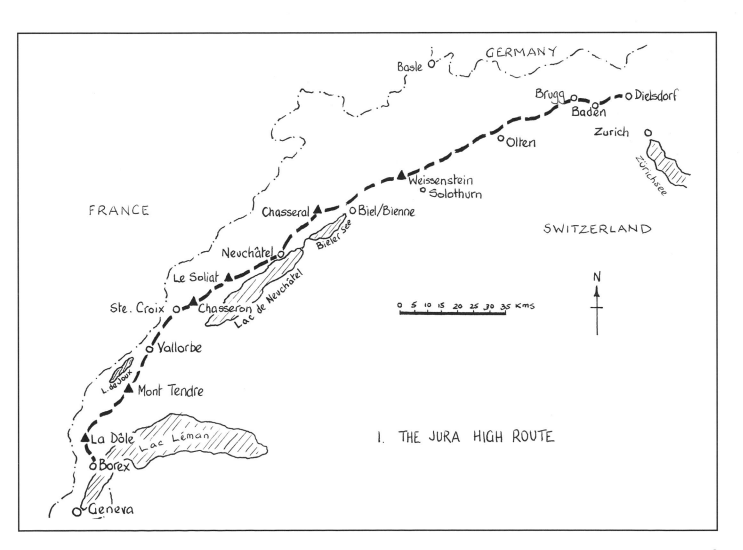

1. THE JURA HIGH ROUTE

Green ridges and views to the Alps

The Jura are Switzerland's unsung mountains. Purist's will argue (with some justification) that they are not the Alps; indeed they are not, but they look to the Alps and are near enough to the big mountains in my estimation to be included in this collection of walks by virtue of the wonderful long distance route that traverses the length of the easternmost Swiss ridge. Walk the Jura High Route in its entirety and I'm sure you will agree with its inclusion here.

Outside of France and Switzerland the Jura are virtually unknown, yet to those who live near them, and to those who have had the good fortune to explore them, they have a unique majesty and appeal, a subtle texture, a pastoral purity, a tended luxury in their smooth green slopes and sweeping valleys; a comb of forest shaved on a limestone crest.

Belloc sang the praises of that quite astonishing view of the distant mountains from the heights of Weissenstein in one of the most frequently-quoted pieces of walking literature when, on his path to Rome, he broke through the forests and saw for the first time the Alps, hanging on a far horizon: "Up there in the sky, to which only the clouds belong and birds and the last trembling colours of pure light, they stood fast and hard; not moving as do the things of the sky."

The Jura are walkers' mountains, let there be no doubt about that. They have their sudden brash limestone cliffs that have great appeal to climbing devotees, it is true, and they also make possible the most marvellous cross-country ski tours. But in summer, when all snow has gone and the meadows are knee-deep in wild flowers, the winding trails beckon and fulfil every promise. You can wander to your heart's content hour after hour, from one isolated farm to another, with only the birds and crickets and butterflies for company. And, if it's not too hazy with heat, capture long views that stretch across the lowlands of Switzerland to the Oberland giants or, farther south, to Mont Blanc whose summit snows imitate the drifting distant clouds.

The Jura consists of a green corrugation of parallel ridges, part French, part Swiss, running in a long arc between the two countries and forming a natural boundary as it does. The Jura High Route wanders south-westward down the length of the Swiss ridge, from Dielsdorf outside Zürich to Borex, a small village to the north of Geneva. It is a route some 299 kilometres long, and along the way it crosses the highest summits—Mont Tendre, La Dôle and Chasseral, each over 1600 metres—and wanders across the linguistic divide from German-speaking to French-speaking Switzerland. It traverses meadowland and forest, visits countless secluded farms and villages well away from the tourist haunts, and takes you through historic small towns and past ruined castles. For much of the time the hills and their valleys are virtually empty of people, and you experience an aura of solitude almost unknown among the higher Alps. As I was to discover, in the Jura it is possible to take a walk in the sky undisturbed by the crowds. The Jura High Route then, is a walk of rich variety and countless rewards. A walk worth being teased into.

Stage 1: 5 days

Dielsdorf squats mid-way between Zürich and the German border in a lowland countryside of farms and market gardens. It's a village of neat houses with neat gardens round them; there are patterns of fields laid out equally neatly and above the village a hillside trim with fruit bushes and small vineyards. The High Route is signposted from the railway station and you strike off up the hillside towards a crown of woodland with views between the trees of a tender land easy to love.

Within the first hour you come to the finest village of the whole Jura route—Regensburg, with its 13th century castle turret, its stone-walled houses, some with timber-framing and three-storeys high, and its superb cobbled square complete with centre-piece fountain. Ducking under the archway of a 16th-century gasthof a lovely gentle view unfolds before you, and if you've not been captured by the character of the Jura by now, you never will!

The High Route is mostly oblivious to the cluster of small towns and villages in this corner of Switzerland, for it steadfastly works a single-minded course along the ridge, in and out of woods and occasionally teetering above steep, plunging slopes with martagon lilies and hare-bells stuttering from the bare limestone ribs. Then suddenly the hills have been cut and the path leads steeply down to Baden, seen dramatically below a grey cliff, with the River Limmat twisting anxiously through. The way-marked route goes into and through the best of the old town, inching past pavement restaurant tables and even wandering along one of the railway station platforms on a most innovative diversion, and you begin to wonder what else is in store before you reach Geneva.

From Baden to Brugg the walk takes you among beechwoods and down beside the urgent swirl of the River Reuss, the air surprisingly cool even on a summer's day, and you realise then that the river brings with it more than just a memory of its glacial beginnings.

The old Habsburg town of Brugg stands astride the Reuss at the end of the first day's trek, and when you leave in the morning it is to wander through an agricultural landscape broken here and there with patches of forest. There are trees heavy with black cherries hanging over the path, and later there will be wild strawberries, raspberries, blackberries and bilberries to feed on as you walk.

This is the shortest and gentlest stage of the whole route, an early interlude of lowland walking before taking once more to the Jura proper near Staffelegg. When you set out from Staffelegg next day the path begins to work its way to the viewpoint of Wasserflue (844m) where, on a clear day, you have your first sighting of the Alps and later, on the wooded summit of Geissflue (963m), a glorious vista of Jura ridges spreading far away to the north-west, the line of the Black Forest beyond, while below the villages of Oltingen, Wenslingen and Anwil lie trapped amid chequer-board fields striped here and there with the cutting of hay.

On the fourth day you come across a well-engineered track that curls its way up the sharply-cut slopes of the Belchenflue (1098m), neighboured by stark limestone cliffs rising out of green pastures. The track was made by Swiss soldiers during the First World War and onto the rock walls that tower over it a number of large regimental insignia have been carved and brightly painted, presumably representing those sections of the military responsible for the creation of the track.

The route suddenly breaks away on a path picked out limestone white through the sloping pastures that adorn the crest, valley to the right of you and valley to the left. Woodland takes over and through this you lose height, cross a clearing with a neat farm set in its midst with a stream bubbling past, and come to a most attractive little hamlet, Bärenwil. There's not much to Bärenwil; a few houses and farms, a gushing fountain and a typical Jura restaurant bright with hanging baskets and petunia-clad window boxes. The continuing path leads right beside the restaurant, goes uphill and soon resumes the easternmost ridge overlooking the *Mittelland*—that low-lying, mostly agricultural plain that stretches from the foot of the Jura to the foothills of the high Alps. I wandered there on a hazy warm summer's day. There were no views of the Alps then, but the air was heavy with the fragrance of new-mown hay, alive with the sound of cowbells, birdsong and the furious buzzing of innumerable crickets. Beside the path martagon lilies, missed by the scythe, were nodding their heads. Butterflies stretched out their wings

On Day 4 of the JHR the path leads among the hills of Challhöchi, so typical of the turf and tree-clothed Jura landscapes. (Kev Reynolds)

upon them and prodded for nectar, thankful for their escape. Below to the right, in the valley cut by the Augstbach river, stood the remains of the castle of Alt Bechberg, and beyond that, the village of Holderbank. Despite the chorus of natural sound I gloried in the peace and tranquility of that crest. All was as it ought to have been. There was nothing out of place.

The ridge steepens towards the Roggen-schnarz and the JHR is aided by hundreds of timber-reinforced steps, more tiring to ascend than any zig-zag path. High woods clog the broadening ridge, but on reaching the Roggenflue (995m) you find yourself on top of a prominent limestone cliff with another huge view to enjoy before tackling the long descent to Balsthal.

South-west of Balsthal the Jura hills rise steeply to Höllchopfli (1230m), on whose slopes there is a hang-gliding school based on the farm of Schwängimatt. Over Höllchopfli you descend a little, then follow above the

thousand-metre contour for the rest of the day, along the Schattenberg overlooking a narrow defile through which a village can be seen, tiny in the distance, and on to the farm of Hof-bergli where you can relax on a verandah in the shade with a cool drink. An hour and a half later—a woodland, pasture and easy climb later—you come onto Belloc's viewpoint of the Weissenstein high above the unseen town of Solothurn, and there join with that brash and bullying man of letters who could, nonetheless, write like a dream and see if your vision matches his: "One saw the sky beyond the edge of the world getting purer as the vault rose. But right up . . . ran peak and field and needle of intense ice, remote from the world. Sky beneath them and sky above them a stead-fast legion." (*The Path to Rome*)

In other seasons this is ski country, a very popular place with local Swiss from the plains who visit winter and summer alike in family groups, school parties and clubs, for the skiing, walking or simply to enjoy a picnic with the

wonderful views (best seen in the autumn when the lowlands are hidden beneath a vast blanket of fog and the Alps rise out of it pure and white). Weissenstein is topped by a large hotel and restaurant, but half an hour further along the ridge at Hinterer Weissenstein there's a smaller, quieter place to stay away from the crowds who ascend to Weissenstein by chair-lift or by car.

Stage 2: 4 days

The walk continues along the ridge on its steady south-westerly course, but passing now from German-speaking to French-speaking Switzerland, and as you do so it is not only the language that changes, but the architec-ture too. The scenery remains as it was, slowly developing and unfolding according to nature's rules, yet wherever habitation is found it becomes evident that there is now an unspoken affinity more akin to that of France than to teutonic Switzerland. Route signs too change from *Höhenweg* to *Chemin des Crêtes*, while the walk itself continues unaffected by these external developments.

At the end of a six and a half hour day you come down off the heights to a shadowed basin scooped from the hills to find the village of Frinvillier tucked beneath a swirl of concrete taking a major road to Biel. But escape from Frinvillier is a strenuous haul up a tree-crowded slope of hillside, making for the summit of Chasseral (1607m), the highest point of the Bernese Jura. Once the forest eases and panoramas show themselves again, this becomes a stage of considerable beauty and interest. Halfway through it the trail goes past one of the few Swiss Alpine Club huts found on the route. Cabane Jurahaus is a fine building, but it is open infrequently—at weekends or when club members have booked it. (The same may be said of other mountain huts here in the Jura. Unlike those of the high Alps, these are only open at certain periods and with no permanent guardian in residence. As a consequence you should not rely upon using them for accommodation, but if you arrive to find one open and with bed space available, non-members may be welcomed. Certainly that was my experience, and the hut in which I stayed was as idyllic as any I've ever been in.)

Chasseral's summit is topped by an enormous transmitter tower, and a short distance beyond it a large hotel looks out to the Lac de Neuchâtel far below, and the Oberland trio of Eiger, Mönch and Jungfrau on the distant horizon. But to the north the views are also rather fine; they encompass secondary ridges, gentle pastures and sparkling hills of green that fold out of Switzerland and into France. It's difficult to say which is finer; both will brighten any walker's day.

On a stage almost entirely dedicated to descent the route leaves Chasseral and drops more than a thousand metres to the lakeside town of Neuchâtel, then next day creeps along the base of the hills for a while to negotiate the crossing of the river l'Areuse where it washes through a dark and deep defile. The Gorges de l'Areuse are cool and shadowed, the rocks green with moss and lichen, the river green too, and the leaf-shade of a million trees casting a green light on everything; the crossing of the gorge on a spray-damp footbridge is almost sub-aquatically luminescent.

A dense forest clothes the hills above the river, but after 2½ hours of steeply-climbing exercise you emerge from the darkness of trees to find yourself on the very rim of a vast natural couldron along which you will walk for another hour. The Creux du Van is a great limestone amphitheatre more than 1200 metres

wide and two kilometres long. Forests clothe the base of it, some five hundred metres below the rim, while the upper reaches spread out to a high moorland-like plateau with sections of limestone pavement exposed and harbouring numerous plants. There's a farm, Ferme du Soliat, not far from the lip of the cirque, with mattresses in an outhouse where walkers can stay the night. On the day that Nigel Fry and I arrived here it rained heavily in the late afternoon and early evening, but shortly before sunset the rain eased and we went back to the Creux du Van to get some fresh air. The cirque was filled with mist—it was indeed just like a couldron—and as we wandered along the rim of it, so the dying sun from behind threw our shadows into the mist and created haloes around us; each to his own brocken spectre.

Section 3: 5 days

After Le Soliat the walk takes you on a middling course away from the ridge, exploring a 'heartland'-like landscape of broad pastures tilted gently by past geological foldings, but then returns to the crest at Le Chasseron for another huge panorama, while the western side of the ridge plunges dramatically in appalling cliffs. Coming off the ridge the trail now leads to a small and attractive town that is the home of the Swiss musical box industry. Sainte-Croix, set in a hollow between Le Chasseron and Mont de Baulmes, is also becoming known today as a first-rate cross-country ski centre and, apart from the single exception of Neuchâtel, is the first place met on the Jura High Route that is motivated towards tourism.

The Jura has narrowed, and as the walk progresses out of Sainte-Croix so you become aware of just how close France is—in some cases only a meadow or so away. As a reminder of Switzerland's vulnerability in times of war there are plenty of signs of military defences—tank traps and a farm virtually festooned in concrete blocks! But before you come to this the path takes you up onto the crown of Le Suchet (1588m) with a 360° panorama worth savouring. It includes the Alps, with the Mittelland before them. It includes the Lac de Neuchâtel and the Jura crest stretching from Chasseral in the north to La Dôle in the south-west—and much low-lying fresh green pastureland that is undeniably French. On this stretch of the walk the Lake of Geneva begins to show itself and, on haze-free days, Mont Blanc rises with its garland of ice and snow shimmering out to the south.

Vallorbe is the next town to interrupt the rural peace, but it does so with a certain grace

and style. Through it flows the River Orbe, and as you leave the town bound for Mont Tendre (highest of the Swiss Jura at 1679 metres) and Col du Marchairuz, so the JHR takes you to the Source de l'Orbe in a pleasant woodland whose glades are soggy with new-born streams.

Mont Tendre, six hours and more out of Vallorbe, is something of a disappointment, given its pedigree. There's nothing unsatisfactory about its summit views, just the summit itself. As the highest point, not only of the walk but of the Jura ridge, one would expect something more than a mere hiccup on the ridge adorned with a large metal triangulation marker!

Continuing from it for a further hour you come to another CAS hut, Refuge du Cunay, superbly set on a green shelf of hillside, and after this cross a wide slope of pasture ribbed here and there with a criss-cross pattern of brilliant white limestone walling, and come to Col du Marchairuz (1447m) with a hotel offering dormitory places for the long-distance trekker, as well as standard bedrooms.

Two days are left to reach Borex. Two days along the ridge among flowers—some of the most outrageous flower meadows of all are to be experienced here—as you draw ever-closer to visions of the Alps. On the limestone and turf bluff of Crêt de la Neuve (1494m) androsace form dense cushions of bloom on otherwise naked outcrops; tiny blue stars of gentian and the black vanilla orchid adorn the grass; campanulas peek from benevolent crevices in the rock and the tall yellow-flowered gentian that is almost the symbol of the Jura, line the onward route as extravagant marker wands.

St. Cergue, an attractive village built on slopes overlooking the Lake of Geneva and the Alps beyond, has grown in popularity as both a winter and summer resort without compromising its charm. Thomas Arnold once wrote of its views—which are said to stretch from the Jungfrau to Mont Blanc—"I never saw surpassed." La Dôle, last summit on the long walk, is reached in just under three hours from St. Cergue. Rousseau was deeply moved by what he saw from it. "The moment when from the top of the Jura mountains I discovered Lake Geneva," he wrote, "was a moment of ecstasy and delight."

Then it's down, down, down for 1200 metres and about ten kilometres, through woodland, meadows and a great open plain of wheat towards Borex, Lac Léman and its vine-clad slopes—and the distant mountains shimmering in the afternoon. The Alps, where so many dreams lie.

Walk 2: *Traverse of the Vercors High Plateau in Winter by R Brian Evans*

Location: In the Pre-Alpes of south-eastern France.

How to get there: By super-fast TGV train from Paris to Grenoble; may be reached from many parts of England in a day. From the Channel coast, either Zeebrugge or Calais, the road journey to Grenoble is entirely on Autoroute and takes a day to drive.

Distance: 55 kilometres (34 miles).

Time required: 5 short days, although an extra day in case of bad weather is recommended. Experienced skiers, or summer walkers, will need 3 days.

Type of route: An adventurous cross-country ski trek which demands a good deal of competence in mountain walking and navigation. The level of skiing ability required is low, for any steep descents can be walked if necessary, but ski novices would need to be very careful—an accident on the plateau could be very serious. The route is almost as rewarding in summer, but it is necessary to know the location of water sources (marked on the 1:25,000 maps).

Start: Corrençon.

Finish: Chichilianne.

Best time of year: January—March for skiing. Any time is suitable for walking when the deep snow has melted. May–June for spring flowers.

Maps: IGN 1:25,000 series *Massif du Vercors* (in 2 sheets: *Hauts Plateau Nord; Hauts Plateau Sud*) or Didier & Richard 1:50,000 *Massif du Vercors.*

Guidebook: *The Limestone Pre-Alpes of France* by R Brian Evans (Cicerone Press) (in preparation).

The classic winter route of the Pre-Alpes

The Vercors is one of several *Parcs Regional* in the French Alps. It is an area of unspoilt natural beauty, a most impressive part of the Pre-Alpes; an extensive wedge-shaped plateau of limestone with Grenoble at its apex. Tilted plateaux, peaks and scarps form a wave-like pattern. Forests clothe the lower slopes, grassy prairies mingle with limestone pavements above. The most prominent escarpment runs in an almost unbroken wall of impressive crags

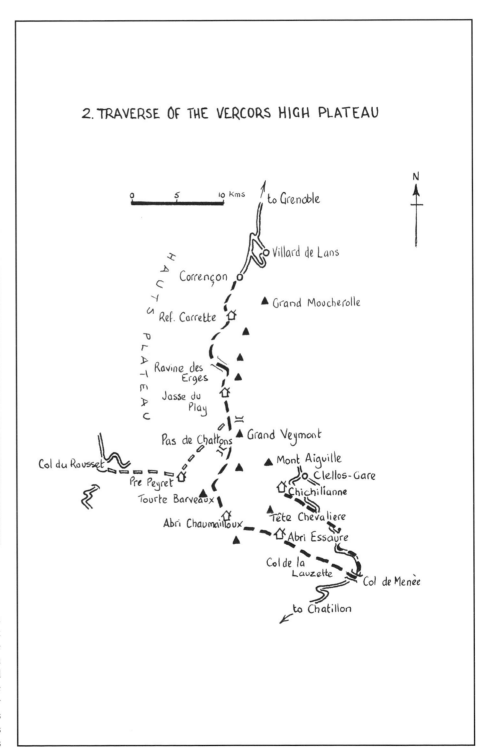

2. TRAVERSE OF THE VERCORS HIGH PLATEAU

and spires along the eastern edge from near Grenoble southwards to the Col de Menèe. An exciting walker's route (described in *Classic Walks of Europe*), traverses below this escarpment, but another classic route, totally different in character, follows the high plateau behind the cliffs.

A summer traverse of the plateau has its attractions, with broad views over roll upon roll of forest and clearing. Snow-covered Alpine giants sparkle to the east, whilst here is dry limestone with rocky paths which twist among tiny tangled pines—the attractive *pin a crochet*—growing incredibly out of pockets and crevices. Summer also sees vast flocks of sheep grazing the clearings. The sheep are brought from the sun-scorched pastures of the Midi to summer amongst the cooler, lusher grasses of the Vercors. Unlike their British counterparts, they mass together, sometimes in flocks of over a thousand, with a *berger* and dogs to look after them. Walkers must give the flocks a wide berth and respect their valuable water supplies. Water is a real problem for backpackers in the Vercors, for many of the sources are feeble and may fail in a drought. Conversely some sources in amazing high places flow strongly all year.

Walkers who are used to being pampered in other parts of the Alps will find no luxurious 'huts' in the Vercors. The PRV authorities look after a chain of simple refuges which form important overnight stops for backpackers. They generally contain a table, a stove or fireplace, and communal wooden-floored sleeping platforms. Originally there were several purpose-built timber cabins, but due to a design fault most of these burnt down. Now only two remain, with modified stoves. The other refuges are substantial stone cottages, similar to a Scottish bothy. These huts are in keeping with the unspoilt atmosphere of the area, well away from tourist paths. At busy times the huts can be crowded and it is wise to carry a lightweight tent, although camping is officially banned in the Reserve Naturel of the Hauts Plateaux. Backpacking is relatively easy, for once up on the plateau, gradients are gentle. There are many other gîtes and guardianed refuges at lower altitudes in the neighbouring villages.

A traverse of the Vercors plateau in winter is the classic trip of its kind in France, or indeed the Alps. Nowhere else has its unique character; a magical blend of intricate route-finding, stunning views if the weather is kind, and a sense of adventure; for the vertical cliffs which edge the plateau give it an isolation which is special. Cross-country skis form the usual means of progression, as walking in deep snow is too arduous. The skis can be the cheapest package available at hypermarkets in the surrounding towns. You will need light-weight skis with fish-scale soles which grip when going uphill. The bindings have a clip which holds the boot toe in place. The boots are light and lined for warmth. Sticks complete the package. Novices have been in the party on several of my trips, and they have coped well and enjoyed it, but any party embarking on the traverse should include a skier experienced in winter hill craft.

More important than cross-country ski skills is mountain sense and experience, for if caught in bad weather it takes real skill to navigate in the confusing maze of the plateau. Full winter backpacking gear is essential: a warm sleeping bag, foam mat, warm clothing, cooking stove and emergency shelter, preferably a lightweight tent. A false sense of security prevails when the sky is blue and a myriad ski tracks point the way. Overnight snow can wipe out all ski trails and mist can make finding the next snow-covered hut extremely difficult. Snow hides many waymarks.

Much of the plateau can be explored in day trips from a valley base in one of several attractive villages, which offer plenty of accommodation. A short version of the traverse, from Col du Rousset to Corrençon, or vice-versa, makes a fine introduction. The following description is based on a week's holiday for an average party. Daily distances are not great, which allows for short winter days and enough time to follow the intricacies of the route, or for novices to pick themselves up after their customary 'sit stop'.

Snow cover varies enormously. Christmas/New Year has provided me with some of my most enjoyable trips on the plateau with continuous sunshine for long periods, but hardly enough snow to warrant skis. When the 'big dump' arrives the plateau is well-covered until Easter, especially in the forested areas, but may be wind-blown on the crests.

Day 1

Corrençon lies six kilometres south of Villard de Lans. A bus service runs from Grenoble to Villard, which is one of the major resorts of the area, summer and winter. There is an extensive downhill ski piste system here, plenty of shops and accommodation. If you have travelled by car from Britain you will have reached Villard in a long day of driving. The vehicle is perhaps best left in the smaller village of Chichilianne at the southern end of the traverse, preferably under supervision. You can then return to Grenoble from Clelles by train and reach Villard by mid afternoon, which will still give enough time to attain the Refuge Carrette in about two hours.

There is a large car parking area at the start of the cross-country ski trails, for Corrençon is one of the most popular centres in the Vercors, with many radiating machine-pisted circuits in the forest. Officially you have to buy a ticket to use the pistes, but our route uses them only for the first few kilometres. If you are a novice on cross-country skis then this is a good place to get your ski legs.

The trail to the Carrette lies straight along the rising floor of a combe, with the steeper slopes of the downhill pistes on the left. Novices will find the going easy, for it is all uphill. Trails fork right and left, but our route continues up the narrowing combe into dense forest, through a defile, the Porte Barnier, where a spur is crossed. The stone Refuge Carrette lies in a clearing just beyond, a little above the main trail.

Day 2

Today provides the first test for ski novices as the trail snakes down through forest to the broad clearing of Darbonousse, where views back over a sea of frosted pines reveal the wave-like mountain crest of the Vercors with hints of huge cliffs falling down the far side. After another clearing the trail forks—straight ahead a way through the forest is a lower traverse of the Vercors. Our route bears left and rises up the Ravine des Erges, a stiff climb and an even stiffer test for anyone skiing the other way. The mountain rim of the plateau dominates the scene above the typical small *pin a crochet* of the higher plateau, now that the denser *epiceas* (the traditional Christmas tree) are left behind. The trees host many tits and you may see the distinctive crossbill eating the pine seeds. The heaped tangle of hillocks and hollows, clearing and forest, is part of the special attraction, with changing views at every turn. Rarely is the trail straightforward. Ahead lies the Grand Veymont, at 2341 metres the highest peak in the Vercors, easily incorporated in a summer traverse.

From the top of the Ravine des Erges to the Jasse du Play is a test of navigational skills even in good weather. In bad conditions it can be daunting. Snow covers the GR (*Grande Randonnée*) markers on rocks, and the number of ski tracks can be confusing. A clearing at the top of the ravine is followed and starts to descend. Leave this to climb higher and make a contorted traverse amongst limestone craglets. In summer I have been amazed to see the roughness of the ground which lies below the snow cover. A small forested dome, the Tête de Cogneaux, is passed to its left and a very steep descent over crags is made into the

The mountain rim of the plateau above the Ravine des Erges. (Brian Evans)

ravine of the Sentier Central. Leave this immediately to gain a large clearing with a huge hollow, on the side of which is the stone refuge of the Jasse du Play, a solid, welcome haven in a delectable setting. (The summer water source is feeble and lies about twenty minutes away.) This is a vital refuge on the route and is very popular. Officially there is floor space for ten, but on almost all my visits there has been at least double that, in an atmosphere of congenial viviality. Note that the French retire early to their sleeping bags and expect visitors from other countries to be as quiet and well-behaved as themselves.

Day 3

This is a challenging day with rewarding high level views and intricate route finding in the latter stages. At first the trail is easy and undulates gently along a high-level shelf (1640m) below the mountain crest. At the far end of the broad clearing of the Plaine de la Chau there is a crossroads of trails near a bergerie. Take the steep track towards a shoulder of the Grand Veymont, into tangled forest. After a rise of fifty metres the trail traverses steep ground. Where it leaves the forest the main track descends towards the Grande Cabane, a large bergerie in the centre of a vast flat clearing, but our route branches left to traverse gently below the steep icy gullies of the Grand Veymont to gain the Pas de Chattons at its southern tip. The last part of the traverse is across steep slopes which, if icy, may prove daunting to novices. The pass proves to be a gateway to another rising combe which in turn leads to a flat crest, at 1935 metres the highest point of the trip. An intervening ridge hides most of Mont Aiguille, which is tantalisingly close. If the day is good and progress satisfactory, then it is worth skiing across the edge for a close-up view of this remarkable fortress-like peak.

Continuing on the trail the end of the narrow crest drops into a broad combe, the Plain of the Queyrie, with its solitary tree a distinctive landmark. The slopes of this south-facing descent are often crusted and can be frustrating in such conditions, when it is best to seek better snow on the left at the earliest opportunity.

At the tree bear left across a low shoulder to the last section of the route—across one of the most tormented sections of plateau in the Vercors, in summer a chaos of bare limestone.

Pass the bergerie of Jasse de Peyre Rouge in a craggy hollow and continue towards the slopes of the conical Tourte Barreaux ahead. Keep well under the slopes of this, to avoid the worst of the hollows, but the final stretch to the refuge is across the grain of the ridges and hollows. The Abri de Chaumailloux is not easy to find in gathering darkness of a winter evening, for it lies hidden below a rocky knoll at the head of a grassy combe, above the ravine of the Pas de l'Aiguille.

The Chaumailloux is yet another popular refuge and you will be lucky to find it empty. The double-tiered sleeping area seems to expand as more and more people appear. Our dismay one bitter winter night as a large contingent of army personnel appeared turned to relief as they continued on their exercise!

Winter brings fog to the valleys and this sometimes creeps up onto the plateau particularly at the head of narrowing combes. On one occasion we reluctantly decided that the time had come to leave the hut in dense mist only to burst out into brilliant sunshine a hundred metres above. The Chaumailloux is in one of the most serious winter situations of all the huts in the Vercors, for escape down the Pas de l'Aiguille is impracticable due to its steepness and avalanche possibilities. I have vivid memories of pulling out to the Pre Peyret and Col du Rousset on an incredibly bad day. To follow a compass course is difficult as the route twists so much, and the possibility of skiing over small cliffs in a white-out is always there.

Day 4

You can lie in this morning, for even with a diversion to a fine viewpoint, this is an easy half-day of only five kilometres. To linger in this delightful spot is a chance to soak up the atmosphere, and is necessary because the final day is long and arduous if conditions are poor.

The monument to the Resistance at the head of the pass is worth visiting, especially the tiny cave where there is a moving précis of the battle in 1944.

The trail traverses across a break in the steeply-forested slopes of the Tête des Baumiers. This leads onto a flat shelf and the Pas de la Chevrerie, a low col at the entrance to a curving combe with a small bergerie, the Chamousset, at its head. If the Chaumailloux is full, this could be used as a shelter, although the room left open in winter is tiny, unsavoury

and cold. I have passed by when it was impossible to locate the doorway in deep drifted snow.

Climb to a col at 1823 metres on the bare plateau above. The Tête Chevalière (1951m) lies close over easy slopes and is a wonderful viewpoint perched on the edge of an impressive void, backed by the stubby Mont Aiguille and the graceful pyramid of the Grand Veymont. South and west the plateau stretches to a fringe of pines on the edge of the great cliffs of Archiane. Everywhere the horizon seems to be defended by escarpments which serve to instill a healthy respect at the prospect of bad weather.

Back on the trail the way descends into a steep valley which emerges suddenly onto a very flat shelf. The stone refuge, the Abri de l'Essaure is a welcome if somewhat spartan haven. I trust that the roof will have been repaired and the primitive fireplace replaced by a stove since my last visit. The Park authorities have improved many of the refuges in recent years.

Day 5

From the plateau edge close to the Essaure you can see the village of Chichilianne directly below, but the summer path is impracticable in winter and anyway, the complete traverse of the Vercors ends at the Col de Menèe. We must take a longer, circuitous, route.

The refuge lies at the head of the long Vallèe de Combau which could provide an easy escape in dire weather. Keep on the eastern side of the valley-head along a shelf which makes easy progress. If the snow is good then a high level traverse of the steep slopes of the Tête de Praorzel is practicable. If there is any danger of avalanche then descend into the valley. Where the valley bends the Col de Lauzette is our objective, high on the mountain ridge. This is the key to the final traverse of a steep-sided crest onto the downhill ski slopes of the Col de Mènee. Cross a col and circle a little hump ahead to enter the forest left above the road tunnel.

You've just completed one of the great ski traverses of Europe!

The road is snowploughed from the west only as far as the tunnel. You will have the pleasure of an easy ski along the snow-covered road as it twists into ravines on the side of the escarpment. Nearer Chichilianne you can join ski trails in the valley left of the road.

Walk 3: *GR5: Traverse of The French Alps by Martin Collins*

Location: South-east France (Haute-Savoie to Alpes-Maritimes).
How to get there: By train from Paris Gare de Lyon to Montreux (for the start), Annemasse (for Samoëns), St. Gervais (for Les Houches and Chamonix), Moutiers (for Pralognan), Bourg-St. Maurice (for the Vanoise), Modane (for the Arc valley), Briançon (for the Queyras) and Nice (for the Alpes-Maritimes).
Nearest international airports: Geneva and Nice.
Distance: 660 kilometres (400 miles).
Time required: Allow at least 4 weeks.
Start: St Gingolph (Lake Geneva).
Finish: Nice.
Type of walk: Long and, at times, arduous, it is nonetheless a magnificent route that explores some superb mountain scenery. In places it is well-trodden, but elsewhere there are some remote and rugged sections.
Maps: Didier et Richard *Itineraires Pédestres et à Ski* 1:50,000 Sheets 3,8,11,6,10,1 and 9 (going north to south). IGN 1:1,000,000 of France showing all GR routes and National Parks—good for planning.
Guidebook: *GR5—Walking the French Alps* by Martin Collins (Cicerone Press).

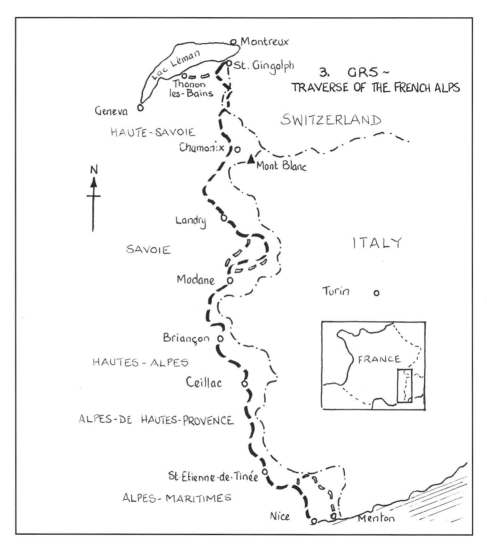

Lake of Geneva to the Mediterranean

Set off south from the shores of Lake Geneva and you will encounter some of the finest Alpine walking in the whole of Europe. A way-marked trail—one of France's renowned *Sentiers de Grande Randonnée*—winds through 660 kilometres (400 miles) of magnificent country to reach the Mediterranean coast at Nice. Bearing the prefix GR5 and known as the *Grande Traversée des Alpes*, the trail is a genuine hiking route through what often amounts to mountaineering terrain. As well as crossing all the principal massifs of the French Alps, it draws tantalisingly close to Mont Blanc, Western Europe's highest peak.

On its way south, GR5 passes picturesque villages, emerald lakes, high refuges and an unfolding panoply of magnificent scenery. The journey is essentially one of transition—from dense forest, Alpine pasture, glaciers and snow-fields in the north, to bare rock ridges, olive

groves and cicadas as you approach the flesh-pots of the Côte d'Azur. Along the way there is a progressive shift from cool to hot, from slate to pantile, from moist luxuriance to aromatic brittleness.

By traversing a succession of passes between valley systems, you are led from one mountain group to the next on a classic trek which will take the fit walker about four weeks to complete. Substantial demands will be made at times on stamina and personal resourceful-ness, but nowhere is the terrain technically

difficult, other than the possibility of snowbanks obscuring the path early in the season when ice-axe security is desirable.

In fact, snowfall closes high ground to walkers during the winter and the trail, along with its complement of accommodation, refreshment and supply points, is not consi-dered fully open until about the end of June. Start then, or a little later, and you will savour the Alpine landscapes at their best, with snowy summits soaring into clear, astringent air above drifts of wild flowers.

Trekkers at Porte du Lac Vert, with the Dents du Midi on the skyline. *(Martin Collins)*

Blisters apart, weather is a great determinant of hiking pleasure. I have known summer storms in the Alpes-Maritimes so ferocious that movement was impossible. Unusually late winter snows will disappointingly block the paths of Haute-Savoie for much of July, while hot winds from Africa can dry sweat before it has moistened the brow. Such exceptional weather occurs from time to time, but in an average year the tendency is towards fine, settled conditions.

Styles of travel vary between individuals. I have always favoured backpacking—self-sufficiency at the cost of a heavier pack— but with a little planning you could overnight at huts and *gîtes d'etape* (a French equivalent of private youth hostels). Equally viable is to split the route into smaller 'bites' which fit more readily into a week or two's holiday. The following stages do just that, but at the end of the day they remain only suggestions—so much depends on individual pace, the weather and unforeseeable delays.

Stage 1: 5–6 days
Lake Geneva, largest of the Alpine lakes and fringed with mellow resorts, provides a fitting start for the trek. Although the initial climb of some 1500 metres (5000 ft) to Col de Bise is a testing one, these first days are spent cross-

ing the friendly limestone Pre-Alpe of Haute Savoie which rise to Dent d'Oche and the Cornettes de Bise. It is a landscape of green pastures, ancient chalets and enthralling views ahead to snow-capped peaks.

A sequence of grassy cols—Bise, Mattes, Chésery, Coux and Golèse—though up to 2100 metres high and strenuous enough to climb, are never far from human settlement. Cheese making is a thriving cottage industry and cattle and goats, brought up to higher grazing in the annual transhumance, announce their presence with jangling bells and biting insects.

Beyond the long descent to Samoëns you

Exciting views ahead from Col des Mattes. *(Martin Collins)*

approach the great mountain barrier of the Northern Alps. The terrain grows perceptibly more rugged, more remote. There are spectacular waterfalls, amphitheatres of rock and permanent snowfields to cross, yet trails are well walked and there is no shortage of huts or wild camping spots. From one such pitch on Collet d'Anterne I witnessed an ethereal vision of Mont Blanc, unveiled from thundercloud and lit pink by a dying sun: one unforgettable experience among many, for it is this mountain above all else that dominates the next few days.

Le Brévent (2526m; 8287ft) is the only summit, *per se*, traversed by GR5, and dizzy views down to Chamonix and across to the glittering snows of Mont Blanc and the Chamonix Aiguilles accompany the big ensuing descent to Les Houches and civilisation.

Stage 2: 3–5 days

The Tramway du Mont Blanc on Col de Voza offers a tempting detour up to the Bionnassay

Glacier, but GR5 stays lower, either crossing Col de Tricot or tracing the Montjoie valley's patchwork of fields and hamlets to Les Contamines, an Alpine town at the threshold of wilder country.

An old Roman road points towards the valley head where the cols of Bonhomme and Croix-de-Bonhomme take you from Haute-Savoie into Beaufortain. Relatively undeveloped, it is a region famed for its cheeses and, more recently, for its hydro-electric power—so-called 'white coal'. Mountains are still lofty (Mont Blanc is just over your shoulder) and wildlife profuse once off the beaten track.

A marvellous hour of ridge walking on Crête des Gittes brings you to a hut near the Roselend dam; gaining height, sheep replace cattle on increasingly sparse pasture. The remote Col de Bresson breaks through seemingly impregnable rock walls and delivers you into Tarentaise, a region that has undergone brutal transformation this century as the age of the mule was superceded by that of the

helicopter within a few decades.

Already there are subtle changes in flora, fauna and architecture which herald a transition from Northern to Southern Alps. South-facing hillsides are noticeably drier, hold less winter snow and echo to the chirping of crickets.

Stage 3: 4–6 days

After plunging into the deep Isère valley, GR5 sets off for the Vanoise. Surroundings grow in stature and beauty, protected from exploitation within the Vanoise National Park, but perilously close to some of the largest ski centres on earth around Les Arcs.

An ambling ascent of Col du Palet confronts you with a choice of three onward routes through the National Park to Modane. The main trail passes Tignes and internationally renowned Val d'Isère—ski resorts both—crosses the high Col d'Iseran (2764m) and follows a natural mid-height shelf (or *balcon*) route to loop round the great Doron Gorge and two artificial lakes, before crossing Col du Barbier and dropping to Modane. There are several huts along the *balcon* trail, but no other supply points without descending off-route into the Arc valley.

GR55—the classic high-level option from Tignes—is to be recommended if fitness and weather are favourable. Mostly staying between 2000 and 2600 metres, you cross Col de la Leisse, the popular Col de la Vanoise and Col de Chavière—the latter 2796 metres (9173ft) above sea level, and the greatest elevation reached by any of France's GR paths: a high spot in every sense! Strategically placed huts and the delightful town of Pralognan allow various overnight options, but this variant is always a potentially serious undertaking, especially under early season snow conditions when an ice-axe will be necessary.

If you tire of the sometimes agoraphobic infinities of land and sky characterising mountain travel, why not try the GR5E which descends from Col d'Iseran to the floor of the Arc valley? Here you will thread through the ancient Haute-Maurienne villages: lots of vernacular architecture and mountainsides to gaze up at.

Whichever way you select through the Vanoise, your senses will be thrilled by Alpine scenery of the highest calibre.

Stage 4: 4-5 days

From the frontier town of Modane, GR5 enters impressively *sauvage* terrain in the Hautes-Alpes; close to Italy's northern conurbations, the country seems more Italian than French. Col de la Vallée Étroite, though not steep, is gained over desolate— almost lunar— slopes. Encircling peaks, no longer hung with glaciers like their counterparts further north, seem ominously barren and hostile, yet on lower, sunny hillsides alpine flowers abound and the Queyras Regional Park is well known for its broad-leaved and conifer forests.

Col des Thures signals a temporary descent from the heights, but beyond Plampinet the trail rises again to Col de Dormillouze and Col de la Lauze. On your way down to Briançon—hub of this stage—you may be walking ankle-deep in crickets, for here the weather is appreciably hotter and drier as

Atlantic weather influences give way to those of continental and Mediterranean origins.

Richly endowed with historical associations, Briançon deserves more than a fleeting visit. I have always found it hard to drag myself away from its fascinating citadel-like old town and narrow streets thronged with visitors. By this point in the trek you too may well be feeling a little deprived of civilised attractions!

The cols of Ayes and Fromage are approached by lengthy, shallow ascents through forest and meadow, yet their southern sides, exposed to relentless sunshine and erosion, are stonily arid.

Stage 5: 4 days

Permanent snow may be absent, but the Alpes-de-Haute-Provence are both high and lonely and should not be tackled casually. Gradients can be steep and sustained, underfoot conditions very rough, yet some of the best mountain scenery on GR5 awaits the well-prepared walker.

Rising at first through forest, past the exquisite Sébeyrand and St. Anne lakes, the trail punctuates landscapes hostile to man, but compelling in scale and feature. Col Giradin (2700m) is a little precarious on both sides, but provides memorable views back across range upon range of sand-coloured peaks into the blue haze of distance. Ahead and more than eight hundred metres below, lies the Ubaye valley whose rough road is tramped from La Barge to Fouillouze. Cols Vallonnet and Mallemort bear signs of old wartime buildings and, indeed, the town of Larche soon reached —not far from the Italian border—was rebuilt after destruction in 1944 by the occupying forces.

Pas de la Cavale, the last major mountain barrier on GR5, demands respect. The going is particularly rugged and route finding not altogether straightforward, so only set off in reasonably favourable conditions.

Higher up the Lauzanier valley, past a couple of delectable lakes, chaotic boulders and coarse scree lead you round a dramatic cirque and up to the narrow col itself. Italy lies down to the east, while the Alpes-Maritimes beckon to the south-west. The descent is extremely steep and loose—dangerous if the 'Lombarde'

wind is blowing hard from Italy and dislodging stones from above. Col des Fourches, Col de la Columbière and Col d'Anelle are tame by comparison—no obstacle to reaching the Tinée valley.

Stage 6: 5-6 days

It is almost—but not quite—downhill all the way to the Mediterranean. The southward trek holds on resolutely to its mountain identity, passing the modern ski resort of Auron, traversing Col du Blainon and terraced hillsides to Roya hamlet. Now in the Mercantour National Park, GR5 climbs to a shoulder of Mont Mounier, the coast at last in view given good visibility. Knee-jarring descent separates you from St. Sauveur-sur-Tinée, the lowest altitude walked since Landry in the Isère valley.

St. Damlas-Valdeblore lies at the northern end of a long limestone chain running down to Utelle and the Mediterranean hinterland. It is also the departure point for GR52, a variant swinging north, then east and south through very remote country, and ending at Menton. Throughout this final stage of the trek water and accommodation can be scarce, temperatures often searingly hot and summer thunderstorms a potential hazard.

South of Mont Tournairet, at Brec d'Utelle, the path has fallen away—just as you think difficulties have relented. However, you are soon negotiating olive terraces, spiky vegetation, village lanes and the flanks of Mont Cima (878m) to arrive at Aspremont, built atop a circular hill. In a celebratory mood I once ate (and drank) too much here—an indulgence I do not recommend if you have a train to catch!

Nice is but three or four hours distant, ups and downs in moderation and the air heavy with the scent of wild herbs. Seen from Mont Chauve d'Aspremont's summit ridge, swimming pools gleam lurid blue in suburban villa gardens, and before long you have reached the upper roads and are striding down broad avenues to the centre of cosmopolitan Nice. You will surely dip a sweaty toe —or more— into the warm Mediterranean, but try to visit the old quarter with its honeycomb of alleyways, shops and stalls, before contemplating the journey home.

Walk 4: *Walliser Wispile by Kev Reynolds*

Location: North-east of Col du Pillon, Bernese Alps, Switzerland.

How to get there: By train to Gstaad via Montreux or Thun, and from there to Gsteig by Postbus. Nearest international airport—Geneva or Bern. By road through Switzerland to Thun and Spiez, then westward along the Simmental to Gstaad and continue to Gsteig. Or alternatively, along the Lake of Geneva to Aigle (south of Montreux), and then east along the Col du Portillon road to Gsteig.

Distance: 11 kilometres (7 miles).

Height gain/loss: 684 metres (low route) 776 metres (high route).

Time required: 4–4½ hours.

Type of walk: Moderately graded walk on mostly good paths, if narrow in places. No difficulties. Splendid viewpoints. No opportunities for refreshment along the way.

Valley base: Gsteig.

Map: Landeskarte der Schweiz 1:50,000 series, sheet no 5009 *Gstaad-Adelboden*.

Guidebook: *The Bernese Alps* by Kev Reynolds (Cicerone Press).

Green ridges and lonely alps above Gsteig

The Bernese Alps have as their last bastion in the west the big massif of Les Diablerets. Although its summits rarely rise much above three thousand metres, Les Diablerets certainly gives every appearance of being a large and noble mountain, broad and substantial as it is and hung about with glaciers on its north and east faces where skiing takes place even through the summer.

The main Oberland ridge extends its wild and rocky tentacles in a long north-east to south-west projection, but elsewhere here the mountains are less severe and they wear their greenery with pride, with meadows and woods to the crest of many transverse ridges, and flowers almost reaching to the very highest and loneliest of their summits.

Below Les Diablerets to the north-east the Rüschbach stream flows down from the Col du Pillon to join the Saane in the low meadows of Gsteig; a soft, lush and decidedly pleasant valley draining north between gentle hills that are generously wooded, their slopes picked out

with patterns of farmland shaved in blocks as haymaking progresses through the long days of summer.

The eastern hillslope rises above the valley to the crest of the Höhi Wispile that effectively divides Gsteig's valley from that of Lauenen. The ridge curves a little at its southern end and slightly overlaps another protruding north from the Spitzhorn (which owes allegiance to the higher Arpetlistock) and then fades in a short spur above Gsteig. The ridge that is overlapped by the Höhi Wispile is initially known as the Walliser Wispile, a delightfully brief stretch of forest and pasture before being overshadowed by the abrupt crags of the Spitzhorn. At the point of overlap between these two crests is the gap of the Krinnen Pass (1659m), traversed on the Alpine Pass Route.

Above the pass, and caught in a fold of hillside, nestles a little alp hamlet enjoying broad views and sunshine. A few paces from the alp will grant secretive views onto the Lauenental and up to the higher peaks, while the main object on show is Les Diablerets itself with its satellite ridges and subsidiary peaks, namely the

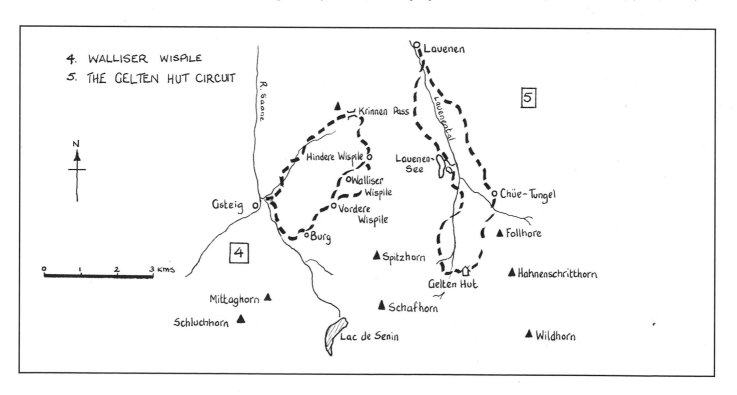

Oldenhorn and Schluchhorn. Then below the alp another, larger, hamlet shelters in a bowl, mountain behind, broad views ahead and woodland below.

This walk takes you from Gsteig up to the pass and on to each of the alp hamlets in turn before descending, ever-interestingly, to Gsteig once more.

Gsteig makes a pleasant base, so long as you don't hanker after evening entertainment. There's very little of the village, but what there is is rather colourful. Its dark-timbered chalets are bright with flowers, its hotel straight off a chocolate box, and its pretty white church, seen with the Schluchhorn and Mittaghorn behind, being immediately photogenic. There are plenty of good walks of all degrees of seriousness to be had from here, including the lengthy crossing of the Col du Sanetsch to Sion in the Rhône valley in canton Valais (about $9\frac{1}{2}$ hours), or over the Blattipass to the west and down to the Arnensee and on through the Tscharzis valley to Feutersory. But the Walliser Wispile loop makes a splendid day's outing too. It's not too demanding, but you should allow a full day to enjoy it properly without haste, giving time to sprawl upon the flowery upper hillsides and simply breathe the fragrance of summer in the Alps. It may be one of the least taxing of all the walks in this collection, but that is by no means to its detriment.

It is a walk I discovered by accident during a summer spent researching the Bernese Alps for another book. I'd been walking in the hills above the Col du Pillon from shortly after daybreak in order to capture the soft early morning light on the snows of Les Diablerets, and descended to Gsteig a little before midday to collect my tent before heading east to meet a friend with whom I was due to climb next day. Rather than eat my lunch on the road, I decided to wander up towards the Krinnen Pass and there to enjoy the peace and the views, the wild flowers and fragrance. But it was curiosity that drew me on. And on and on. And I was led into such welcoming country that the hours were quickly forgotten as viewpoint followed viewpoint, and one landscape of enchantment gave way to another. Dawdling here, side-tracking there, I drained the day without regret and beat a hasty evening retreat with my head a-buzz with memories and the certainty that what I'd discovered purely by chance just happened to be good enough to be classified as one of the classic walks of the Alps.

Gsteig has a partial village square with a couple of small food stores and a footpath signpost opposite the attractive Hotel Bären. The

From the ridge above the Krinnen Pass a clear view may be had down to the Lauenensee in the next valley. *(Kev Reynolds)*

The alp of Hinderer Wispile, with the bulk of the Diablerets massif ahead. (Kev Reynolds)

walk begins here, taking to a side street between bright troughs of flowers adorning chalet windows, but soon breaking away from habitation with meadows on either side. Before long you desert the lane and take to a footpath cutting straight ahead through sloping meadows and among trees to cross and recross another lane winding up the hillside. With customary Swiss efficiency waymarks in the form of paint flashes, and the occasional yellow footpath signpost, keep you on course for the Krinnen Pass. It is an easy path to follow and you gain height without difficulty, sometimes alongside a shaded stream with jays shrieking a warning among the trees, and if you walk quietly you may catch sight of red or roe deer in the woods.

As you draw near to the pass, so you find yourself enclosed between two minor hillside spurs, both wooded and restricting views. However, immediately below the pass an open meadowland (somewhat marshy in places)

makes a fine sheltered place for a picnic, for suddenly the views back towards Gsteig and the mountains above it are shown quite clearly. There is a farmhouse set in this meadow as if to add scale and balance to the view, while the ridge above it is lined with pine and fir trees and consequently blocking all views into Lauenen's valley to the east.

The Krinnen Pass is a mere dip in the wooded crest, meadow to the west, thick woodland to the east. Go through the fence to a junction of paths and immediately bear right on a narrow trail twisting among the trees as it climbs along the very edge of the crest. In places the path lurches steeply and the views to the right, at first very fine, become distorted and lost for a while. Then there's a brief clearing, thoughtfully provided with a bench seat to entice you to relax and enjoy the sudden explosion of light that comes flooding from east and west with tight panoramas of distant hills and hinted valleys soft and pastoral ahead.

Still the ridge entices you on, again among trees with more height to gain. Then the trees thin out and there's a meadow lush with wild flowers throughout the early summer, and simply glorious views to the east and southeast. It's a perfect place to rest, to sit among the grasses and absorb the loveliness of the world about you. This is not dramatic scenery. The drama of the high Alps will be found elsewhere. The mountains near to hand are friendly and unassuming. The Wildhorn, for example, is wild in name only when seen from this view, its snows and modest glaciers draped round its shoulders in order to add stature, not severity, to its appearance. Green ridges splay opposite—countryside explored on the Gelten Hut Circuit (Walk 5), while down below, set in a nest of greenery, the sparkling lake of the Lauenensee shines as a mirror to the drifting summer clouds.

When at last you manage to drag yourself away from this sloping balcony of flowers,

Hotel Bären in the heart of Gsteig is so typical of the flower-girt buildings of the Bernese Alps. *(Kev Reynolds)*

continue along the crest for another five minutes or so and you will come to the alp of Hinderer Wispile (1868m). It's only a tiny hamlet consisting of a handful of farms, cattle byres and haybarns built around a rough shoulder of hillocks and hollows (token of its limestone origins). One or two of the hollows contain pools to reflect the mystery of the surrounding peaks. Again, views are quite delightful, especially to the outliers of the Diablerets massif rising stubbornly to the south-west.

From the alp there are two routes to choose from, both of which will lead to the lower alp of Vorderer Wispile. The high path continues along the steadily rising ridge heading south, and then swings down a minor hillside spur to the alp, while the alternative trail stumbles over rough slopes, round the edge of more limestone pits, and down to another tiny collection of huts on the way to Vorderer Wispile (1756m). There's not a lot to choose between them; the upper route perhaps wins with its extensive views, the lower route by way of its additional alp of interest.

From Vorderer Wispile a broad track winds on down the hillside all the way to Gsteig, but there are footpath short-cuts that drop through forest to yet another alp, Burg (1507m), which allows a sneak preview of the route to Col du Sanetsch and the Sanetsch waterfall bursting from a rocky cleft to the south.

At Burg look for a signpost indicating the path to Burgfäller and Gsteig. It leads down a tight, tree-crowded gorge where a series of cascades paint rainbow patterns of spray. The path is a sheer delight, at times almost a catwalk of little bridges and balconies over deep pools and long drops, and it comes into the bed of the valley among trees still, with just a short stretch of lane left to wander back to Gsteig.

Walk 5: *The Gelten Hut Circuit*
by Kev Reynolds

Location: Bernese Alps, Switzerland.
How to get there: By train to Gstaad via Montreux or Thun, and from there to Lauenen by Postbus. Nearest international airport—Geneva or Bern. By road through Switzerland to Thun and Spiez, then westward along the Simmental to Gstaad. From Gstaad a short drive to Lauenen.
Distance: 16 kilometres (10 miles).
Time required: 6–7 hours.
Height gain/loss: 790 metres.
Type of walk: Visually rewarding, ever-varied. The route is never difficult, although there are steep sections and in places the path is rather narrow and exposed. An exceptionally fine walk, highly recommended.
Valley base: Lauenen.
Map: Landeskarte der Schweiz 1:50,000 series, sheet no 5009 *Gstaad-Adelboden*.
Guidebook: *The Bernese Alps* by Kev Reynolds (Cicerone Press).

On the flanks of the Wildhorn

This walk has everything you could possibly wish for on a day out in the Alps. It has a clear lake with a partially reed-fringed foreshore, a superb cascading waterfall, flower-strewn meadows, a nature reserve and a mountain hut charmingly set below a sheen of glaciers. It has long views, green ridges, remote alp hamlets and a lovely unspoilt village to begin and end in. And it's not difficult. Quite long, certainly, and with some steep sections of path. But there's nothing about it that a normal active walker would shy away from.

The walk starts in Lauenen, that delightful little village without pretention found near the head of the Lauenental some seven or eight kilometres to the south of Gstaad. The valley is a green and gentle swathe of pastureland, a soft and seductive vale whose southern limits are somewhat marshy and whose upper slopes are neatly shorn in summer. To east and west the walls of the Lauenental have easy shoulders with tempting passes that lead to Lenk in one direction (via the Trüttlisberg Pass) and Gsteig (by the Krinnen Pass) in the other. There are paths that follow along these gentle grassy crests with fine views to enjoy, and there are several modest peaks to climb, especially those of the Lauenenhorn (2477m) and Gifer-

spitz (2542m) to the north-east; all of which combine to give Lauenen a head start as a centre for a walking holiday.

Lauenen is not so well known as many another Oberland resort, and in some ways that is to its benefit. It stands well to the west of the main tourist villages of Grindelwald, Mürren and Kandersteg, and but for the sole exception of Gsteig, is the last walking centre in canton Bern. It has a lovely 16th century church and a house dating from 1765 that graphically reveals the quality of local craftsmanship of another age. In common with many a Swiss village it is lively with flower boxes at its windows, its main street quietly attractive without concession to the rash of featureless architecture that has spoilt so many Alpine resorts. From the village you gaze south to where the mountains close off the end of the valley, and there, rising in a snowy mass, is the Wildhorn with its glacier-etched ridge leading westward to the neighbouring Arpelistock. It cannot stand comparison with the major massifs further to the east, but the Wildhorn massif has an undoubted charm all

its own. In the basin rimmed by these mountains there sits, unobserved from here, the Geltenhütte, an enchanting timber and stone-built mountain refuge that serves as a focus for this walk.

Some might be tempted to take a local bus from Lauenen to the Lauenensee at the roadhead and begin their walk from the lake itself, but that would be a mistake. The lake, about three kilometres south of the village, is the first major feature of the walk and it should be approached with stealth in order to gain maximum effect. So ignore temptation and start from Lauenen to follow the road up-valley a short distance until a minor road forks off to the right. This winds up among sloping pastures with a number of handsome chalets set in their midst, and then deteriorates to a track heading along the edge of pinewoods, and out again to a scattering of farms, each one enjoying views over the valley and up to the higher mountains gleaming ahead.

In about an hour the track swings round a slope enlivened with a frieze of trees, and there below stretches the green lake of Lauenensee.

The Gelten Hut, with its blankets out to air on a bright summer's day.
(Kev Reynolds)

It is a green lake, too. Clear, certainly, but with reed-lined banks and grass and trees reflected in it the water shimmers with a mirror of greenery.

At the far end of the lake, and set upon a bluff, a small restaurant offers refreshment to those who have travelled this far by bus. If you've walked from the village and have intentions of reaching the Gelten hut, you'll no doubt be keen to continue and save refreshment for later.

Beyond the restaurant a path begins to climb the hillside in tight zig-zags. It leads through patches of forest, climbing steadily all the while, and finally emerges to a delightful open pastureland hemmed in by sharp mountain walls, sliced by a cornflower-blue stream and with the double cascades of the Geltenschuss waterfall streaking the bare rocky hillside ahead. This is a delectable spot and it is understandably very popular as a site for family picnics.

This magical bowl of pasture, known as Feisseberg, marks the start of the Geltental, a nature reserve noted for its extravagant Alpine flora.

Wandering through pastures such as these, with an impression of remote seclusion, it is tempting to stray off-course to study garlands of wild flowers, to dawdle beneath the waterfall and capture rainbow patterns of spray dashing against the cliffs. And why not! Days in the hills should allow time to gather as many experiences as possible and on this walk there are so many aspects, so many features of mountain terrain to absorb. But back to the path, for it now breaks away to the right to climb rockier slopes by long zig-zags, bears left, crosses a stream and, climbing still, ducks behind a waterfall where it's almost impossible not to be dampened by spray. Alpenroses sprawl across the steep slopes beyond the waterfall and from here wonderful views are to be had looking back down-valley.

The path veers sharply to the right and takes you along a narrow cleft beside the stream that has successfully bored great roundels in its limestone bed. Then across the stream by way of a footbridge and the trail heads over a large grassy bluff, summer-bright with flowers, and at last reaches the hut (2002m), perched on a natural shelf with the Wildhorn rising behind it.

This is a splendid place to be on a clear summer's day with huge views to enjoy, for in three and a half hours you've wandered through one patch of paradise after another to reach a site of near-perfection. Back the way you have come you can see far out to the shrinking mountains of middle-Switzerland; a

The Wildhorn massif, and much of the route followed on this circuit, is seen to good effect from Lauenen.
(Kev Reynolds)

streaking of green tended valleys and blue undemonstrative peaks. But immediately behind the hut the hillside falls away sharply into a deep and secretive bowl of pasture with another waterfall crashing into it. Streams come pouring from the snow-and-ice-fields of the Wildhorn massif to join forces in those soft luxurious meadows, before breaking free through a minor gorge that then takes the new-born Geltenbach out to its tumultuous cascades, seen on the walk up to the hut.

Everywhere you look from the Gelten hut there is something rather special to focus attention on. It's a lovely place to be, and a difficult site to leave. The hut can sleep nearly a hundred in its dormitories, and from here mountaineers set out for routes on a variety

of neighbourhood peaks. But for those of us calling by on our walking route, it makes a convenient lunch stop, and when the guardian is in residence food and drinks are usually available.

Rising as a natural protective wall to the north-east of the hut a steep grassy knoll has a narrow path slanting up to its crown. The continuing route follows this, in preference to a return to Lauenen on the same trail as the upward route, and then heads northward high above the valley with a magnificent vista drawing you on. It's a narrow path, but not difficult. Along a grass-covered ridge the way then loses a little height and comes to an isolated alp hut, marked on the map as Usseri-Gelten, and continues round the slopes of the Follhore from

Having left the hut, the route then traverses the steep Gelten Alp with its fine view down to the Lauenensee.
(Kev Reynolds)

where, if you stop to gaze back towards the Arpelistock, stunning views are to be had. The Lauenensee can also be seen quite clearly, a pool of blue (no longer appearing green from here) glinting in a peaceful landscape.

The path descends steeply in places, once aided by a metal ladder, then veers round to an undulating scoop of hillside with the alp hamlet of Chüetungel nestling among the hummocks. Above the farms on the far side of the rough pastures a stony saddle offers a way to the Wildhorn hut, and from there down past the Iffigensee to Iffigenalp and eventually to Lenk. Following this would have the effect of extending the walk to a two-day outing or, for those with plenty of time at their disposal and energy to match, a three-day loop by return-ing from Lenk to Lauenen by way of the Trüttlisberg Pass.

There is a junction of paths by the stream which runs through Chüetungel, with a sign-post giving directions. There are two paths leading to Lauenen and the one to take is that which branches off to the left once you've crossed the stream.

At first it leads over more rough pastures, then descends tightly against a rock wall with a steep and exposed drop to the left. This is the most potentially dangerous section of the whole walk, and yet it is safe enough for those unaffected by exposure. Although it is a very narrow stretch of pathway there are fixed cables in the worst places as a safeguard. Even-tually the path eases and heads through forest, but when it emerges there are open pastures again with solitary alp huts and farm buildings on a natural shelf, or terrace, of hillside, giving them a human scale. Along this shelf it is worth pausing for a while to enjoy a backward view to the Geltenschuss and the Wildhorn snows above it. It all looks so far away.

Once down in the valley all that is needed is a gentle level walk down-valley a short dis-tance to Lauenen once more where you can relax with a cool drink on a café terrace and see the whole circuit of your walk laid out before you. There's something very satisfying in that.

Walk 6: *Diemtigtal to Simmental*
by Kev Reynolds

Location: Bernese Alps, Switzerland—to the south-west of Spiez.
How to get there: By train to Spiez via Thun, and train from there to Oey. Nearest international airport—Zürich or Bern. By road through Switzerland to Thun, Spiez and Oey.
Distance: 13 kilometres (8 miles).
Height gain: 818 metres.
Height loss: 1049 metres.
Time required: 4½–5 hours.
Start: Grimmialp.
Finish: St Stephan.
Type of walk: Moderately demanding, but the paths are not always well-defined. Some of the steep grass slopes could be very slippery when wet, and caution is then advised. No opportunities for refreshment along the way. The countryside explored during this walk is quietly lovely.
Valley bases: Oey, Diemtigen, Zweisimmen.
Map: Landeskarte der Schweiz 1:50,000 series, sheet no 5009 *Gstaad-Adelboden*.
Guidebook: *The Bernese Alps* by Kev Reynolds (Cicerone Press).

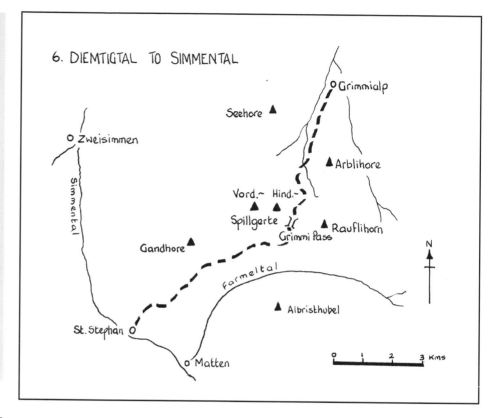

High pastures in a secret land

Almost every Alpine district has its own classic walk, many of which will be familiar (by repute at least) to most mountain wanderers, and I've sought to include a number of these in this collection. But it has been my aim to introduce lesser-known areas too, not simply long-time favourites. Hence the inclusion of this route which explores a quietly unassuming valley that just happens to be one of the loveliest in canton Bern, crosses a gentle ridge and descends through pasture and forest to the Simmental. Such a walk will give a great day out far from the crowds that throng some of the better-known footpaths.

The Diemtigtal cuts into a modest mountain landscape to the south-west of the lake of Thun, and too far north of the main Oberland crest to retain the glaciers and large snowfields that give other regions their instant appeal. This is a pastoral valley, green and lush, that is heavily wooded in places but with several little hamlets so unspoilt and attractive that in 1986 the Diemtigtal won an award for its architectural heritage. A number of shapely

peaks giving huge views embrace the head of the valley (Spillgerte, Männliflue and Seehore among them), and under them high alps, seemingly remote and isolated from the world, are open to the sun. This walk passes one of them on its way to the Grimmi Pass (or Grimmifurggi as it is also known).

To the north and west of the Diemtigtal the Simmental makes a long bow-like curve on its journey from the mountains above Lenk to the balmy idyll of the Thunersee at Spiez. It's an important valley for communications between the lakes of Geneva and Thun with the Jaun Pass and Col du Pillon completing the cross-mountain link; one joining the Simmental at Reidenbach, the other at Zweisimmen by way of Gsteig and Gstaad. Several other valleys flow into the Simmental, while the Diemtigtal is one of its major tributaries joining at the village of Oey, a neighbour of Latterbach a few kilometres west of Spiez.

For walkers tackling this route Oey is accessible by train on the Speiz-Zweisimmen line,

and from Oey there is a Postbus service to Grimmialp where the walk begins. If you have your own transport it is best to park in Oey and take the Postbus, returning to your vehicle by train from St Stephan at the end of the day.

The journey through the Diemtigtal is a delight. It's only about twelve kilometres from Oey to Grimmialp, but every kilometre is interesting. At first woods come down to the river, but these soon give way to neat pastures and meadows dotted with hamlets and secluded farms. Here and there sub-valleys are cut back, enticing and full of promise for other days. Then, just before reaching Grimmialp the valley divides. From the south-east flows the Fildrich stream, with the hamlet of the same name at the head of this branch of the valley, while from the south-west flows the Senggbach; the way to Grimmialp. The Postbus ends its journey outside the Hotel Spillgerten, which is the roadhead also for private vehicles. Once you have left this there will be no further opportunities for refreshment until the walk is concluded, other than goats' cheese for sale at a high alp just below the pass.

There's not much to Grimmialp, but the pastoral simplicity of it is full of charm. Broad and open here, it is an instantly attractive landscape that surrounds and as you set off to explore further, so the valley's charm becomes even more appealing. The hamlet sits in the heart of splendid walking country and from it there are other passes to tackle, other hillsides to visit, other alps to wander to. Apart from Grimmifurggi the crossing of the Scheidegg (1991m) to the south-west of Grimmialp is also worth considering. With more magnificent views from the pass, the route descends to Blankenburg in the Simmental down-valley of St Stephan, which marks the conclusion of this walk via Grimmifurggi.

The Grimmifurggi walk, signposted from the hotel at the road-head, takes you up-valley a short distance on a lane between meadows, then onto a grassy footpath beside a clear bubbling stream. This makes a gentle prelude, wandering on soft turf with the rich fragrance of pine in the breeze and the friendly chortle of stones shifting under the rush and wash of the stream. A rutted track then heads among trees and over rough pastures to link one or two farm buildings before another footpath with white-red-white bergweg paint flashes cuts uphill to yet another farm.

Above this the hills are clothed in mature pine forest, damp and cool with permanent shade and with a track winding through. Alongside the track wild flowers and soft fruits add variety and colour in season, while one can imagine any number of deer watching your progress from the anonymous shadow of the trees.

It's an easy track to follow and it emerges at last above the treeline to a good clean view of the steep limestone walls of the Spillgerte Rothorn and Chalberhorn; walls to set a rock climber's fingers itching. Below these walls an isolated farmstead nestles among the undulations of a pitted pastureland. In early summer, before the cattle are brought up to graze, flowers are everywhere; fragrant, colourful and a sheer delight to see. Streams come dashing in narrow clefts, and hillocks and small grassy bluffs are covered with alpenroses.

We came here in mid-July and grew heady with the natural perfume, sat upon a bluff to eat an early lunch and gazed with undiluted pleasure at the long shaft of the Diemtigtal below winding peacefully into the haze, its upper alps far off picked out by the sun and promising more good walks to reach them. Alpine choughs croaked among the high crags and crickets set the grasses alive with an elec-

An old barn door seen at Grimmialp in the Diemtigtal. (Kev Reynolds)

tric buzzing. There were butterflies drifting from one flower head to another and the day was blessed with beauty.

The pass is obvious and detected above the alp. It is reached by way of a narrow, often faint, path that crosses and re-crosses little streams and winds up hillocks bright with yellow flowers. Grimmifurggi (2057m) is an open, gentle saddle between the Spillgerte Rothorn and the Rauflihorn, a green-slung saucer of buttercups with views overlooking fresh valley systems to the south and snatches of snowpeaks far beyond them, notably those of the Wildstrubel.

On the southern side of the pass a steep grass slope (slippery after rain) leads down to

South of the pass the trail cuts across steep grass slopes way above the Fermeltal. (Kev Reynolds)

The steep walls of Spillgerte lure the walker up towards the pass of Grimmifurggi. (Kev Reynolds)

another lone farm, Obere Bluttlig (1983m), clustered with cowbells hanging from its eaves and with a tremendous panorama from its windows. The path forks here with one branching off to the left on a steady contour leading towards the head of the Farmeltal, while ours continues its descent. A second farm (Untere Bluttlig) sits two hundred metres below and here the path forks once more. This time it is necessary to branch off to the right on a westerly descending traverse that takes you through steep woodlands below the south-west ridge of the Spillgerte massif.

This woodland stretch crosses several gullies and streams and finally comes out to an open spur of mountainside at the Dachbode alp whose large farmhouse is served by a broad track. The track leads on and eventually goes down into the valley by way of innumerable hairpins, but there is a waymark to direct the continuing path away from the track soon after leaving the farm and this heads across meadowland again to pass another isolated farm, this one marooned in the midst of pastures starred with huge white daisies.

Farm leads to farm and the panorama grows in scale as the Simmental comes fully into view below. The mountains are not massive, nor intimidating. They are not slung with glaciers and snowfields, nor adorned with jagged aiguilles. These are friendly mountains walling a friendly valley. A living, working landscape. Farms reassure. Summer-only in occupancy they sit upon the hillsides and smile at the sun. Window boxes brighten otherwise dark timbers and small garden plots are fenced against night-marauding deer.

Down in the Simmental various small ham-lets and villages make patterns against the shorn meadows, the river linking one with another lined by the railway. Down there lies St Stephan, a small village yet much larger than Grimmialp at the start of the walk, and a narrow road goes to it from some of these upper farmsteads. Happily it is not necessary to follow the road all the way, for there are footpath short-cuts through yet more pastures and woods, familiar paint flashes directing the way at road crossings.

Then at last you reach the bed of the Ober Simmental not far from St Stephan's railway station, exchanging steep turf for level tarmac, the peace of the hills for a modest valley industry. It comes not as a rude awakening, but as a gentle reminder that there are two sides (and more) to life in the Alps. Yet neither is more real than the other.

WALK 7: *The Petersgrat Crossing by Kev Reynolds*

Location: Bernese Alps, Switzerland.
How to get there: By train to Kandersteg via the Bern-Brig (Lötschberg) line. Fast, efficient service. The nearest airport is at Zürich or Bern. Minibus taxi from Kandersteg to Selden.
Distance: 20 kilometres (12½ miles).
Height gain: 1570 metres (5151ft).
Height loss: 1335 metres (4380ft).
Time required: 2 days.
Start: Selden (Gasterntal).
Finish: Fafleralp (Lötschental).
Valley base: Kandersteg.
Type of walk: Strenuous; a glacier walk only to be attempted by experienced mountain walkers (or under their guidance) equipped with rope, ice-axe and crampons—and the knowledge of how to use them.
Map: Landeskarte der Schweiz 1:50,000 series. Sheet no 264 Jungfrau.
Guidebook: *The Bernese Alps* by Kev Reynolds (Cicerone Press).

7. THE PETERSGRAT CROSSING
8. THE LÖTSCHENTAL HIGH ROUTE

A glacier trek in the Bernese Alps

The Bernese Alps have a heart of ice. Behind the stern north faces of Eiger, Mönch and Jungfrau there lies a vast tract of snowfield and glacier moulded together like a displaced Polar ice-cap, a monochrome wonderland of great beauty, a landscape consisting of huge jutting peaks above a scene of permanent winter.

There are icefields on the northern flanks of the Oberland, too, but these are mostly hanging glaciers draped down the face of the mountains—the last remaining vestige of those huge rivers of ice that long ago carved some of the loveliest valleys in all of Switzerland—if not in Europe. But on the western edge of the Oberland crown there is one particularly large sheet of snow and ice that is a remnant of an ice-cap that once adorned much of the Bernese Alps. This is the Petersgrat, running in a long, high and narrow plateau at more than 3100 metres to the west of the Jungfrau, between the valleys of the Gasterntal to the north and the Lötschental to the south. This ice-cap feeds the easy glacier of the Kanderfirn which flows down to the Gasterntal, while to the south it drops steeply with several

smaller glaciers into the head of a number of sharp, but delightful little valleys that in turn feed the Lötschental.

The crossing of the Petersgrat, first made in 1712 by Samuel Bodmer, makes a superb outing, a two-day expedition that takes you from flower pasture to flower pasture with an arctic wasteland in between. Although the Kanderfirn is an easy glacier without major crevasses to negotiate in a normal summer, all standard safety precautions—which implies the use of rope, ice-axe and crampons—should be adopted from the time you gain it at the head of the Gasterntal, to the time you desert the Petersgrat's ice at the head of the Uister Tal.

There is a mountain hut conveniently situated under the small island lump of the Mut

thorn right at the head of the Kanderfirn in a wild and desolate (yet utterly magical) spot, and this makes an ideal overnight's resting place. The Mutthorn hut (2898m) is set in a sea of ice overlooking the much steeper icefield of the Tschingelfirn which pours away from its door towards the unseen Lauterbrunnen valley. Ice is all around, in bold forms of towering cliff and in deep craters with the under-blue exposed to the levelling rays of the evening sun. A night spent in the Mutthorn hut will undoubtedly be a night to remember.

This walk is best considered by those having a base at Kandersteg, for there's a minibus taxi service running most mornings from the town's railway station as far as the hamlet of Selden in the Gasterntal, and at the end of the walk one can easily return to Kandersteg by way of the railway from Goppenstein which feeds northward through the Lötschberg tunnel.

Day 1

At the southern end of the long Kandertal, three or four kilometres beyond Kandersteg, the valley is blocked by a sudden upthrust of mountains, but out of a narrow and shadowed ravine comes bursting the wild Kander river, a frantic thrash of spume and spray as the torrent finds escape between steep and overhanging walls of permanently-wet rock. This is practically the only indication one has that a valley is to be found there. The Gasterntal holds its secrets well.

A footpath climbs up beside the river from Eggeschwand in the damp shadows of the ravine to enter the valley, while a narrow private road winds in a tortuous zig-zag through the same ravine, but on the opposite bank. Path and road unite where the valley opens to level pasture and forest with streams flowing in undisciplined waywardness across the meadows and invariably amongst the trees too.

Given an extra day it would be worth forsaking the minibus ride to walk from Kandersteg as far as Selden (a three-hour walk, but worth taking four in order to explore the valley) and to spend the night in one of the rustic mountain inns there prior to going up to the Mutthorn hut. Indeed, it would be possible (but not advisable) to make an early start and to walk all the way from Kandersteg to the hut in one go, but that would be rather foolish. This is a route to enjoy at an unhurried pace. After all, the very best of the mountains, like a gourmet meal, should be savoured, not bolted. Indigestion of the spirit is as unwelcome as indigestion of the stomach!

The minibus taxi, then, leaves Kandersteg railway station around 9.30 in the morning and bumps its way into the Gasterntal. Almost at once the valley captures your imagination with its long ribbons of waterfall sprinkling the steep rocky walls, the streams winding through the bed of the valley, the dark intensity of the forests, the snowpeaks hinting above and the full-blown extravagance of its flower meadows. Oh, in early summer the Gasterntal is a wild garden of great beauty.

Selden seems not to belong to the twentieth century. The two mountain inns there are romantic places of weathered timbers, of creaking floors and an outlook straight from the brothers Grimm. From the hamlet a path branches south to Gfällalp and on to another classic crossing of the ridge to the Lötschental by way of the Lötschenpass. Taken in reverse, this would make an obvious return route from the Lötschental, given time and favourable weather, thereby creating a three or four-day circuit.

The track/road (but not the minibus) continues beyond Selden and goes as far as the farm of Heimritz (1632m), one of those farms that could so easily have featured in *Heidi*, with goats grazing all around and nothing but raw mountain scenery from its doorway. A path continues, goes through an idyllic region of dwarf pine, soft turf and boulders stationed among them as if put there by the hand of a landscape gardener, and then crosses to the true left bank of the Kander stream. On a clear day the icefall at the southern end of the Kanderfirn, here called the Alpetligletscher, can be seen some way ahead, and as the walk progresses so the ice cliffs grow in stature and severity.

The walk to the head of the valley takes you through some rough country undermined by the burrows of marmots and, higher, coloured by alpenroses. But no matter how rough the country is, the path itself, though narrow in places, is never less than adequate. On one crossing I came up here to meet an elderly Englishman wandering alone at a sedate pace. We chatted for a few minutes and he confessed with a certain nostalgia in his voice that this was his first year in the Alps without his ice-axe, explaining that he was now too old for any guide to take him on. "They're afraid I might die on the spot," he said. Nevertheless, even in advanced old age he was still able to find pleasures in following valley footpaths into the inner recesses of the mountains. No doubt he had his memories of the high places, but he found plenty of rewards too, simply in being there. There was a lesson or two to be learnt from his example.

The path goes up onto a moraine wall and on to a steepening bank bright with alpenroses in mid-summer, with the glacier's icefall seen above to the left. Looking back the view is splendid to the large mass of the Balmhorn and its close neighbour Altels apparently blocking the south-western end of the valley. Steeper and steeper the trail zig-zags over a bluff and then levels to draw alongside the glacier. This is the place to tie onto the rope.

Initially you ascend smooth terraces of rock that are often coated with grit, before getting onto the glacier proper, then head straight up the gently-sloping icefield keeping more or less to its right-hand side, and with an upper tier of ice above your right shoulder. Bordering the Kanderfirn on the left rise the steep cliffs that form the southern flanks of the Blümlisalp—those fine peaks that plunge dramatically into the Oeschinensee above Kandersteg on their far side.

The ascent of the Kanderfirn is uncomplicated and, by virtue of its easy angle, not too demanding. Given good conditions it will take about $2\frac{1}{2}$ hours from the end of the glacier to the hut. But should clouds begin to fall and visibility falter, it could be quite another story, for it is important to locate the correct route to the Mutthorn hut.

As you approach the broad head of the glacier with the Tschingelhorn off to the right, a minor peaklet appears like a cock's comb ahead. This is the Mutthorn. The hut is found immediately below its right-hand broken rocks, but the first view you have of it is only a few moments before you actually reach it. It lies below, on the north-eastern side of the saddle and apparently half-buried in a chilly basin of ice—a memorable setting.

From the Petersgrat ice cap you gaze across to the Bietschhorn and the snow-peaks of the Pennine Alps. (Kev Reynolds)

Day 2

With the minimal amount of time required to mount the Petersgrat from the Mutthorn hut, it is hardly necessary to join the climbers in their pre-dawn starts, but my advice would be to rise early anyway—before first light—in order to have breakfast and to be away as the sun comes up. There is an indefinable magic to be experienced at these altitudes at dawn, with the pure light draining into far-off valleys lost still in the misty coverlet of night, with individual peaks and peaklets rising like islands of an archipelago from a froth of vapour. A magic that never fades no matter how many times you encounter it, no matter how often you crunch over the ice with frost crystals dancing before your eyes as you peer at the sun-stained mountain tops, at the chasing shadows and the voiceless beauty of the lost world below. And from above the Mutthorn hut you have all that and more. The Eiger is seen side-on, sharp as a spear, the Jungfrau unrecognisable from here, the back of the Breithorn and the Tschingelhorn (first to catch the sun), while out through a scoop in the mountain wall the modest Faulhorn stands proud above other peaks of the middle ranges. It's a grand way to start a day.

From the hut you head almost due south, rising steadily towards the lowest point of the vast Petersgrat ice-cap which is found just to the right of the Tschingelhorn's south-west ridge. It will take less than an hour to reach it, but you will be in no hurry to depart, for the views are again staggering to contemplate.

As you gain the *grat* you gaze straight across the hinted gulf of the Lötschental to the lovely Bietschhorn (3934m), a graceful pyramid of rock and ice with its north-eastern ridge leading the eye irresistibly to the Lötschentaler Breithorn and the Schinhorn. But it is out to the south that your attention is suddenly drawn, for way off on the far side of the imagined Rhone valley the whole incredible line of the Pennine Alps stretches from the Dom to the Mont Blanc range. Only Monte Rosa and the Matterhorn appear to be missing from that glittering array, hidden shyly behind other intermediate peaks. But the Weisshorn is seen, as are the Zinalrothorn, Ober Gabelhorn, Mont Blanc de Cheilon, Pigne d'Arolla, Grand Combin, Grandes Jorasses and dozens more. The whole magnificent world of the high Alps, it seems, is laid before you. Without question it is a panorama worth striving for.

From the Petersgrat two small but distinctive valleys fall below into the Lötschental. That to the left is the Inners Tal, while that

The Bietschhorn, first climbed by Leslie Stephen in 1859, seen from the lower reaches of the Uister Tal. (Kev Reynolds)

On the descent to the Lötschental the huge wall that links the Bietschhorn, Lötschentaler Breithorn and Schinhorn is seen in all its glory. *(Kev Reynolds)*

directly ahead is the Uister Tal. Either may be descended, but for the purposes of this route the choice is the Uister Tal. You slant down the steep icy slope making towards the left-hand side of the valley head, and soon come to the edge of the glacier and onto rocks. From here the narrow valley plunges wild and steeply, at first rough with boulders and scree, with streams racing and rocks clattering under-foot, but lower down, on a path at last, you come to the first grass, the first tangle of alpen-roses, the first small flower—and a stunning

view ahead to the Gletscherstafel wall framed by the sharp V of the Uister Tal's slopes. It is an amazing piece of natural architecture, and to my mind it offers one of the very best views on a morning of unimaginable beauty.

Near the base of the valley you leap over the stream and meet a crossing path which you can either take to the left, which leads down to Fafleralp near the head of the Lötschental (for the bus to Goppenstein and the return to Kandersteg by train through the Lötschberg tunnel), or to the right, following the *Lötschen-*

taler Höhenweg on a long and tiring walk to Kummenalp, where you can spend the night prior to tackling the crossing of the Lötschen-pass back to Selden in the Gasterntal. But whichever route you decide to take back to Kandersteg, the crossing of the Petersgrat will remain a spectacular highlight to savour in the long dark winter evenings at home.

Memories, of course, can be almost as rich as the magic of making dreams come true.

WALK 8: *The Lötschental High Route by Kev Reynolds*

Location: The Lötschental, north of the Rhône valley in Switzerland.
How to get there: By train via Bern through the Lötschberg tunnel to Goppenstein. International airports—Geneva, Bern and Zürich. By road through Switzerland to Kandersteg and then through the rail tunnel to Goppenstein, or across either the Grimsel or Furka Passes into the Rhône. Past Visp turn north on the sign to Goppenstein.
Distance: 18.5 kilometres (11 miles).
Height gain: 731 metres.
Height loss: 319 metres.
Time required: About 7 hours.
Type of walk: Apart from the initial steep ascent to Faldumalp, this is a mostly gentle, easy-angled walk with the possibility of breaking it at Lauchernalp with cable-car down to Wiler.
Start: Ferden.
Finish: Fafleralp.
Valley bases: Ferden, Kippel, Blatten, Wiler or Fafleralp. Camp site in Kippel.
Map: Landeskarte der Schweiz 1:50,000 series. Sheet no 264 *Jungfrau.*
Guidebook: *The Valais—Switzerland* by Kev Reynolds (Cicerone Press).

High alps and magnificent views

Of all the spectacular valleys draining into the Rhône, the Lötschental, the longest flowing from the north, is unquestionably one of the loveliest. There are many well-travelled wanderers who reckon it to be among the finest of all the valleys of the Alps, and I am inclined to agree with them.

The Lötschental came late into the twentieth century and, either by divine providence or careful forethought, it hasn't quite caught up yet. That is one of its charms. A number of its villages have a spirit of unworldliness about them; a sense of unhurried antiquity coupled with a traditional folklore symbolised by grotesque masks of the *Tschaeggaettae*—carved from wood and with animal hair or fur attached, and with cows' teeth fixed to gaping mouths. There are the 'Toy Town' soldiers who parade in scarlet tunics and white trousers

for civic ceremonies and local weddings, and there is the neat traditional architecture of its houses, typical of the Valais.

Narrow cobbled alleys make a maze of every village back-street. Houses and hay barns lean one against another, many raised on staddle stones. Their churches are slender-spired, white painted and delicately handsome against the dark timbers of neighbourhood homes. Yet darkness is not a feature that remains in the mind, because flowers brighten window boxes and surround the fountains that grace each village square. Flowers are in the meadows and on the hillsides, and peace washes the valley in a grace of calm.

At its head the retreating tongue of the Langgletscher pokes over the saddle of the Lötschenlücke, beyond which lies that great arctic basin of converging glaciers that forms the icy heart of the Bernese Alps. Yet the Lötschental is not an icy world at all. In fact it is a sun-trap of a valley. A blissfully warm glen of unparalleled loveliness with its shorn meadows dotted with hay barns, its dark forests, black-timbered villages above a clear-running river and a southern wall of impressive peaks dominated by the immaculate Bietschhorn, first climbed in 1859 by Leslie Stephen. And half-way along the northern wall which divides the canton of Valais from that of Bern, there's a green shelf speckled with eight little alp hamlets linked by a magnificent pathway: the *Lötschentaler Höhenweg.*

The *Höhenweg*, or high path, is the classic walk of the valley and one of the very best in all the Valais. Every one of the alp hamlets visited along the way has its own special character (a number of them have places of refreshment, too) that helps to enliven the route with interest and colour. The path itself is a carefully graded trail that undulates along a vague terrace of hillside, and it is only the initial climb to it from the valley that is particularly steep or strenuous. And there are, of course, the views; wonderful views that encompass the whole majesty of the Lötschental in a single glance. Views that insist on drawing your attention away from the pathway to gaze on the Bietschhorn opposite—or way back to the south, far beyond the suggested gulf of the Rhône valley, to where Monte Rosa stubs the horizon with a glistening crown of ice.

It's a fairly long day's outing—starting from Ferden in the bed of the valley, it will measure just over 18 kilometres and require around seven hours of walking, without rest stops—but it is sometimes eased by being tackled in two separate trips with the mid-way use of cable-car from Wiler to Lauchernalp. The walk described here is the full route, ending near the head of the valley at Fafleralp from where a Postbus serves the rest of the valley's villages.

Ferden to Fafleralp

Ferden is the last village in the valley before it curves southward to Goppenstein, noted as the southern opening of the Lötschberg railway tunnel. Ferden itself is an attractive place with a pretty church and a friendly cluster of houses backed by a steep slope of forest below a grassy hillside, and it is this slope that has to be tackled first to reach the start of the *Höhenweg.* A signpost in the village square by the church directs the path to Faldumalp, the first of the alp hamlets on the high path.

It's a steep haul with more than 660 metres of height to gain before the route levels, but it is made with many windings, first through forest shade, then out to sloping pastures with a surprise of a view along the length of the valley, now some way below. This view more than repays the effort required to win it and sets a seal of approval on the day's walk.

Faldumalp is gained after about an hour and a half; a glorious little hamlet of snug chalets and barns, and a simply delightful timber chapel perched on a knoll overlooking the valley and guyed down against high winds. I know of few habitations more idyllically set than this, the panorama from every doorway sufficient to answer all one's dreams.

From it there are other good walks to entice you to return. One leads up to the lofty summit viewpoint of Niwen (2769m); another much-lauded route goes over the Restipass to Leukerbad, and the first stretch of this latter route is taken by the high path as far as Restialp. To walk from Faldumalp to Restialp is an easy stroll along a narrow, and in places exposed, pathway that dodges in and out of larch trees and shrubs of bilberry and alpenrose. It takes you northward round the slope of the Alplighorn, beyond which a stream is crossed in the bed of a combe coming from the Restipass. Just beyond the stream the path winds up to the hamlet of Restialp (2098m) where refreshments are available.

One of the good things about walking in the Alps is the frequency with which one has the opportunity to break for refreshment; sometimes at a secluded farm that doubles as a restaurant, sometimes at a little alp hamlet such as Restialp. There will be plenty of other temptations along the *Höhenweg*, too. Temptations to sit in the sunshine with a cold drink before you, beautiful views wherever you look, and the winding trail teasing you on when the bill has been paid.

The route continues, now heading northeastwards to round the spur of a mountain with the Bietschhorn dramatic-looking across the depths of the valley. In half an hour from Restialp you come to Kummenalp in a bowl of pastureland at the foot of a hanging valley, at the head of which is the Lötschenpass, a classic crossing that leads to the Gasterntal and Kandersteg. Kummenalp has a *gasthof* with beds and dormitory accommodation, and refreshments may also be had here too.

The path is broader now, the angle steady as it follows a contour at just over 2,000 metres and heading a little north of east. With views dominated almost every step of the way by the Bietschhorn, forty minutes will see you to the next alp on the route, Hockenalp (2048m). This little cluster of timber chalets and hay barns is situated on a shelf of cricket-busy pasture directly above Kippel, one of the main villages of the Lötschental from which it is reached by an extremely steep trail, and beneath the Hockenhorn, unseen from the hamlet through the foreshortening of the slope above. Once more, refreshments may be had here.

Faldumalp, with its little timber chapel perched above the Lötschental, one of the loveliest valleys in the Alps. *(Kev Reynolds)*

For much of the walk the lovely Bietschhorn is in your sights across the valley. (Kev Reynolds)

On the next stage, the twenty-minute stroll along the path to Lauchernalp, you cross the valley's only ski region, where there is cable-car access from Wiler. If there is any threat to the continued Shangri-La-like existence of the Lötschental, it will surely come with an expansion of this ski development, and those of us who have known the valley idyll at its best will watch the future here with anxious eyes.

Leaving Lauchernalp behind, and with the glacier at the head of the valley gleaming bright in the afternoon sunlight, the path slopes down a little, still edging the hillside above shrubs and trees, the low valley pastures making neat patterns far below where they have been cut and raked. Then the red shutters of Weritzalp (Weritzstafel on the map) appear ahead. Yet again it is possible to buy refreshments at a modest little hut perched on the steeply-sloping hillside; a few tables and chairs squashed against one another on a handkerchief-sized terrace above the pathway. The chalets here are accessible from the valley by a narrow, twisting private road, but you'd hardly know it, and you wander through on the continuing path that slopes down again, now among trees, to reach the few hay barns and alp huts of Tellialp (Tellistafel—1865m).

To one side of the hamlet a stream comes dashing down the hillside, having been born among the shallow glaciers that form the southern edge of the great Petersgrat ice-cap high above. The path crosses the stream, rounds another spur and follows an undulating course among patches of larch and pine before coming to a little teardrop of a tarn (Schwarzsee) trapped in a narrow trough at 1860 metres.

From Tellialp to Fafleralp the path keeps mostly to the shade of pinewoods, and views are caught as brief snatches of wonder between the trees. On the way, easing round the hillside, the route crosses another boisterous stream coming from the wild-looking Uisters Tal down which the Petersgrat Crossing emerges (see Walk 7), and shortly after slopes down to Fafleralp (1787m).

Fafleralp is another interesting and ancient-looking cluster of chalets near the road-head. There is a large hotel tucked against sparse woods, and a superb modern chapel nearby that is well worth visiting before catching the Postbus back to your valley base. The chapel makes a stark, but not unlovely contrast to that other chapel seen at the beginning of the day in Faldumalp, while if it's spiritual uplift that you seek, you'll have had more than your fair share on the walk leading from one to the other.

Here on the Lötschental High Route, as much as anywhere I know of, you'll have had a glimpse of heaven on earth.

WALK 9: *The Rottal Hut by Kev Reynolds*

Location: High on the south-west flanks of the Jungfrau at the head of the Lauterbrunnen valley in the Bernese Oberland, Switzerland.
How to get there: By train to Interlaken, and from there to Lauterbrunnen. Postbus from Lauterbrunnen to Stechelberg. Nearest international airport—Zürich or Bern. By road through Switzerland to Bern, Thun, Interlaken and through the Lauterbrunnen valley to Stechelberg.
Distance: 12 kilometres (7½ miles).
Time required: 8 hours (5 hours up, 3 hours descent).
Height gain/loss: 1845 metres.
Start/finish: Stechelberg.
Type of walk: Extremely steep and strenuous, some short stretches require scrambling—but aided by fixed cable. The paths are mostly clear, if narrow, but are often rough under foot. Magnificent high mountain views.
Valley bases: Stechelberg, Lauterbrunnen.
Map: Landeskarte der Schweiz 1:50,000 series, sheet no 264 *Jungfrau*.
Guidebooks: *The Bernese Alps* by Kev Reynolds (Cicerone Press). *Bernese Alps Central* by Robin G Collomb (Alpine Club) (Climbing guide).

On the flanks of the Jungfrau

There are several steep walks in this book, but few that are steeper than the approach to the Rottal hut. One section of the route involves the use of fixed cable to aid the ascent of a rather severe gully, a short stretch of scrambling that requires a little care to negotiate, especially if others are on the grit-and stone-littered rockbands above, but the remainder of the walk will be straightforward enough—if somewhat strenuous to tackle, and demanding about five hours or so from valley to hut.

At the southern end of the Lauterbrunnen valley a great amphitheatre of snow and ice peaks forms a stupendous north-facing wall, guarded by the Gspaltenhorn to the west and the Jungfrau to the east. Going anti-clockwise from the Gspaltenhorn there is the glacial saddle of the Tschingelpass, then the rocky lump of the Mutthorn—unseen from the valley

At the foot of a rock band that is overcome with the aid of a fixed chain, you gain an idea of how steep the walk has been so far. The Lauterbrunnen Valley is seen far below. (Kev Reynolds)

as it is hidden behind the higher, curious ear-like horns of the Lauterbrunnen Wetterhorn, with the Tschingelhorn immediately next to it. Then comes the saddle of the Wetterlücke and the lovely Breithorn (not to be confused with the Breithorn above Zermatt, nor the Breithorn a short distance to the south across the depths of the Lötschental). The Lauterbrunnen Breithorn is a true 'character' mountain that commands attention from the valley itself, but following the great wall eastwards there are plenty of other fine peaks to admire, too. From it the next peak of note is the Grosshorn, neighboured by the Mittaghorn, the splendid Ebneflue and Gletscherhorn, the Rottalhorn and, finally, the Jungfrau itself. Each of the summits on view, save for that of the Gspaltenhorn, is well above three and a half thousand metres, and bearing in mind the comparatively low altitude of the valley, the height of these peaks seems quite astonishing.

The Rottal hut is perched high above the upper basin of the Lauterbrunnen valley under the south-western arête of the Jungfrau. All around there are high peaks and plunging precipices; hanging glaciers, snowfields, rubble slopes and rock faces. Directly opposite the hut to the south, across the magical cirque of the Rottal, the north face of the Ebneflue (or Äbene Flue, 3962m) gleams like a mirror of ice. It's a superb location with stunning Alpine vistas, given favourable conditions, and the walk up to it and back to the valley again, will provide a good day's exercise filled with a high degree of visual enjoyment.

The road through the Lauterbrunnen valley ends at Stechelberg, a small farming hamlet with camp site and hotel accommodation, that is served by Postbus from the railway station in Lauterbrunnen village. Despite its small size it makes a good (if low-level) base for a walking holiday, for there are some tremendous routes available from it. The route to the Rottal hut is just one of them.

It begins by following a broad paved footpath heading up-valley beyond the roadhead with the Weisse Lütschine river boiling through its channelled bed below to the right. Immediately away from the road, and despite the company of the many people who wander along the initial stretch of this path, one gains a gathering sense of remoteness, of intimacy with the mountains that seem to girdle themselves around you. There are short but steep pastures rising above, and for a while plenty of trees and bushes with birds darting among them. Then, immediately before the path crosses a stream, a second, much more narrow path breaks away to the left, signposted to Stufenstein and the Rottal hut.

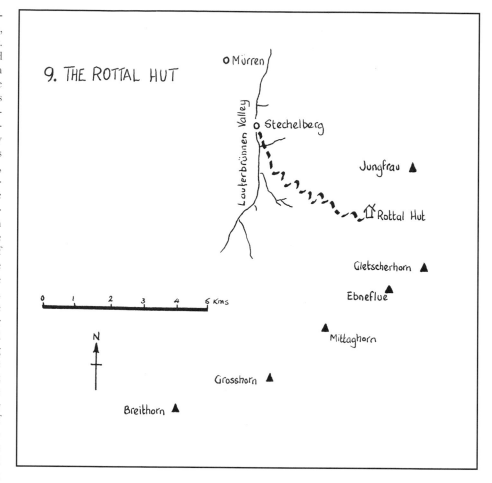

At once you realise that there's a certain determination required for this walk; the way makes no concessions to tired legs or untrained bodies, for it rears up the hillside in a series of tight zig-zags. None of this should come as a surprise, for if you study the map in advance you will notice that while Stechelberg lies at an altitude of a modest 910 metres, the Rottal hut is at 2755 metres—that leaves a difference of 1845 metres, or 6053 feet, to make up in a horizontal difference of only about four kilometres! It is, not surprisingly, a very steep walk.

The first hour is almost entirely in the shade of trees, but with views between them to the big mountains ahead. Now and then there are open sections, and having at last left the woods behind there is a lovely view of the Breithorn forming a backcloth with a solitary alp hut perched upon a slope of pasture as a foreground.

Up and up the path continues, goes through a fenced pasture and then bears right to cross a stream draining through its steep, stony bed.

On the far side the way maintains its punishing angle, now with the icefall of the Rottal's glacier seen way above and the icy face of the Mittaghorn off to the right. Sheep graze the monstrous slopes here, and on my way down from the hut one hot summer's afternoon I stopped to rest on a grassy bluff, draped my sweat-soaked shirt over a rock to dry and wandered around taking photographs. With my back turned, one of the sheep took my shirt between its teeth and made off with it!

Pastures give way to a wilderness of rock and scree, vertical crags running in a line above that are split here and there by dark-shadowed gullies. The route to the hut formerly cut off to the left to pass below the cliffs of the Bäreflue, but this was swamped by a huge avalanche in 1976 and is today threatened by icefall from the glacier seen above, so the path was re-routed. Now you go up to the base of the cliffs, some of which are overhanging, and follow them to the right until coming to a neat gully with a fixed chain hanging down it. Paint flashes are a reasonable.

The hut, perched above a sea of ice, gazes across to the Lauterbrunnen Breithorn. (Kev Reynolds)

guide as far as the gully, but once you arrive there it is advisable to listen for the sound of anyone descending. If there are others above you, stand clear of any stones being knocked down and wait until the rock face is empty before taking your turn. There is nothing difficult in this short ascent for those with a little scrambling experience, but the narrow shelves of rock are invariably littered with grit and stones, and it is important not to dislodge any of these onto people below.

Having overcome the rock face you rejoin an obvious path. This swings in easy windings up a boulderscape that was once a huge moraine. Marmots may be heard or seen here, as well as chamois and even ibex. Glacier crowfoot, saxifrage and gentians brighten the way, but it is the presence of those huge mountains, now so close, that dominates the walk as you work a way up onto the crest of moraine that has been bulldozed over countless centuries by the glaciers that converge in the braw scooped bowl of the Rottal below to the right. This bowl is draped with ice; contorted ice whose bucklings and sawn-off sèracs give zebra-patterns of blue amid a sea of white, with the north wall of the Ebneflue rising so dramatically above it.

The path heads along the top of the moraine wall with the tiny glimmer of the hut

All the way to the hut eyes are inevitably drawn towards the great bevy of peaks blocking the head of the Lauterbrunnen Valley. (Kev Reynolds)

now seen for the first time ahead. But it will take a while yet before you reach it. Rising high above it, but seriously foreshortened from this angle, is the Jungfrau, virtually unrecognisable as the graceful snow-draped monarch that is seen to such effect from Wengen and other points north. From here it is a jumble of rock and ice, misshapen and confusing.

At the end of the moraine a steep snow slope has to be crossed, tucked high against a band of cliffs, then onto rocks for a short and easy scramble, aided by another length of fixed cable. More flowers adorn tiny crevices in the rock and melting snow drips from lip to lip while the sun shines—but if you leave the hut early on a morning sharp with frost, these rocks may be glazed with ice and quite lethal under foot.

The Rottal hut is found nearby, set among the boulders of a slope of rock and rubble overlooking the glaciers. There are towering mountains all around, reflecting the sun off their blank ice walls, cornices curling from lofty ridges and picked out clearly against the deep blue sky. There are snow cols and icefalls, darkened walls of rock and ancient moraines slowly absorbing vegetation. There is a herd of ibex here too, and some individuals have sufficiently overcome their shyness to stray near to the hut and if you are quiet you may well be able to watch them at close quarters.

It is a delightful setting for a delightful hut. Owned by the Interlaken Section of the Swiss Alpine Club, and with a guardian in residence during the main summer season, the hut can officially accommodate 46 in its dormitories, but like so many others in the Alps there will be periods when three times that number of climbers will be claiming a corner in which to sleep, and it is on occasions such as these that

mountain huts quickly lose their appeal. But go there all the same, for the approach to it, though strenuous and demanding, is a real joy, and the growing intimacy with the high mountain environment that is achieved, both on the approach and at the hut itself, will repay any effort involved in getting there. Go there and sit in the sun with a flask of the guardian's tea replacing some of your lost liquids, and gaze at the stunning views, and be thankful.

The return to the valley will necessarily be the same as that taken on the ascent, but special care should be given to the crossing of the snow slope just below the hut, and to the descent of the gully in the cliffs of the Bäreflue. In many ways the descent is as tiring as the way up, and by the time you reach level ground once more in Stelchelberg, you'll know you've had a day out. But what a day that will have been!

Walk 10: *Schynige Platte To Grindelwald by Kev Reynolds*

Location: Bernese Oberland, Switzerland.
How to get there: By train to Interlaken, and change there for Grindelwald.
Nearest international airport—Zürich or Bern.
By road through Switzerland to Bern, Thun, Interlaken and Grindelwald.
Distance: 19 kilometres (12 miles)—the full walk. 15 kms to First.
Time required: 6-7 hours.
Height gain: 693 metres.
Height loss: 1646 metres.

Type of walk: Easy but long, on good paths most of the way. Most height gain is achieved effortlessly. Splendid views elevate this to one of the finest day walks in the Alps.
Valley bases: Wilderswil or Grindelwald.
Map: Landeskarte der Schweiz 1:50,000 series, sheet no 5004 *Berner Oberland.*
Guidebooks: *The Bernese Alps* by Kev Reynolds (Cicerone Press). *100 Hikes in the Alps* by Ira Spring & Harvey Edwards (The Mountaineers/Cordee).

A ridge walk in view of the Eiger

Any book of selected walks in the Alps should include this one. And no wonder, for it's a true classic which gives one of the loveliest days out you could possibly wish for. The views are stunning. The paths are well-marked and adequately signposted. There are opportunities for refreshment along the way. The scenery constantly changes; there's the chance to stand on a minor summit that is a major viewpoint, and you end with a choice of either riding Europe's

Soon after leaving Schynige Platte the path edges along a ridge that drops in the north towards the Brienzersee.
(*Kev Reynolds*)

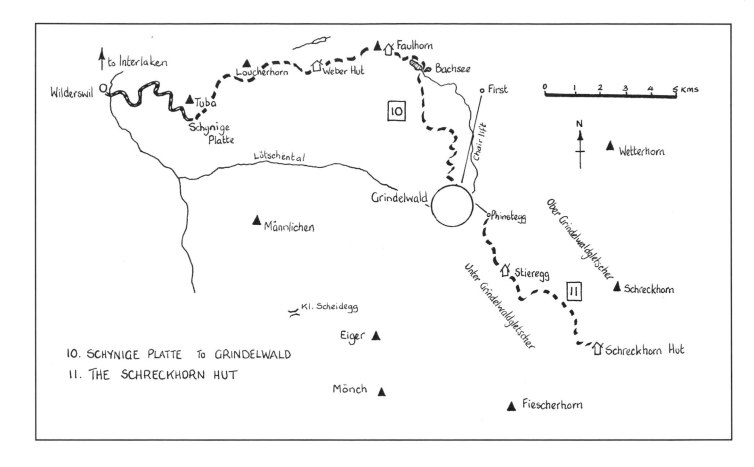

10. SCHYNIGE PLATTE TO GRINDELWALD
11. THE SCHRECKHORN HUT

longest chair-lift, or walking down through rich pastures to Grindelwald, whose scattered chalets lounge in view of the Eiger.

Grindelwald looks to the mountains from its generous green slopes where once flowed huge glaciers. In fact in Victorian times Grindelwald was known as the 'glacier village'. That epithet is perhaps not quite so applicable nowadays since the icefields have retreated somewhat, but the mountains will have lost none of their majesty or appeal and the crowds who flock there, winter as well as summer, are united almost as one voice in appreciation of the beauty of the area. It certainly has much to offer.

The head of Grindelwald's valley—more properly known as the Lütschental from the Schwarze Lütschine river which flows through it—is a vast tilted bowl of pasture backed by the immense glowering grey cliffs of the Wetterhorn, Mättenberg and Eiger, each separated from the other by the Oberer or Unterer Grindelwald glaciers. The outstretched arms that wall the valley are, however, of a more friendly disposition than these frowning mountains. They are more gentle and rounded, with grass growing over all but their brief rocky crowns.

In summer neat stooks of hay stand out like freckles down their slopes. Cattle, with bells clattering at their necks, graze the rich, well-watered meadows and farmers occupying isolated alps spend their summers making the cheeses for which Switzerland is justly famous.

The southern wall is that which divides Grindelwald's valley from that of Lauterbrunnen. It has the saddle of Kleine Scheidegg at its mountain end, and the nobbly tops of the Lauberhorn and Männlichen spaced out along it. Beyond Männlichen the slopes plunge to the village of Zweilütschinen where merge the valleys of the Schwarze Lütschine and Weisse Lütschine. There are popular trails leading all along the upper slopes of this ridge, and cableways strung from both Grindelwald and Wengen which grant easy access to it.

The northern wall of the valley extends farther westward than its opposite number and only comes to an abrupt halt above the shores of the Brienzersee, which has the busy town of Interlaken sprawling nearby. This mountain wall has been rucked and moulded over untold millenia to create subsidiary spurs that project valley-wards, while on the northern side of the crest small but attractive hanging valleys hide

their virtues in the shadow of several minor peaks that jut out from the ridge.

At the Grindelwald end of this long wall the First chair-lift rises over the meadows in four stages, and makes easily accessible the magnificent lakes of Bachsee, and the summit of the Faulhorn (2681m) above them. At the western end, the ridge of the wall at Schynige Platte is reached by funicular railway from Wilderswil, the village that guards the entrance to the valley.

Between Schynige Platte and First there winds one of the finest footpaths in all of Switzerland. It is a path known and loved by thousands of visitors, and one that bears repeating many, many times over. It is almost guaranteed to give five hours of delight—or nearly seven hours if you continue the walk down to Grindelwald. The walk, of course, may be tackled in either direction, but I favour heading eastwards from Schynige Platte, for that way you walk into the views. And what views they are!

If your holiday is based in Grindelwald take an early train down-valley to Wilderswil (direction Interlaken) and from there catch the funicular to Schynige Platte. But do make sure of fine weather. Check the forecast and choose your day well, for this is a walk that really needs good conditions to draw out the full glory of the mountain landscape.

The ride on the funicular gives unbelievably beautiful views; breathtaking is a cliché that comes into its own here, for as you gain height so the head of Lauterbrunnen's valley rises as though on a pedestal. The Breithorn looks superb. Then comes the Jungfrau in all its majesty, snow and ice in a dazzling cascade; then the graceful Mönch and the Eiger's great triangular face of shadow, standing back ready to be admired; and this is undoubtedly one of the best places from which to admire these fabled Oberland summits—as impressive a collection of peaks as any you might hope to find outside the Himalaya. In truth, they stand comparison with any mountain group in the world, and it doesn't matter how many times you've seen photographs of them in books or on calendars, the reality of being there, of seeing them 'in the flesh' so to speak, is never less than awe-inspiring.

The station at Schynige Platte stands at 1987 metres, which gives a boost to the start of the day's walking. From here the sight of those great snow-and-ice-draped mountains hanging in the sky above the unseen depths of the valley is almost certain to delay your departure, but when you finally manage to tear yourself away onto the path signposted to the Faulhorn and Grindelwald you are presented with a choice. That route which is marked as the *Panoramaweg* is the one to take. It leads initially round an upper scoop of grassland and in half an hour or so brings you to the very edge of a steep cliff that falls dramatically on its far side towards the Brienzersee. A fascinating panorama is to be had from this cliff-edge, but despite its drama there's nothing remotely difficult about the route along it.

The first stage of the walk takes you towards the Laucherhorn, a modest summit of 2230 metres, but then you skirt below it across a slope of scree to enter a hidden region of bare limestone ribs and walls, now temporarily out of sight of the Eiger, Mönch and Jungfrau. The path is clearly marked and it leads over a minor col between the Laucherhorn and Ussri-Sägissa to emerge at the head of the little moorland-like valley of Sägistal, trapped by encircling mountain walls. Sheep graze here,

and it is not unusual to find snow patches lying throughout the summer. At the far end of the valley is a tarn, the Sägistalsee.

The right-hand wall of the Sägistal rises in a series of limestone terraces with the continuing pathway wandering along one of them. The path then rises gently and turns a spur, crosses more bare ribs of the mountain and brings you into a narrow cleft of hillside with a tiny privately-owned mountain hut tucked into it, marked on the map as Männdlenen. This is the Weber Hütte (2344m), a cosy if crowded place situated just at the right place and time to tempt with its offer of refreshment.

From the hut the way now climbs sharply, then eases along the flanks of Winteregg with the summit of the Faulhorn seen ahead. But of more interest than that is the resumption of views to the Eiger, Mönch and Jungfrau, seen from a slightly rearranged angle, yet just as lovely and welcoming as the last time you saw them. And after a short stroll farther along the ridge you begin to see the stiletto points of the Schreckhorn and Finsteraarhorn sharp above a mass of other summits locked in a world of snow and ice. The panorama is stunning.

The Faulhorn is sometimes adopted by paragliding enthusiasts as a launching pad, and it is entertaining to sit on the ridge and watch them take off and then glide effortlessly in the breeze over the valley until they become nothing more than tiny specks of colour against the stark mountains that form such a delightful horizon.

It is not necessary to climb the zig-zag path to the top of the Faulhorn, as a path skirts below it and descends to a saddle to the south of the peak. But if you have both time and energy, it is worth the extra effort for the fresh panorama that greets you there. Tucked under the actual summit is a restaurant and hotel attached, a popular place from which to view both sunset and sunrise.

Continuing to Grindelwald the path now slopes down to a saddle where you have a choice to make of either breaking off to the right to descend to Bussalp, from where buses run to Grindelwald, or left to Bachsee and the First chair-lift.

Taking the left-hand pathway the trail takes you down over rough slopes of rock, scree and meandering streams to reach the large tarn of

Bachsee (2265m), with its amazing spectacle of the Wetterhorn first, then the savage-looking Schreckhorn, and then the Finsteraarhorn rising above the huge ice-plastered face of the Fiescherwand. It is perhaps the most splendid of all the panoramic views won on this walk, and it is truly memorable.

The first time I walked to the Bachsee I was caught in a short but vicious storm that effectively denied me any views. On the second occasion I went there on a morning bright with promise, but arrived just in time to have all views of the mountains stolen by a vagrant black cloud that stubbornly refused to leave. Then on the third occasion I walked from Schynige Platte with hopes held high, but by the time I reached the Faulhorn clouds had gathered yet again and were snuffing out the mountains like candles in the darkness. However, just as I reached the first of the two lakes a wind came from nowhere and began to shift those clouds from the distant summits—and the place shone in glory. It was worth waiting for.

At the far end of the first lake you must decide whether to continue the walk into Grindelwald itself, or take the chair-lift down. If you choose the latter you should continue along the main path for a further ten minutes or so to reach the large restaurant at the First chair-lift station. But to walk down is to prolong the day's enjoyment, and you bear right to pass between the lakes, then cut off leftwards into a deep and grassy scoop of hillside with streams racing through to pour over a lip in a thundrous waterfall near a farm. As you wander down into this scoop, so the Wetterhorn pulls itself up to full stature, and a moment or two later the Eiger reveals itself side-on, the impressive Mittellegi ridge appearing to be razor-sharp as it climbs to a surprisingly pointed summit. Not from here a full view of the notorious Nordwand, but the mountain is no less majestic for that.

Wandering down across one slope of pasture after another is a continuing pleasure. Slowly Grindelwald comes into view and one feels almost reluctant to reach it; reluctant to finish this walk in full view of the Eiger; a walk that is quite justifiably one of the classic walks of the Alps.

WALK 11: *The Schreckhorn Hut by Kev Reynolds*

Location: Above Grindelwald, Bernese Alps, Switzerland.

How to get there: By train to Interlaken, and change there for Grindelwald. Nearest international airport—Zürich or Bern.

Distance: 17 kilometres (11 miles)—the round trip.

Time required: 8 hours (1½–2 hours may be saved by the use of the Pfinstegg cable-car.)

Height gain/loss: 1486 metres (1138m if cable-car is used).

Type of walk: Strenuous and exposed, but safe and visually spectacular to the Rots Gufer where rock scrambling with the aid of ladders, fixed cable and metal pegs elevates the route in seriousness. For those who might be uneasy on this section the walk is worth tackling as far as this point. Some small amount of objective danger, with possibility of stonefall in places. But a magnificent outing nonetheless.

Refreshments available at Pfinstegg and Restaurant Stieregg.

Valley base: Grindelwald.

Map: Landeskarte der Schweiz 1:50,000 series, sheet no 5004 *Berner Oberland*.

Guidebook: *The Bernese Alps* by Kev Reynolds (Cicerone Press).

View from the Schreckhorn Hut. The Finsteraarhorn, highest peak in the Bernese Alps, is seen at far left, appearing lower than its neighbour. The glacier is that of the Obers Eismeer. (Kev Reynolds)

Into a world of glaciers

This walk leads into a landscape of savage beauty. Into a world of permanent winter where huge glaciers scour the heartland of the Bernese Alps, and where the mountains themselves rise as islands of rock in a stormy sea of snowfield and ice-cliff.

It is not a walk for those who suffer from vertigo, nor for those who would be nervous on delicate ledges aided by fixed cable. There are one or two very steep sections of the route, too, that have steel ladders and metal pegs fitted to aid the crossing of difficult passages of rock face directly above the icefields. That being said, so long as necessary precautions are taken there should be no untoward difficulties experienced along the way, and for most of the time the path is easy and gently graded.

It might be worth noting that the walk is perfectly safe and easy as far as the Rots Gufer,

the rock face where the fixed cables are found, about 45 minutes from the Schreckhorn hut. Should you be nervous about tackling the complete route, it is certainly worthwhile going as far as this.

As its name implies, the Schreckhorn hut is situated below the beautiful prong of the Schreckhorn peak (4078m) above Grindelwald, and was built by the Basel section of the Swiss Alpine Club in order to provide accommodation for climbers tackling routes on a number of surrounding mountains. It replaces another hut, the Strahlegg, that was destroyed by an avalanche in 1977. From it there are magnificent views across the steepening glacier of the

Obers Eismeer to the spiky summit of the Finsteraarhorn (4274m), highest of all the Bernese Alps, and of an overall scene of arctic splendour.

It will take nearly five hours to reach the hut from the centre of Grindelwald, and another three and a half for the return, but an hour or more may be saved by taking the cable-car to Pfinstegg at the start of the day, and this is also useful in offering a speedy return to the valley afterwards, thereby making the walk there and back more feasible for a day's outing.

From Grindelwald's green and pleasant slope there are two main glacier systems in view. That to the east is the Oberer Grindel-waldgletscher which flows from the steep glacial cirque rimmed by the horseshoe of peaks dominated by the Wetterhorn, Bärglistock, Schreckhorn and Mättenberg. That to the south is the Unterer Grindelwaldgletscher which squeezes from a dark defile sliced between the sheer walls of the Mättenberg and the Mittellegi ridge of the Eiger. It is through this gorge and following this glacier that the route to the Schreckhorn hut goes. From Grindelwald the gorge hints at mystery, and it is the unravelling of that mystery that makes this walk so very special.

The Pfinstegg cable-car station is located on the southern, lower, edge of Grindelwald below the pretty white-walled village church, and the cableway whisks you in about seven minutes up to a lofty perch four hundred metres above the valley. Pfinstegg is set in a convenient position to begin the route to the Schreckhorn hut. On the ride up you gain a preview of what is to come, as you gaze through the cleft of mountains to the great wall of the Fiescherhorn catching the sun that is denied to the gorge below. However, for those who would prefer to walk all the way, follow signs for the Gletscherschlucht. Nearby you will find a winding lane that climbs into forest, and in a short distance a footpath breaks away from it and goes steeply up the hillside, eventually bringing you onto the Pfinstegg-Stieregg path.

The path at first wanders among pines and shrubbery at the upper limits of the tree-line, then eases round the steep slopes of the Hohturnen which serves as the eastern gateway to the glacier gorge. Now the cliffs plunge dramatically to the torrent thrashing its way between the awesome walls. Opposite, on the western side, a face of huge slabs rise and taper to the Mittellegi-Hörnli ridge of the Eiger; an amazing piece of mountain architecture planed smooth by the ceaseless industry of the glaciers over innumerable centuries. In places the path is extremely exposed, but is safely guarded by a wire and rope fence, the upper cliffs overhanging, and one grows in admiration for those workmen of old who were responsible for carving this open gallery of a path out of the raw cliff face.

Then the gorge is passed; the walls are spaced farther apart and light comes flooding from the south. Ahead the tumultuous hanging Fieschergletscher, and above that the Fiescherhorn itself forms a vast, gently-curving wall, generously coated with ice and pillows of snow.

The way continues, up and down, still with a severe drop to one side. Then there is a stream to cross, the Hohturnenlamm, draining down from a high corrie under the Mättenberg, and beyond it you wander along an old moraine thrown up long ago by the passing glacier, turn a cliff and there before you, in some surprise, you see a little meadowland with a trim building set upon it. This is the understandably-popular Restaurant Stieregg, boasting a stunning panorama from its terrace.

From Stieregg the view is indeed one to remember. It is dominated by ice, but it is not a sterile view. It is rich with contrasts, with movement and colour, with such a variety of shades of blue, of white and browns and grey; a wash of light and shadow; a landscape of grace and majesty. Huge mountains loom all around to form almost a complete circle. Glaciers have carved it. They have given shape and form to this vast bowl of glory and continue their toil day and night, year in and year out. The works of man are laughably insignificant by comparison.

Tearing yourself away from this brief interlude of grass the route resumes over glacial moraine, rough in places and diverted here and there from its original course where the bank has crumbled away. Ahead now you have a direct view of the ice-fall of the Obers Eismeer, with the prong of the Agassizhorn just seen above it, with the Finsteraarhorn behind that. It is a fascinating view and one with which you will soon become almost intimately familiar.

A second poor pastureland is reached near the lower part of the ice-fall. This scanty patch of grass, pocked with boulders and rocks and with its southern limit disappearing into moraine debris, often has a few sheep grazing there. After this the climb to the hut begins in earnest, for ahead rise the cliffs of the Rots Gufer with their safeguarding fixed cables, metal pegs and sections of iron ladder.

It is an interesting, ever-varied obstacle to overcome, with the marked route leading up rock slabs and gullies directly above the toppling sèracs that creak and groan and crash as they shuffle themselves in a constant act of rearrangement. Blue-green chasms appear steeply below your boots, or off to one side as you draw level with an upper section of the ice-fall. Ice particles dance and glitter in the sunlight and the sun's heat reflected from the glacier is felt even on the cool, damp rocks.

Above the barrier of the Rots Gufer the path continues, now crossing gullies with streams hurtling down them, now over a patchy snowfield or two, then across more streams, gaining height all the time. Icefields stretch far ahead; glaciers hang perilously from the faces of mountains to right and left and the glare of sun on snow and ice makes you squint even behind the protection of sunglasses.

Finally you come to a cone of moraine and rocks spreading from the left. Ahead the way seems to be blocked by converging glaciers feeding the Obers Eismeer. There are the ruins of a stone hut, and here the path forks. The Schreckhorn hut at last comes into view, and you bear left and wander up the slope of moraine to the top where the hut is found tucked against the lower cliffs of the western arête of the Schreckhorn. Unfortunately from this point this otherwise beautiful mountain is grossly foreshortened.

None could spend time in this remarkable place and remain unmoved by the panoply of rock, snow and ice mountains that are spread before you. It is one of those rare settings straight out of dreams; a gleam and a dazzle of pristine beauty. The Finsteraarhorn, of course, draws the eye by its fin-like delicacy, but the lesser-known Agassizhorn is also worth noting, as is the upthrust of ice that conceals the true summit of the Fiescherhorn almost opposite the hut. But then you sweep all before you in a panning gaze until your eyes rest on a snow peak off to the west, rising out of a vast glacial amphitheatre, and realise that this is the Mönch, the central figure in the classic Oberland tryptich, of which the only member absent from this view is the Jungfrau. For next to the Mönch to the right is the brief east face of the Eiger. How different this is to the monstrous and notorious north face! You'd hardly dare believe it to be part of the same mountain. Then the Eiger's wall slants northeastwards, and you remember that this rises to the knife-edge of the Mittellegi, seen earlier in the day from the approach walk near the gorge.

All is as it ought to be, yet the scale is difficult to comprehend and it is only when you catch sight of a couple of other walkers approaching by the path along the moraine cone, that you can suddenly arrange some degree of perspective. Then, and only then, does the full awesome majesty of this heartland of the Bernese Alps impress itself upon the senses. It is quite something to absorb.

Eventually, of course, it will be necessary to retrace your steps back to Grindelwald, and this in itself is an opportunity for another bite at the cherry. If the upward route was full of joy, then the downward journey will be no less pleasurable. For now you can see the ice-falls, the glaciers and mountain walls under a different light, from a different angle and with renewed perspective. And by the time the pavements of Grindelwald are trod once more, you'll have a fresh understanding and appreciation of the mountain world. This walk will have ensured that much, at least.

WALK 12: *The Alpine Pass Route by Kev Reynolds*

Location: Switzerland. Sargans to Montreux.

How to get there: Flight or train from London to Zürich. Train from Zürich to Sargans. For the return journey trains run to Zürich from Montreux via Lausanne.

Distance: 325 kilometres (202 miles).

Time required: 15-16 days.

Start: Sargans.

Finish: Montreux.

Type of walk: Long and strenuous, but with numerous transport options for those who need relief on some of the longer or more arduous sections. Accommodation is available at the end of every stage, so backpacking is unnecessary. The ever-changing scenery makes this a magnificent trek. (Several commercial trekking companies use the central portion of this route for a fine two-week tour, with days off to explore particular areas.)

Maps: Landeskarte der Schweiz 1:50,000 series Nos 237 *Walenstadt* 247 *Sardona*, 246 *Klausenpass*, 245 *Stans*, 255 *Sustenpass*, 5004 *Berner Oberland*, 5009 *Gstaad-Adelboden*, 262 *Rochers de Naye*.

Guidebooks: *The Alpine Pass Route* by Kev Reynolds (Cicerone Press). *The Alpine Pass Route* by Jonathon Hurdle (Dark Peak). *Alpenpassroute* by Arnold Fuchs (Kümmerley + Frey) (in German).

A classic traverse of the Bernese Oberland

The Alpine Pass Route is a splendid route, one of the longest traverses in Switzerland and without doubt one of the most scenically spectacular. It begins in the little town of Sargans on the borders of Liechtenstein, and finishes in Montreux on the banks of the Lake of Geneva; 325 kilometres of mountain and valley, sixteen passes and some 18,000 metres of height-gain in fifteen day stages. Yes, the Alpine Pass Route is an epic walk; truly, one of the classic walks of the Alps.

The central section takes in the much-loved Bernese Oberland where footpaths lead beside the Wetterhorn, in the shadow of the Eiger, and within sight and sound of the avalanches that strip the beautiful snow and ice walls of the Jungfrau. But elsewhere, to east and west, there are other mountains too, not so immedi-

ately recognisable, perhaps, but no less lovely for that: among them Tödi and Titlis, Gspaltenhorn, Blümlisalp and Wildstrubel and the great mass of Les Diablerets—and dozens more besides. There are distinguished resorts like Grindelwald, Lauterbrunnen, Wengen and Mürren, and quiet 'backwater' villages such as Weisstannen, Elm and Griesalp to visit; long vistas of snow peak and glacier, of meadow and forest and glistening tarn, of scree slope and stark moraine and some of the most exquisite valleys in all of Europe. The Alpine Pass Route enjoys them all.

Such a route through such a country is made less demanding than otherwise it might be. Being Switzerland it is quite unnecessary to shoulder a towering rucksack in order to tackle the APR as a backpacking exercise—although, of course, there's no reason why not, if that is your wish. For at the end of every stage there are prospects of overnight lodging, either hotel, hostel, mountain hut or *matratzenlager* (dormitory accommodation usually in a farm outhouse, but sometimes in part of an hotel). There are villages with food stores and restaurants and, in some of the more popular areas, alp farms also double as restaurants to tease the perspiring walker with their offer of refreshment. On some days there are transport options, too, such as cable-cars or chair-lifts, funicular railways or buses that could be adopted as a means of bad weather escape or in case of injury or just plain weariness.

The Alpine Pass Route may be an epic walk, but it does not offer a wilderness experience. Undeniably there are many sections of the route where you will probably see no-one at all for two or three hours at a time, and a number of the high passes are taxing enough for most walkers to cross, yet the footpaths are clearly defined, waymarked and signposted with typical Swiss efficiency—although nowhere will you see a single sign specifically announcing the direction of the route of the APR. Unlike most British long distance trails there is no single line of the Alpine Pass Route and with various alternative stages available, it would be possible to return two or three times to the APR and each time experience a slightly different route. The APR described here, however, is the more logical way; that followed by the guidebook.

Stage 1: 4—5 days

Sargans is a small town nestling at the junction of the Seeztal with the Rhine Valley, with the mountains of Liechtenstein breaking away behind it, and a suggestion of valley opposite where the route begins. There's a fine castle overlooking the town and a major road leading tourist traffic away from its centre. Its mountains are modest mountains, but it has easy access that makes it a convenient place from which to set out on a long trek, for it is served by a direct rail link with Zürich, and with the first day's stage being a fairly short one, it is quite feasible to catch an early flight from London to Zürich and be in Sargans at lunchtime in readiness for a four-hour afternoon walk. Those four hours are full of variety that manage somehow to give a flavour of what is to come.

In a little over half an hour after setting out the route takes you through the charming village of Mels, backed against a steepening hillside and with the river Seez foaming through in a torrent as it escapes the constrictions of a gorge at the entrance to the Weisstannental. Postbuses wind in long loops of narrow road into this valley, but the walkers' route ignores the road and climbs steeply instead to the hamlet of St Martin, with views overlooking vineyards, the rooftops of Mels and across to Sargans and the Rhine Valley. There follows a woodland stretch, high above the mouth of the Weisstannental, and then a gentle descending traverse over pastures leading into the bed of the valley by the string of barns and farms of Schwendi. Forty minutes later you come to Weisstannen itself, a quiet and pleasant village with good walking country on its doorstep and hotel and gasthof accommodation available.

The Weisstannental is one of those little-known valleys off the tourist route. It's a cul-de-sac, boasts no popular resort, has neither lake nor dramatic glacial scenery, no major snowpeak nor great waterfall to attract visitors. But as the first valley on the Alpine Pass Route, with the first pass at its head, he would have to be a very myopic walker indeed not to fall for its simple charms. The upper part of the valley is heavily wooded, opening here and there to pastureland with streams draining through, the mountains ahead closing in a neat amphitheatre that denies all hint of the Foopass (2223m). But from the end of the track at the farmstead of Untersass a footpath begins the steady climb that will eventually lead to it.

The path is well-graded and brightened at first with shrubs and wild flowers, but then as you gain height and are led into the cirque of mountains that trap the valley, so vegetation becomes less extravagant and the trail narrows and steepens, with slender cascades pouring down the crags opposite, and you then emerge onto a brief levelling where sits a solitary farm and cattle byre; Fooalp. I came here one bitter September morning to find a herd of sorrowful-looking cows knee-deep in a khaki mixture of mire and overnight snow. Snow lay on the hills above and across our path, but a pair of chamois hunters had gone ahead and broken trail for some of the way, leaving us with only the last few hundred metres to the pass to locate.

Foopass is a slender saddle in the ridge linking the Foostock with Chli-Schiben, and from it views stretch out to include the long ridge of the Hausstock in the south-west where the next day's pass is to be found.

The way down to Elm is likely to take nearly four hours. It begins steeply at first, then eases to a more gentle descent, passing farms and crossing streams and meadows—a rich green hillside with Elm's valley gradually easing into view far below. Elm itself is a ribbon of houses alongside a quiet dead-end road. As you wander along the street, neighbourhood dogs asleep in the gutter, it is hard to imagine the terror that struck here more than a hundred years ago when a steep, 500 metre buttress

rising above the village, which had been badly eroded by quarrying, suddenly collapsed on the community killing 114 inhabitants.

The continuing route takes you up-valley alongside the river and through the lovely pastoral Sernftal with the snows of the Hausstock ahead, before climbing into a hidden pastureland basin with the Richetlipass (2261m) beckoning from above. Like that of Foopass, the Richetli is a narrow one and a joy to reach. In many respects it appears to be one of the most remote of all the passes on the route, with views over a veritable maze of ridges and hinted valleys stretching far off. If the way up to it is tiring and quite strenuous in places, the way down is even more so. There is a cone of a spur to aim for, with the narrow path leading along its very crest before plunging steeply down beside broken crags to gain a high hanging valley. There are farms linked by a broad track in this hanging valley, but the track suddenly gives out and the only way down from it to Linthal is by a wild, twisting path through jungly forest. (There is a mechanical hoist used by the farmers, which explains how it is possible for there to be tractors in the upper valley, but no driveable route to it!)

From Linthal to Altdorf is a very long stage indeed, but it is possible (and perhaps advisable) to break it into two by going first up to Braunwald and then taking a superb belvedere trail high on the hillside with views south to the snowy mass of the Tödi, and round to Urnerboden in the valley of the same name, and the next day continue over the Klausenpass to Altdorf. If this method is adopted there is much to be gained by it, for time spent in

the valley of Urner Boden will be time well spent. It is a glorious flat-bottomed plain of lush meadows bordered by spectacular mountain walls, and with the shapely Clariden (3267m) focussing attention to the south. Clariden's north-west ridge drops to the easy crossing of the Klausenpass, a road pass with opportunities for refreshment at the summit.

West of the Klausenpass (1948m) the highlight is the descent to Äsch, a simple, tiny hamlet of haybarns and farmers' wooden chalets with an impressive water spout gushing from the mountain wall behind it, and it makes an astonishing contrast with the bustling town at the end of this stage. Äsch is like a forgotten village, a place which time has passed by; but Altdorf, several hours' walk away, is a century and more away in terms of commerce, architecture and style. Altdorf is William Tell's town; the local hero is depicted everywhere. But despite its charms there's a snarled funnel of traffic in its streets, and after a night spent here it is good to escape to the peace of the mountains once more.

Stage 2: 2 days

As enjoyable as the days were to Altdorf, they may be seen in retrospect as just a prelude to the real Alpine Pass Route. There was nothing insignificant about the crossing of either the Foo, Richetli or Klausen passes, but as you set out for the Surenenpass (2291m) it becomes evident that this is a crossing of a different order.

Above the village of Attinghausen, just thirty minutes' walk from Altdorf, the mountainside rears dramatically, the path climbing very

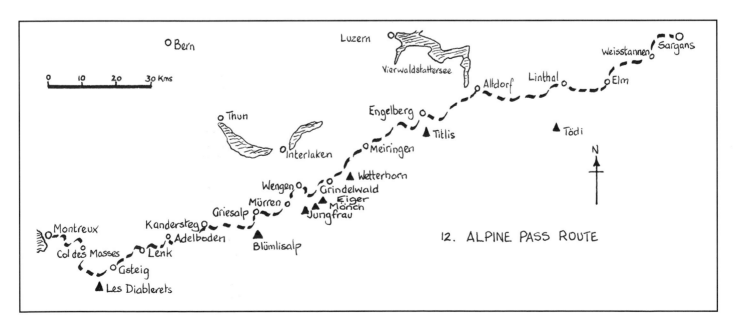

12. ALPINE PASS ROUTE

steeply up tilted meadow and forest alike. There is a cable-car as far as Brüsti that offers a saving of about $2\frac{1}{2}$ hours of effort, and since there will still be about seven hours of walking from Brüsti before you reach Engelberg, there should be no shame in giving in to this temptation. From Brüsti the path to the pass leads along a green ridge with a wonderful view over the distant blue sparkle of the Vierwaldstattersee, a fjord-like lake at the very heart of the founding of the Helvetic Conferation, seen trapped among friendly mountains.

Above the green ridge the way takes you up and over long strips of scree with a final sharp pull onto the actual pass. And there you catch your breath with wonder, for ahead the mountain plunges to a clutch of tarns while far-off rises the square-cut bulk of Titlis, across whose shoulder tomorrow's route will lead. It's a fabulous view and one I never tire of, while the long walk down to Engleberg gives pleasure with every step.

There are several remote farms along the path that offer refreshment and simple accommodation, and it is tempting to give up on prospects of Engelberg and spend the night here, with a stream for company and the stars lighting the topmost peaks like candles on an extravagant cake.

Crossing the Jochpass (2207m) between Engelberg and Engstlenalp is something else. There are cableways almost the whole way, and the footpath is forever in the shadow of either cable-car or chair-lift, the path itself being among the busiest of the APR. But it remains a fine walk all the same, with the shining glacial ice of Titlis above, and the gleaming waters of Engstlensee below the pass.

Once down at the Engstlenalp two options present themselves. One is to drop straight into the Gental, with its spray of waterfalls bursting from a grey rockface, the other is to follow a high terrace path way above the valley for nearly four hours all the way to Reuti above Meiringen, there to descend on a steep zig-zag forest path to the very edge of town. Having walked and enjoyed both I would slightly favour the high belvedere route. But consider returning another year to walk the valley route too!

Stage 3: 4 days

Having reached Meiringen you've at last entered the Bernese Alps, and on the walk to it from Engstlenalp the Wetterhorn was in view almost the whole way. On the first day's walk out of Meiringen the route takes you over the Grosse Scheidegg right beside this easily recognisable cornerstone of the Oberland and down to Grindelwald, sprawling over flower-bright

Trekkers pausing for a breather on the way from Grindelwald to Männlichen. The Eiger's great North Face is half-sheathed in morning mist. (Kev Reynolds)

Between Mürren and the Sefinenfurke the APR heads across beautiful alpine meadows and alongside the Gspaltenhorn.
(Kev Reynolds)

pastures with the Eiger frowning at you. Then there's another choice of crossings to be made on the way to Wengen and Lauterbrunnen. The obvious route to take is by way of Alpiglen, where so many Nordwand adventurers have set out, and then over Kleine Scheidegg (2061m), through the much-loved Wengernalp (loud with the boom and roar of avalanches pouring from the Jungfrau) and down into the gulping shaft of Lauterbrunnen's valley. But the alternative is equally worth considering: it goes up and over the western meadows with beautiful views directly onto the Eiger's notorious north face, and back to the Wetterhorn and Schreckhorn as you climb up to the Männlichen ridge (2229m). From Männlichen the Lauterbrunnen Valley is unbelievably far below, but what a viewpoint as you gaze up at the Jungfrau and to the great wall of peaks heading the valley! Then down, dramatically down the mountainside into Wengen's main street before tackling the final

descent to Lauterbrunnen village. Both routes will leave your knees trembling by the time you've reached the valley!

Lauterbrunnen lies at an altitude of less than 800 metres, and since the next pass is more than 1800 metres above it, it would be worth considering going up to Mürren to spend the night there (if you've energy to spare) in readiness for the crossing of the Sefinenfurke next day. Hotels in the village are generally more pricey than elsewhere, but half an hour above it there are two gasthofs with *matratzenlager* accommodation, and the most glorious views of the Eiger, Mönch and Jungfrau high above the unseen valley. Being there of a summer's evening to catch the alpenglow staining the distant snows is one of the lasting memories of the Alpine Pass Route, while setting out in the crisp morning to gaze on the long and lovely ridge of the Gspaltenhorn is an added bonus.

The Sefinenfurke (Sefinen Furgge) is a classic pass at 2612 metres; a narrow nick in a lofty

ridge, all crag and schist and raw panorama. There is a fixed rope on the western side to aid the initial descent, then it's a case of slip and slither on seemingly endless slopes of scree. But the scree does give out at last, and you wander down over rough hummocks of grass and boulder following a stream, until suddenly you gaze across a fresh landscape towards the big, brazen massif of the Blümlisalp. It's an intimidating scene, but you continue down, heading away from reality, to find the little hamlet of Griesalp at the upper end of the charming Kiental. Should the weather turn threatening here, on no account should you tackle the Hohtürli (2778m) by which you gain access to Kandersteg. This is the highest pass on the whole route and is no place to be caught in a storm. So if the weather does turn bad whilst at Griesalp, an escape may be made by bus through the Kiental to Reichenbach, and from there to Kandersteg.

Hohtürli, then, is the high point of the walk,

and its crossing puts two thirds of the route behind you. There is something rather significant in that, but the climb to the pass from Griesalp is a strenuous one even by APR standards, even though by now you will be well-used to 'pass-bashing'. There is one section that tackles the steepest cone of black schistose grit I've ever come across. So steep is it in places that no path can be made and you lower your head and simply kick your way up it. By the time you reach the pass the additional few metres of uphill to the Blümlisalp hut will be well worth tackling for the promise of refreshment it offers.

The hut sits in a wild but remarkable position, perched as it is on the very ridge and with the glaciers of the Blümlisalp massif just behind it. The views are so splendid that it's tempting to ignore the long descent to Kandersteg in order to spend the night here, just for the experience.

A good three hours or so will be needed to complete the descent, but they are ever-interesting hours, for they begin with scree slopes, then tackle a moraine wall below the green ice tongues of the glaciers, then over a wide hummocky basin before dropping to the much-loved Oeschinensee—a gem of a lake trapped in a horseshoe of huge peaks. It is no surprise to find that this is one of the most popular tourist haunts in all of Switzerland.

Kandersteg has a small camp site situated on the approach to town from the Oeschinensee. It has no shortage of hotel or gasthof accommodation, and there are plenty of shops for the backpacker to restock with supplies for the onward journey.

Stage 4: 5 days

Having now crossed the highest pass on the route, it is easy to imagine that the remainder of the walk to Montreux will be an anti-climax. None of it. In fact the day leading from Kandersteg to Adelboden via the Bunderchrinde (2385m) is a classic, with wild views and a chance to see herds of chamois grazing high up near the pass. Adelboden gives the impression of having all-but lost the big mountains, but the scenery is delightful anyway, dominated as it is by the snowy mass of the Wildstrubel standing back among soft pastures and with a foreground of grass-covered fells.

To reach Lenk from here the walker has another choice of crossings. The normal route is to wander up among a tracery of cableways to the easy Hahnenmoos at 1956 metres, but there is a better way which maintains the spirit of the APR, and that is to tackle a green ridge (the Tronegg Grat) between the valleys of the Geilsbach and the Engstlige—a remote and

Having emerged from a cloud-sea swamping Altdorf's valley, this backpacker pauses for a drink by the green ridge of Grat. (Kev Reynolds)

lovely stretch—then up to the saddle of Lüegli (2080m) to the north-east of the Regenboldshorn, round the slopes of this graceful peak and over the Pommernpass (2055m) where a welcome landscape is spread before you. Green hills, green valleys, dark green woodlands. But above them all rise craggy lines of peak and ridge, spattered with snow, their slopes sliced by streams; nothing so awe-inspiring, perhaps, as the Oberland giants further east, but utterly delightful in their overall effect. The descent to Lenk is as lovely as any downhill walk on the APR.

There is a short stage after Lenk; the crossing of the Trüttlisberg Pass (2038m) to Lauenen, and it is worth continuing from there over the modest Krinnen Pass (1659m) all the way to Gsteig. Two passes in one day at this stage of the long walk should not be too taxing, especially passes like these, for by so doing you will be in a good position to tackle the next long stage that leads to Col des Mosses.

First the Trüttlisberg Pass; a green and flowery gem of a crossing—more a slight dip in a ridge than a real pass. The way to it is a pastoral symphony of colour, fragrance and the sound of crickets in full summer; the long line of larger mountains now far enough away not to intimidate, but rather to add a backcloth of grandeur to a foreground of gentility. Cattle and sheep graze up here. Farms lie scattered along the transverse crests, the sides of which are scythed and shorn into patterns of shade. This is limestone country, and all around the pass the hillsides are pitted and pock-marked with curious undulations. The Krinnen Pass is quite different. It's a wooded pass, forested all

along its eastern approach from Lauenen, but open with meadows on the west before you drop into forests again. From the pass you gaze across a fine scoop of valley to the steep rise of Les Diablerets, the last of the big mountains of the Bernese Alps, and which marks the boundary between German and French-speaking Switzerland.

Gsteig is the overnight stop here. A small village astride the Col du Pillon road, there's rustic accommodation to be had, while there's a simple camp site a short distance uphill on its south-western side. Climbing out of the village is a shock to the system. One imagines all major effort to be over now, but the path to the Blattipass (1900m—unmarked on the map) is steeper than many so far met since leaving Sargans, despite the lush vegetation. And Blattipass is no craggy nick in a wild mountain ridge, but a mere dip of a saddle where trees and shrubs and flowers grow, and there's the most incredible panorama that includes most of the major Oberland peaks in it, from the spiky meringue-like tips of the Wetterhorn, past the arrow-blade of the Eiger to a succession of cream-topped waves of snow-peaks crowding the horizon round to Les Diablerets. This is a pass on which to spread yourself in the sunshine and draw breath, drinking in the majesty of the mountains. But don't dream too long as there are many hours of walking left before you reach the village of Col des Mosses.

From Blattipass to Col des Andérets (2034m) will occupy an hour and a half of pleasure, then you enter a new valley system and follow a high-level trail along the hillsides directly opposite Les Diablerets, passing alp after alp on a belvedere of delight. Far away Mont Blanc shows itself between other peaks on other intervening ridges, and the unmistakable outline of the Dents du Midi gives the first hint that the Lake of Geneva is not so far away now. Eventually you come to the end of a spur of mountain at the huddle of buildings of Chersaule, and bear round to the north-west, then over another minor saddle to descend among forest and pasture all the way to Col des Mosses.

One final day remains; a day of eight hours' walking. A day that will lead alongside the large Lac de l'Hongrin, into the heartland of the lovely Vaudois Alps and up and over Col de Chaude (1621m), the last crossing on the Alpine Pass Route. From it you peer down 1200 metres of forested hillsides to the gleaming Lac Léman. It's a view worth waiting for, and the walk down to it, taking all of three and a half hours, maintains the interest to the very last step.

WALK 13: *The Tour Of Mont Blanc by Andrew Harper*

Location: France, Italy, Switzerland.
How to get there: By train from Geneva to the Chamonix valley where the convenient start/finishing place is Les Houches. The Tour may easily be started and concluded at other places, particularly if joining the route from the Swiss side via Martigny. Nearest international airport—Geneva.
Distance: 190 kilometres (120 miles).
Time required: 10-11 days.
Best time: End of June—early October. Preferably end of August—early September.
Total height gain/loss: 10,000 metres (33,500ft).
Type of walk: Waymarking falls short of being 100% complete, but route-finding is not unduly difficult. The terrain is mainly exposed with limited opportunity for shelter. No insurmountable difficulties in good conditions.
Maps: IGN 1:25,000 (2 sheets) *Mont Blanc* Nos 3630 *Ouest* and 3531 *Est*—'Blue' series.
Didier & Richard 1:50,000 series *Massifs du Mont Blanc & Beaufortin* No DR8.
Guidebook: *Tour of Mont Blanc* by Andrew Harper (Cicerone Press).

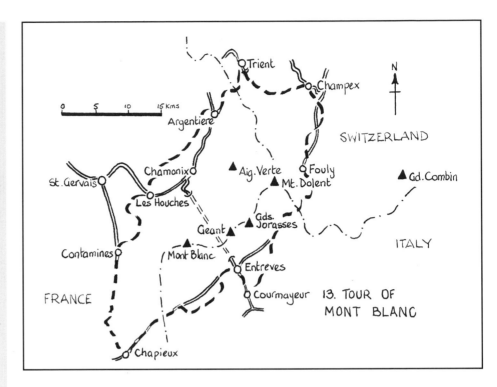

Round the Monarch of the Alps

Everyone will have their favourite walk, but surely the Tour of Mont Blanc is a contender for being the Classic of the Classics? Apart from being a most fulfilling and satisfying Alpine walk, it is ideal in its length with ascents and descents idyllically phased, producing a continual parade of beautiful viewpoints.

The Tour of Mont Blanc (TMB) is the name given to a route that plies a series of valleys connected by high passes, or cols. It is circuitous, which implies that wherever the route is joined, steady progression will return you to the same place. The Alps have their nearest point to Britain roughly at the corner at which Mont Blanc is situated and access by boat/train, air or car are all relatively convenient.

As good a place as any from which to commence is Les Houches, a village at the lower end of the Chamonix valley. From its confines one gets a splendid view along the flanks of

the main chain, the glaciers that divide the panorama being more than obvious. The little railway station at Les Houches is still rather twee and is isolated from the village by the valley's outgoing river, the Arve, whose bridge is actually the lowest point of altitude on the whole route. The roadway here is very busy with the continuous traffic associated with the Mont Blanc tunnel—one of the main arteries of commerce between France and Italy—and some care will be needed to cross safely. The busyness of this spot should be the last reminder of the world being left behind and, if things go to plan, the only intrusion of modern life into your everyday activities will be the occasional contrail left along the overhead air routes.

Stage 1: 1½ days

Starting at Les Houches has two advantages in addition to its convenient access. It permits an impression of the Chamonix valley before commencing the Tour which gives a 'reference' to the scale of things in the knowledge that there will be ample opportunity for a more detailed examination during the last few days

of the holiday, when it will be re-entered from its other end. It is also a convenient place for the Tour to end, allowing any time in hand to be played out in Chamonix itself.

Les Houches is a very attractive village with hotels in all categories, restaurants, shops and supermarket. The path to the first col starts adjacent to the cableway station at the far end of the village, and immediately gains height through its upper pastures, passing close to holiday chalets and shepherds' cottages. With every foot of increased height, the surrounding views become more and more interesting. Entering thin woodland here and there, the path is substantial and the air invigorating. The odd scar created by the need to cater for skiers in the winter will be excused for what it is, and examples of this kind of thing will be more than offset by the unaltered natural attractions of the landscape.

Ascending to the Col de Voza takes no more than three hours, but its ascent starts from an altitude equivalent to Scafell at the bridge over the Arve, and passes the altitude of Ben Nevis at the half-way point, evidence that the scale of things is rather different from

On the French side of the Col de Balme. (L to R: Aig. Verte, Drus, Mont Blanc.) *(Andrew Harper FRPS)*

that encountered in Britain. The actual altitude of Mont Blanc's summit is under review, thanks to modern techniques involving lasers and military satellites, but when a conclusion is reached it will only be a slight variant on 4810 metres (15,781ft) and there will be no threat to it remaining the highest point in Western Europe.

Once at Voza the landscape beyond comes into view where the Bionnassay Glacier tumbles down from Mont Blanc's south-west corner to divide the hillsides which are crossed by the continuing path. There is a snack bar of sorts at the large building at Voza, its prestige days as a hotel long since over and nowadays run as a holiday home. A narrow-gauge railway line serves to fetch tourists from St Gervais and continues through Voza to a point called Nid d'Aigle high above the glacier. The footpath ascends in the same direction as the railway, but only as far as the dilapidated refuge at Bellevue which is run by a dedicated old lady who can come up with ice-cool beer

and substantial food. Entering into her premises is like taking a step backwards into the last century. Whatever your opinion of the place, there is no denying that its situation must represent one of the very best in the whole of France for, from it, the entirety of the Chamonix valley is on proud display.

The path goes past the snout of the glacier before crossing the grassy slopes which lead to the Col de Tricot. No longer can the Chamonix valley be seen, although the significant summits of Aiguille de Goûter, Dôme du Goûter, Aiguille de Bionnassay and Mont Blanc are clearly visible above the Bionnassay Glacier.

The Col de Tricot is a particularly nice place to linger and the severity of the breeze will play its part in dictating the length of stay. The path down is fairly steep, made safe by a series of zig-zags, although it takes longer than imagined to reach the cluster of premises at the bottom of the bowl. Here will be found the welcoming hamlet called Chalets de Miage,

with food, accommodation and (evenings only) fresh milk from the most heavenly-looking cows to be found anywhere.

Up and over the intervening hillside, passing another significant resting place called Chalets du Truc, then down a steep forest track takes the hillwalker to the large-ish resort of Les Contamines.

Stage 2: 3 days
Getting this far will be confidence boosting. Sleep well, eat well and stock up as necessary for the days ahead where little opportunity presents itself for obtaining provisions until reaching Courmayeur, although there will be occasional opportunities to obtain provided meals.

The path meanders through exquisite pastures before ascending in earnest up a flag-stoned mule path that has its history stretching back to Roman times. At its head will be found, surprisingly, more lush meadows amongst which is situated the lovely old Bonant hôtelerie with appetizing meals and sleeping accommodation. Above this the wide path reaches the treeline and then crosses open meadow where the bald steep slopes of the ranges on either side confine the valley in an eerie manner. It rises slightly to draw level with the Chalet Hôtel la Balme, although 'Hôtel' seems rather an extravagent claim, even though there are bedrooms in a turn-of-the-century style at extra price compared with the dormitory bedding more readily available.

The upper end of the Montjoie valley is devoid of any shelter until reaching the first col, the Bonhomme, where there is a very small wooden hut. It is not unknown for the weather to go from one extreme to the other in as little as twenty minutes and to get caught on the almost-level stretch between here and the Col de la Croix du Bonhomme (where there's a refuge just over the brow) can have serious consequences. Although it is possible to walk the route in the most appalling conditions, I am still of the opinion that first-time buyers should have bright skies.

On quitting the refuge at Croix du Bonhomme the path descends to cross the odd water chute, dips and dodges until finally going through healthy pastureland before descending to the valley floor at Les Chapieux. Here will be found the Hotel la Soleil where beds of various sorts are available along with food beyond criticism: a real gem of a watering hole.

The narrow road passing through the village offers carefree walking up a ravine in the early approaches to the Col de la Seigne, passing the small but useful refuge at La Seloge before reaching the roadhead at Ville des Glaciers where the valley widens. The path commences on the other side of a small wooden bridge, shortly passing in close proximity to the enormous refuge at Les Mottets. The ascending path crosses attractive streams in following its winding way with excellent views towards the Glacier des Glaciers on the left, eventually drawing level with the cairn at the col itself.

Mont Blanc is seen to perfection here, its double rounded summit appearing high above all its supporting ramparts. The enormous valley stretching downwards is the Val Vény into which the continuing path descends. What is seen, though, is not solely Val Vény as at some halfway point it continues as the Val Ferret as far as the Grand Col Ferret at its far end.

Even late in the season the bowl on the Italian side of the Col de la Seigne is often covered by snow. In these conditions it is advisable to go along the ridge to the right of the col for about a hundred paces, until seeing a

Grandes Jorasses as seen from Monte de la Saxe. *(Andrew Harper FRPS)*

derelict stone building from where a better path starts its descent to the valley floor.

A nice thing about the Tour of Mont Blanc is that it takes the visitor into Italy and a corner of Switzerland in addition to its slice of France, affording the opportunity to sample the lifestyles appropriate to each. Apart from the language, an inconvenience will be the need for three currencies. Whilst there are adequate opportunities for changing money, enough cash ought to be carried so that the holiday is not interrupted too often by the need to change travellers cheques.

Passing a gutted barrack-like building, the path weaves a little before going along the left-hand side of the valley to get to the vicinity of the imposing Elisabetta refuge. At this point there is an abrupt change in the altitude of the valley floor, and fifteen minutes or so will be engaged in effecting the drop by a succession of paths which bisect the jeep-track hairpins. The lower valley is ravaged by a series of inter-weaving streams, generally known as Lac Combal, at the far side of which will be seen the enormous lateral moraine of the Miage Glacier.

The confine imposes a constriction on the water flow out of Lac Combal where a wee stone bridge allows access from one side of the outlet to the other. From here down there is a narrow roadway which edges past the massive graveyard of boulders dumped at the glacier's terminal moraine. Walking down this can be pleasant enough and, once through the defile, the valley widens again to permit a parallel path for most of its remaining length.

In good weather a preferable path goes up the right-hand hillside just prior to the bridge and ascends to eventually traverse the hillsides high above Val Vény, permitting the most wonderful views of the main massif, and this ought not to be missed.

Col Chécrouit is at the far end of the traverse where there is a group of very old wooden shepherds' shacks, one of which has been converted into a refuge and restaurant. Set in the most magnificent surroundings, its view of Mont Blanc is superb and, as if that were not enough, it affords a commanding view over a significant length of the Val d'Aosta heading east-south-east.

The way down to Courmayeur goes sharp left at the refuge to cross a small marshy area, at the other side of which a path goes steeply down through a bushy hillside until getting to a roadway, which descends the remainder of the way. Walking down this road is far from unpleasant as there is normally little traffic and the trees give the air a wonderful fragrance.

To get into Val Ferret it is necessary to cross the river Dora Baltea which combines the out-pourings from the two valleys. There is a suit-suitable bridge at Entrelevie and, once across this, immediately turn left and walk up the minor road to Entrèves which will be found to have an adequate provisions store and the odd restaurant facility. Whilst there is more choice in Courmayeur, the hotels there are becoming prohibitively expensive and the opportunities for the economical short stay are accordingly lessened. Entrèves is smaller and somewhat nicer in character and, linked with neighbouring La Palud, accommodation will be found at more reasonable terms.

Stage 3: 3 days

La Palud is at the very entrance to the Ferret valley, its twisting and awkward road at that point being home to the base station of the cableway system that rises to the high-altitude Torino refuge. With interchange, it continues over the high snowfields to reach Aiguille du Midi on the French side, and from where it is then possible to extend this fantastic mechanical journey down into the heart of Chamonix itself.

If it is excellent weather, consider allocating a half-day for ascending to the Torino and the slightly higher Pointe Helbronner where there is a terrace with views that will astound you. The main attraction is Mont Blanc's summit, but at the extremes it is possible to recognise the characteristic shape of the Matterhorn away to the east, the Dauphiné Alps around Chambéry and Grenoble to the south-west, the nearer-at-hand Aiguille Verte and the Drus and beyond them the Dents du Midi. To the south is the permanent snow region of the Gran Paradiso National Park.

But to continue with the TMB: once at La Palud, one is generally committed to plying the pleasant road up the valley floor to La Vachey, where two hotels and a dormitory offer a suitable staging. Better, though, is the high-level alternative which starts in the centre of Courmayeur by the church. Passing through the village of Villair, the path ascends to the newish Refuge Bertone and slightly higher to the grassy rounded crest of the Monte de la Saxe.

It is arguable where Mont Blanc is seen at its best, for there are so many excellent view-points. The crest of Monte de la Saxe is certainly a contender! The dominant feature of this walk will be the Grandes Jorasses and it is with this that the slightly more distant Mont Blanc adopts a visual balance that enhances the appearance of the chain.

Guidebooks and maps are necessary in continuing the walk which first curves round by following the ridge to reach Col Sapin and sub-sequently down the length of a sub-valley after passing the cowsheds at Sécheron. The Grandes Jorasses assume an additional prominence for the final stroll down to the valley floor close to La Vachey.

The rebuilding of the refuge at Elena just above Pré de Bar will significantly alter the staging of the TMB. Since the original Elena was destroyed by avalanche there has been no accommodation higher than La Vachey in the Italian Val Ferret. This has made the premises here a bit of a catchment and forced people to end their walking day unnecessarily early, particularly if the nearest accommodation on the Swiss side has been just that bit too far away to contemplate.

The route from La Vachey through Pré de Bar and past the Elena is easy to follow, although after the refuge it begins to ascend with determination until levelling on the final approach to the Col de la Seigne. The ascent allows the unusual shape of the Pré de Bar Glacier to be admired and studied.

The Grand Col Ferret is on the frontier separating Italy from Switzerland, following which is the Swiss Val Ferret. The path gradually loses height as it first sweeps generously round the left-hand side of the upper bowl before cutting down an eroded path amongst the most attractive grassy banks. The significant snowy summit ahead is the Grand Combin and this sits in the distance behind the ridge wall that hides the famous Alpine highway which crosses the Grand St Bernard Pass.

The main descent ceases with the crossing of the bridge spanning the clear and swift-flowing waters of the young Dranse, after which the gradient lessens for the short walk down the tarred road to Ferret. Here will be found a hotel, restaurant and lodging place in addition to the unusual Chapelle de Ferret. La Fouly is farther down the roadway, offering facilities on a much greater scale in addition to boasting an enormous and useful camp site which is nicely positioned away from the village where it occupies a large meadow.

From La Fouly, the next point of significance will be the village of Praz de Fort. One can follow the general line of the roadway, but a more passive way to go starts at the campsite, treading a very pleasant footpath within close proximity of the attractive river for almost the extent of its length. At places the path narrows to round a cliffside and eventually issues onto the defunct lateral moraine of an old glacier to enter Praz de Fort with its colourful wooden buildings.

The stores at Praz de Fort are not extensive, but can easily cater for the average ruck sack. There is at least one modest hotel, but after leaving here there is no guarantee of accommodation being available until Champex.

The next hour should be extremely pleasant, as the still-descending path cants across simple meadows before going through the heart of one of the nicest of old mountain villages, Les Arlaches. Issert follows soon afterwards, although slightly more modern and suffering the fate of being bissected by a highway. At a point where a signpost indicates 'Champex: 2h' the luxury of the gentle downhill jaunt comes to an end, although even the weary should be able to improve on this timing forecast.

Champex is very, very tidy. The hotels are—in the main—pretentious and expensive, whereas the shops are well-stocked with first-class products and produce. All this would be of little consequence without the jewel in its crown: *the lake*. It is a veritable paradise, set amongst steep wooded hillsides, making it a pleasant place for a stopover. There is a campsite in addition to a very useful dortoir.

Stage 4—Champex to Les Houches: 3½ days

The next stage of the TMB can be conducted by two distinctly different routes. The first, which should only be attempted in good weather, soon gets above the tree line and progresses through barren landscape to cross into the Trient valley by way of the Fenêtre d'Arpette. The choice presented by the alternative route through the Bovine is by no means an easy stroll although, by comparison, it is notably pastoral and is certainly not without its compensations.

Adjacent to the chair-lift station at the far end of the village, a service road goes off to the left signposted 'Val d'Arpette'. Just behind the buildings a very pleasant woodland path leads up to the hotel and restaurant building at Arpettaz, a clearing at the start of the scree-ravaged Val d'Arpette. The hotel offers basic accommodation as well as standard bedrooms, is usually well-subscribed with the walking fraternity and its evening menu is invariably substantial; a good springboard for approaching the Fenêtre.

The path is fairly well-trodden and eventually climbs to negotiate a large boulder field before getting to the foot of an escarpment which leads directly to the col. If a prize was needed to tantalise people for this final difficulty, then it is surely the sighting of the magnificent Glacier du Trient which certainly won't go unnoticed.

The way down seems somewhat precarious

but is safe and easy enough when taken with care. Throughout the descent the glacier will continue to provide interest, the camera once more being called upon to provide a lasting impression. Just among the trees will be found a collection of shacks at a spot called Chalets du Glacier where cool drinks can be purchased. The day is finished by walking along the shaded and level path to the Col de la Forclaz.

Forclaz is also the landfall for the alternative route from Champex, the start of which is also at the upper end of the village. Instead of going towards the Val d'Arpette it is necessary to continue on the main road, following it over the brow of the hill and then breaking off to the left onto a minor road which services Champex d'en Bas. The route is marked throughout and it leads from farm pastures, through woodland, over streams, crosses water chutes, climbs the odd escarpment and gives increasingly good views as height is gained.

It rises to a point where it traverses an enormous curved shoulder and it is along this section where some of the best views are obtained, notably the extent of the Rhône valley between Martigny and Sion. Once over an insignificant little ridge, the path loses height relentlessly until drawing level with the highway col at Forclaz where its hotel offers typical Swiss hospitality.

Col de Balme can be approached by either going down to Trient by using a path short-

cutting the highway, or by going to the makeshift bridge at Chalets du Glacier along the level path that starts in the meadow opposite the hotel. Going by Trient is the easier and shorter of the two and is pleasant enough, continuing through the village to where a path slants off over meadows to the right to cross a narrow stream. Here it enters woodlands and zig-zags to emerge on the side of a ravine, where the well-worn path continues to the refuge on the saddle.

The other route is preferable for those who like wider views and a slightly more fulfilling experience. It rises through sparse woodland, giving the occasional commanding view over the Trient Glacier and surrounding landscape. Getting above the trees, attractive shrubs cover the hillside and it is through these that the path winds to gain height until slanting up a bannistered crack to overcome a vertical cliff. At the top of this cliff there is a collection of picturesque shacks, and soon after the path levels to contour three or four sweeps in the hillside and, after passing at least one attractive waterfall, draws level with the refuge at Col de Balme.

My chapter on the Chamonix–Zermatt walk describes a visit to the same venue when approached from the other direction, but the walker gets an entirely different sensation coming up from Trient. Only with the final paces to the col does the confronting panorama featuring Mont Blanc and the Chamonix valley

Walkers relaxing at Col de la Seigne with a fine view of Mont Blanc.
(Andrew Harper FRPS)

begin to appear. To say that it can take one's breath away is certainly not an over-use of the cliché.

With this grand vista for company the drop to the upper end of the Chamonix valley is best accomplished by first going over the Col des Posettes, the highest point seen on the continuing ridge round to the right. The path is one of the nicest in the whole area and ought not to be missed by taking the more direct route down to La Tour, the alternative recommended in extremely bad weather because it is slightly less exposed.

The way over Posettes gives commanding views—particularly towards the Glacier du Tour—that the other route is denied, and is much more pleasant. Eventually reaching the valley in the vicinity of the highway at Col de Montets it continues its descent by going via Trélechamp where simple accommodation is available, although shopping is only feasible at Argentière which is slightly further on.

The Aiguilles Rouges is the name given to the hills and mountainside flanking the northern side of the Chamonix valley which offers a wonderful stretch of walking territory and it is over its length that the final paces of the TMB are taken.

The path starts at the Montets pass and its persistent climb will taunt even the strongest thigh muscles. Approached with a slow determination height is soon won and there are one or two places suited to short breaks which give ever-widening views, particularly the increasing aspects of the beautiful Aiguille Verte and the now-visible Glacier d'Argentière.

Eventually the path levels to contour the hillsides and, as the whole walk is abundant with five-star views, it will only be the insensitive who won't be thrilled by the experience. The buildings on their promontory position at La Flégère are clearly visible from afar, although it will take longer than imagined to get to the spot. The place is served by cableway from Chamonix, a by-product of which swells the numbers in the restaurant. Don't resent this, though, as it is unlikely that the restaurant would be viable without these extra people. There is the opportunity of a worthy diversion to the revered Lac Blanc, a particularly attractive spot higher up the mountainside.

The path continuing past La Flégère is one of the most prestigious in the Alps and is known as the Grand Balcon. Being open throughout, and as it is symmetrically opposite the main chain of Mont Blanc, it certainly lives up to its name for the two hours it will take. The Mer de Glace seems to bisect the range, the sheer north wall of the Grandes

Sunset on the Aiguille Verte and the Drus, seen from the Chamonix valley near Argentière. *(Andrew Harper FRPS)*

Jorasses visible in the distance behind. Further along, the dagger-like Bossons Glacier becomes a dominant feature.

With its stubby TV tower being an aid to recognition, the Aiguille du Midi is one of many spiky summits that are collectively called the Chamonix Aiguilles. To their right, Mont Blanc appears serenely confident with its gently-curved white mantle, its associated satellites the Dôme du Goûter and Aiguille du Goûter being old friends remembered from Day One.

Passing Plan Praz the route continues by ascending the spur leading to Col Brévent. Accessible only by walkers, the col can be quite a wind trap given the wrong conditions, but it certainly represents one of the nicest vantage points for observing Mont Blanc. From its gap, the hillsides to the north also come to view.

The Brévent is the highest point reached during the day and only needs a little sunshine

for its small terrace to become crowded with tourists who have arrived by cableway. Downhill for the rest of the way, most folk usually find they have had enough by the time they reach Les Houches. The path first goes along a ridge and drops slightly to the nicely-positioned refuge at Bellachat. Descent is fairly rapid for a short while after that and once down the bare mountainside, the path levels (by comparison!) to get amongst the bushes, dips into ravines to cross under attractive waterfalls and finally through an increasing density of trees to arrive at the valley bottom adjacent to the railway station.

It comes as a surprise to most people that Chamonix is not on the TMB route, but the merit of keeping high when plying the length of the valley has definite values. Chamonix is not without its interests and time spent there at the end of the holiday can be a suitable way of winding-down from the exhilarations.

WALK 14: *Col De Riedmatten by Kev Reynolds*

Location: Between Val des Dix and Val d'Arolla in the Pennine Alps of southern Switzerland.

How to get there: By train along the Rhône valley to Sion, and by Postbus from there into Val d'Hérens. Privately operated bus from Vex to Le Chargeur; or continuing Postbus to Arolla. Most convenient international airport—Geneva. By road through Switzerland to Sion in the Rhône valley, then head south into Val d'Hérens and/or Val d'Hérémence.

Valley bases: Pralong, Evolène, Les Haudères or Arolla.

Distance: 14 kilometres (9 miles).

Time required: 5-6 hours.

Height gain: 817 metres.

Height loss: 921 metres.

Type of walk: Strenuous in short sections, but mostly easy-going despite some rough patches under foot. Visually spectacular, and on a bright summer's day protection against the sun is strongly advised. Do not set out if there is any chance of bad weather, as there is no shelter to be had along the route, nor any chance of refreshment. Carry a lunch packet and sufficient liquids.

Start: Le Chargeur, Val d'Hérémence/Val des Dix.

Finish: Arolla.

Map: Landeskarte der Schweiz 1:50,000 series, sheet no 283 *Arolla*.

Guidebook: *The Valais—Switzerland* by Kev Reynolds (Cicerone Press).

From Val des Dix to Arolla

Val d'Hérens feeds into the long, flat-bottomed valley of the Rhône outside Sion. But while the Rhône is a hot and sometimes sultry valley, Val d'Hérens is moderated by the crisp, vibrant air of the high mountains that block it to the south. Journeying into it a twist of road climbs steeply away from low-growing orchards and vineyards, and once the necessary height has been gained, the valley then forges ahead in a shaft of delight towards an Alpine wonderland. A third of the way in the valley forks just below the village of Euseigne, which is noted for the pyramids of morainic debris topped by caps of stone deposited there by long-gone glaciers. The western fork of the valley, drained

Mont Blanc de Cheilon seen from the path above the Cheilon Glacier shortly before climbing to the pass. (Kev Reynolds)

by the Dixence river, then becomes the Val d'Hérémence while the main, continuing, valley remains as the Hérens as far as Les Hau-dères where it forks once again. The upper, western branch of Val d'Hérens then becomes the Val d'Arolla, while the upper section of Val d'Hérémence is known as Val des Dix. Between Val des Dix and Val d'Arolla, and running in a long, craggy, dividing line of rock, is the high ridge of the Aiguilles Rouges and Monts Rouges.

In his chapter on the Chamonix to Zermatt High Route (Walk 20), Andrew Harper describes the crossing of that ridge by way of the Pas de Chèvres—one of the highlights of the long trek. It is a fine crossing, of that there can be no doubt, the valleys on either side of the pass offering dramatic and spectacular views of the snow peaks of the central Pen-nine Alps.

But Pas de Chèvres is just one of two neigh-bouring passes; the other being the Col de Riedmatten (2919m), slightly higher but no more difficult than Chèvres, and this too is a classic crossing. It would be a shame then, not to include this passage in a collection of clas-sic walks in the Alps, for it undoubtedly deserves a chapter all its own. From start to finish the route is full of grandeur, packed with interest and variety, and should be on the 'tick list' of all mountain walkers heading for the Alps.

My first crossing was made some years ago now, in a summer not noted in Switzerland for its balmy days. In fact the first few days of that trip had been unbelievably wet, and two or three valleys away from our soggy camp-site a flash flood had wrecked a village and washed away great sections of road. But when the rain did ease off at last the sun came out to smile its benediction and, full of apologies, attempted to make amends for its over-long absence.

We drove round to Le Chargeur at the base of the huge dam above Pralong in Val d'Héré-mence, but if you are based in the nearby Val d'Hérens and need public transport to Le Chargeur, it is best to take a Postbus down-valley to Vex, and from there catch a privately-operated bus as far as the roadhead in Val d'Hérémence. Alternatively, take a Postbus as far as Euseigne and walk the short stretch of linking road to Mâche, from where the pri-vate bus may be taken for the last uphill sec-tion to Le Chargeur.

It was in the 'sixties that the Val des Dix was dammed as part of the impressive Grande Dixence hydro-electric scheme, and the mas-sive barrage at Le Chargeur (Barrage de la Grande Dixence) now towers over the woods

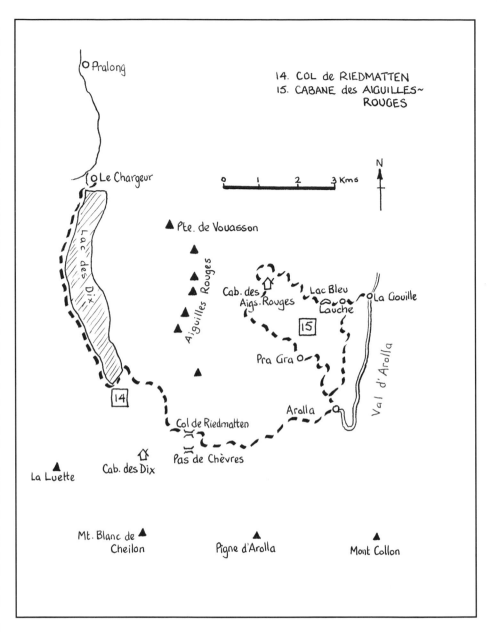

14. COL de RIEDMATTEN
15. CABANE des AIGUILLES~ROUGES

and little meadows of the upper Val d'Héré-mence like something from a science fiction movie. It is a stupendous piece of engineering, the scale difficult to comprehend, while offi-cial statistics merely hint at its size: from base to barrage crest it stands twice as high, with twice the volume of the largest of Egypt's pyramids. To build it took 5,960,000 cubic metres of concrete, and it holds back some 400 million cubic metres of water. It is, apparently, the highest dam in the world—but it gives me the horrors! There is an hotel in the shadow of the dam wall, but I'd have to be dragged screaming to spend a night there with that oppressive monster looming outside.

A cable-car swings up from a car park to the top of the dam wall, thereby saving a steep climb of about thirty minutes or so up a narrow twisting pathway. We walked.

From the top of the dam there stretched a vast sheet of water almost six kilometres long, discoloured from the weeks of heavy rain, but at the far end of the valley a most magnifi-cent backcloth of mountains rose full of snow-gleam against a cloudless, deep blue sky. It was a magical view and one that we would be delighted to walk into as the day progressed. But what, I wondered, would the Val des Dix have been like before the hydro engineers came to reshape the landscape?

From the western end of the dam wall a clear, broad track leads alongside the lake and passes through several tunnels. The first of these is the longest and darkest, but it has a string of electric lights to illuminate the way. There is a switch at the tunnel entrance timed to give five minutes of light, and this enables you to avoid the large puddles and potholes that form obstacles along the track.

We emerged squinting in the bright sunlight, following the track as it continued to the south, green meadows to the right, snow-peaks ahead and dark walls of rock on the far side of the lake where the mountainside rose steeply to the crusty ridge of the Aiguilles Rouges. That ridge directed our route southward, towards snow domes and glaciers dominated by the great wedge of Mont Blanc de Cheilon (3870m) and La Ruinette (3875m), with Le Pleureur (3703m) slightly nearer with its glacier peeling down towards the far end of the lake. A third of the way along the lake we passed an alp off to our right, cattle grazing, their bells clattering in the still morning air.

At the southern end of the man-made Lac des Dix a breakaway path went off towards the Cabane des Dix which is perched above the Cheilon Glacier in an astonishingly beautiful setting, and from which a number of fine mountaineering routes are made accessible. Ignoring this option we crossed a metal footbridge slung across the end of the lake where a spume of water was bursting from a ravine, and took the Col de Riedmatten path climbing over rough slopes starred with edelweiss and the massed purple trumpets of the field gentian.

Side streams were rushing through barren gullies and over our path, and we leapt from rock to rock to avoid the worst of their excesses. There were snow patches dirtied by stones and grit from mountains that towered above us, and we heard the hollow clatter of other stones bouncing through distant clefts as overnight ice melted to aid the slow destruction of every peak around.

The path rose, topped a bluff and there before us was the full unchallenged glory of Mont Blanc de Cheilon, its vast triangular north face rising from a snake of ice. From the pyramid another wall folded fan-like to the east, the structure of its rock seeming to ripple in the perfect, clear light of September, and above it all ran the delicate line of a virginal cornice, wave upon wave against the deep blue sky.

Below the mountain and below our path, the Cheilon Glacier eased its way through the valley, drab and drear without the covering of snow it required to make it properly attrac-

Lac des Dix, with Mont Blanc de Cheilon the great wedge-shaped peak in the background. (Kev Reynolds)

tive, and this late in the summer it was grey with grit and rubble.

Our route followed the line of the glacier, but some way from it. It took us across a rough boulder-and-scree landscape, in places climbing steeply, sometimes passively on the level, and always with Mont Blanc de Cheilon drawing us on. Then we caught sight of the metal ladder that eases the approach to (and descent from) Pas de Chèvres, and spied a tiny figure dressed in red gingerly descending to the rocks below.

The path suddenly swung left and began its sharp ascent to our pass in tight zig-zags, the walls on either side narrowing to constrict the trail and denying us the views we'd become accustomed to. But this was to lead to a most satisfying col; not a broad grassy saddle, not an open glacier pass nor a bowl of dazzling snow, but a brief slice, a rocky cleft unseen and undetected until the very last moment.

Col de Riedmatten presents those who gather there with a gift, a window onto a brave new world.

A last few steps in the shadows and light suddenly flooded ahead of us, washing a landscape of snow, ice and rock, and a distant slope of grass. Below at our feet the mountain fell

into a basin of rocky debris beyond which swept the Glacier de Tsijiore Nouve. But our eyes were momentarily ignorant of these things for all our attention was captured by the crest of Pigne d'Arolla, by the great iced gateau of Mont Collon, by the sharp spike of the Matterhorn's upper reaches far off, by the dark wall of rock topped by the Aiguille de la Tsa and by the snow-wrapped Dent Blanche beyond that.

It is an astonishing view, but there is even more to be seen if you scramble up the rocks to the left of the col and wander along the ridge a short distance where the panorama of such a well-ordered landscape is quite unrestricted. (But take care, for a slip could have fatal consequences.)

Since leaving the lake we had had the path to ourselves, but within moments of our arrival at the col we were joined by a German couple who had come that morning from Arolla. Together we shared an enthusiasm for this magical place and helped each other identify peaks on a serrated horizon. With the aid of their extremely powerful binoculars we could make out the gleam of one or two remote huts otherwise lost in the dazzle of mountains far away. Ah, the world would be grand from

Having passed through a handful of tunnels, the lakeside track leads deeper into Val des Dix. (Kev Reynolds)

those distant lodgings, I thought, but harboured no twinge of longing for our perch on the Col de Riedmatten gave as much grandeur as I could take for now.

The descent to Arolla is straightforward and follows a clear path. At first, of course, there is a steep drop to the rough bowl of debris, but beyond this the trail from Pas de Chèvres is joined and the way continues as a dance over vagrant streams, across a few rocky patches then soft turf and former moraine banks now green with age and bright with flowers. There were Alpine asters and starry saxifrage, more gentians and boulders daubed with the rich patterns of lichen.

But more than anything else, it is Mont Collon that holds your attention all the way down. On the western side of the col it had been Mont Blanc de Cheilon, but now the world is dominated by the great snow-daubed island peak of Mont Collon. From the pass it had appeared majestic and regal, yet as we descended towards Val d'Arolla with Pigne d'Arolla shining over our right shoulder, so Mont Collon grew more and more elevated above its ice-moat. We wandered down towards it, spellbound.

Passing ruined huts and still leaping streams the path forks. Straight ahead the way continues down to Arolla, but the left branch leads

over a shoulder of pastureland and on to the delectable little alp hamlet of Pra Gra, and if you have no business to attend to in Arolla, it might be worth squeezing the day dry by taking this route beyond Pra Gra and on up the hillside to the Aiguilles Rouges hut, as described in Walk 15, there to spend the night.

But Arolla itself should not be dismissed lightly. Small though it is, it has much to commend it. Not least are the continuing views up to Mont Collon as you slump at a café table and down a welcome cool drink as you reflect on the day's pleasures.

WALK 15: *Cabane Des Aiguilles Rouges by Kev Reynolds*

Location: Val d'Arolla/Val d'Hérens, southern Switzerland.

How to get there: By train along the Rhône valley to Sion, and by Postbus from there to Arolla. Most convenient international airport—Geneva. By road through Switzerland to Sion in the Rhône valley, then head south into Val d'Hérens.

Valley bases: Evolène, Les Haudères or Arolla.

Distance: 10 kilometres (6 miles) to La Gouille, or 13 kms for the loop back to Arolla.

Time required: 4–5 hours.

Height gain: 812 metres.

Height loss: 966 metres.

Type of walk: Fairly strenuous—especially on the descent. Some rough sections of path, but nothing notably difficult.

Start: Arolla.

Finish: La Gouille (or Arolla).

Map: Landeskarte der Schweiz 1:50,000 series, sheet no 283 *Arolla*.

Guidebooks: *The Valais—Switzerland* by Kev Reynolds (Cicerone Press). *Walking Switzerland the Swiss Way* by Marcia & Philip Lieberman (Cordee).

A high walk from Arolla

The village of Arolla, set at the head of the long Val d'Hérens in the Pennine Alps of southern Switzerland, has been a particular favourite of British climbers and walkers for something like a hundred years. Going back to Victorian times there was an English church there, the very symbol of respectability and proof, if any were needed, of its acceptance as a centre of note. "In spite of its great height," said R L G Irving, tongue in cheek, "I have known people who found this church disappointingly low."

Climbing higher towards the hut the wall of peaks on the far side of the valley seem to grow in stature. (Kev Reynolds)

Whilst it is easy to appreciate the full charm of Arolla and its surrounding mountains, it is less simple to explain why the British should have adopted it so open-heartedly. That they did, and that Arolla has not outgrown its charm in the many decades since, is to its credit. It has grown, of course, but not to the extent that St Moritz, Zermatt, Grindelwald or Mürren—to name but a few other centres adopted by the Victorians—have grown, and it remains a small, unpretentious base for walkers and mountaineers attracted by the simple beauty of its setting and by the wide range of outings available there.

Quoting R L G Irving again: "Arolla is still small and the hills around it are big, so that even if the weather is so fine that it chases every visitor out of doors, it is easy to find solitude. May peace remain with it and the hoot of cars be never heard!" Fifty years on, all that is still true, save for the hoot of cars. Motor traffic has now replaced the mules that twice daily brought the village its post, although the road up from Les Haudères was not built until well after the second World War. Despite this 'modernisation' Arolla remains untroubled and quietly comfortable with its superb backcloth of 'big hills'— Mont Collon, Pigne d'Arolla, L'Evêque and their sweeping glaciers—as guarantors of its continued popularity.

The village is trapped at the end of a long mountainous trench, known here as the Val d'Arolla since its branch extension from the Val d'Hérens at Les Haudères, and nestled among its scattered woods of larch and Arolla pine. Above it to the south rise the snow peaks of the main Pennine crest, none of which reach the elevations of those better-known peaks above Zermatt, for example, but it is nonetheless a lovely collection of mountains that offer moderate ascents for moderate mountaineers cutting their teeth on their first Alpine summits. From them sweep the converging glaciers that add an undeniable grace and splendour to the scene.

To either side, to east and west, long northward projecting ridges have produced steep walls of rock that cast morning and evening shadows over the valley. The eastern ridge has as its most prominent focal point the sharp little finger of the Aiguille de la Tsa (3668m) jabbing skywards, but along the same ridge there also rise the Pointe de Genévois and Grande Dent de Veisivi as if to underscore its style. The western wall, which divides the Val d'Arolla from the Val des Dix, is buffed by the Monts Rouges and the crest of the Aiguilles Rouges d'Arolla— their highest point being 3646 metres. But whilst the eastern wall remains almost entirely the preserve of the rock climber, the western wall, being more open and a little less severe in its contours, offers some enticing outings for walkers. The route to the Cabane des Aiguilles Rouges is perhaps the best of them all.

This is a day's walk, strenuous at times but not unduly difficult, and one that will give several hours of the most wonderful mountain views. It's a walk to wander slowly, giving time to admire the views, the wild flowers, the alp hamlets, a small blue tarn and the overwhelming peace of it all. There are two alp hamlets to visit, and at one of them it might be possible to watch cheese being made. Marmots and chamois may well be seen, while the hut itself, coming in the middle of the walk, will provide an ideal opportunity to have lunch in a memorable setting. (Food and drinks are available when the guardian is in residence, and you can check this in Arolla before setting out.)

If you are based in Arolla, then this walk can be made into a loop trip to bring you back to the village. If, however, you are staying down-valley in Les Haudères or Evolène, you can start by taking a Postbus to Arolla and ending the walk some way north of the village at La Gouille, from which point you can wait for the Postbus home again.

From the main square in Arolla, near the Post Office, the walk begins by heading uphill along a surfaced road following signs for Lac Bleu. After passing a few hairpin bends a broad track leads off to the right and winds steadily uphill. By this time Mont Collon has become very much a feature in the landscape to gaze at with great pleasure. It is a lovely mountain, shapely and ice-crowned, with bold rock ridges and buttresses and glaciers forming a moat on either side.

After passing a few wooden chalets it is best to leave the track in favour of a path climbing steeply up the grassy hillside, and you will soon emerge onto a neat shelf of pasture where the few houses, barns and cattle byres of Pra Gra are gathered closely together to compose a superb picture.

This little hamlet, with its dark timbers and grey shingles, its water trough and gliding stream, is one of my all-time favourite summer communities to be found anywhere in the Alps. It is in one of the most picturesque settings imaginable, smiling out across the pastures to those great snow peaks that make an icy amphitheatre to the south. Not only does Mont Collon appear so regal from here, but the graceful Pigne d'Arolla (named after the Arolla pine), raises a great wave of snow and also catches the breath with delight.

From Arolla to Pra Gra will take no more than an hour, and from here to the Cabane des Aiguilles Rouges will require perhaps another hour and a half. On this continuing section of the route the way becomes rather rough underfoot, but not sufficiently so to make for difficulties.

A clear, broad path leads round the hillside from Pra Gra heading north so that Mont Collon and its neighbours are now behind you. You will come to a wide plateau where the trail curves leftwards into a wild region of boulder slopes and gravel beds, with streams running through and marmots calling their shrill warnings from observation posts on the boulders. On the slopes above there are sometimes chamois to be seen, and draped in the upper reaches of a minor hanging valley a small glacier and patches of last winter's snow form a solemn picture as they drain down into the stony basin. At the head of the glacier lies Col des Ignes, which marks the divide between the Monts Rouges to the south and the Aiguilles Rouges to the north, and which offers a strenuous and challenging crossing to the lake-filled Val des Dix on the far side.

The continuing path to the hut, picked out with red and white paint flashes, takes you across the gravel beds and over a stream well below the glacier and its col, and swings to the right to make a rising traverse of the rough boulder and scree slopes that lie at crazy angles below the Aiguilles Rouges glaciers. (These glaciers are either hidden or foreshortened from the path, caught as they are in shallow corries above.) At one rather delicate and exposed place the path is safeguarded by a fixed chain—this section is only difficult when icy—and the final pull up to the hut is steep, but straightforward.

Cabane des Aiguilles Rouges (2810m) is loftily perched on the edge of the steeply plunging hillside nearly a thousand metres above the valley, with magnificent views across to the Aiguille de la Tsa and its neighbours opposite, the Dent Blanche tipped white beyond the intervening ridge, and up-valley to Mont Collon again, while behind the hut the long rock wall of the Aiguille Rouges presents a temptation to climbers. The hut is a sturdy stone-built affair, owned by the Academic Alpine Club of Geneva, but is open to all.

This is a stern countryside, so different from that around Pra Gra, yet it is not without charm and a night spent here would surely be a night to savour as you watch the valley below fill with mist and darkness while the aiguilles opposite hold on to the very last stain of a dying sun.

Leaving the hut to continue with the walk the way rises a little, directed by arrows painted

One of the most picturesque alps in Switzerland: Pra Gra, with Mont Collon appearing like a giant iced gâteau behind.
(Kev Reynolds)

on the rocks, then drops steeply, at first towards the east in order to cross a stream, then veering south-eastwards on a clear path once more. The descent is testing on knees and thigh-muscles as the way maintains a steep angle, and if your boots are a little on the small side you'll be cursing them all the way down! Yet tiring though it may be the interest never wanes, for there are many new and varied vistas to enjoy—variations on a now-familiar theme—as well as pleasures to be gained as you pass from one vegetation layer to the next, flowers become more profuse and now and again you wander near colonies of marmots.

Having lost more than seven hundred metres of height since leaving the hut, you come to Lac Bleu, a charming little tarn, clear, cold and sparkling, set in a bowl of greenery and with a waterfall cascading into its western end. This makes a popular and easy outing from Arolla, whose path gives the opportunity to return to the village, thus making the day's walk a circular one. If this is your plan cross the log bridge at the eastern end of the lake, turn right and follow an unmarked path which wanders southward, contouring along the hill-side among trees and shrubbery all the way to Arolla.

For those whose aim is to continue from Lac Bleu down into the valley as far as La Gouille, cross the log bridge at the opposite end to the waterfall and descend to another little alp hamlet (Louché) where a notice board announces that it is sometimes possible to watch cheese being made here. The path continues to descend, still steeply and now among woods, and finally comes onto the valley road at the tiny village of La Gouille with its little circular pond and opportunities for refreshment while you wait for the Postbus to return you to your base.

WALK 16: *Roc De La Vache*
by Kev Reynolds

Location: Val de Zinal/Val d'Anniviers, canton Valais, Switzerland.
How to get there: By train to Sierre in the Rhône valley, and by Postbus from there to Zinal. Most convenient international airport—Geneva. By road through Switzerland to Sierre, then south into Val d'Anniviers.
Valley base: Zinal.
Distance: 11 kilometres (7 miles).
Time required: 5 hours.
Height gain/loss: 906 metres.
Type of walk: Moderate, but with steep sections, on clear paths all the way. No route finding difficulties, but choose a clear day. Carry a lunch packet and a flask of liquid refreshment.
Map: Landeskarte der Schweiz 1:50,000 series, sheet no 5006 *Matterhorn—Mischabel*.
Guidebook: *The Valais—Switzerland* by Kev Reynolds (Cicerone Press).

Alps and glaciers—under the Weisshorn:

Two valleys to the west of Zermatt's valley, the Mattertal, runs the glorious Val d'Anniviers, considered by many to be the grandest or greatest of all the Swiss valleys of the Pennine Alps. "This supremely lovely district" is how J Hubert Walker described it, and that simple phrase makes an adequate précis of its charm.

There are many contrasts to be discovered between the heavy warmth of the vine-clad Rhône at its northern outflowing and the great amphitheatre of peaks at its southern head; tremendous peaks such as the Grand Cornier, Dent Blanche, Pointe de Zinal, Mont Durand, Ober Gabelhorn, Zinalrothorn and Weisshorn, each with its own glacial drapery. And as you journey south through the lush green valley towards that amphitheatre, so an assortment of rocky spires and gleaming snow-heads lures you on into a wonderland.

Sixteen kilometres or so from Sierre the Val d'Anniviers divides into two distinct branches. The main valley continues slightly east of south and is known as the Val de Zinal, while the alternative fork, heading south-west, becomes the Val de Moiry. Both are worth exploring,

The Moming Glacier seen from the tarn at Ar Pitetta. (Kev Reynolds)

Afternoon clouds partially obscure mountains at the head of Zinal's valley. (Kev Reynolds)

both have lovely villages and superb walks; but the route about to be described is tackled from Val de Zinal, the branch named after the last village in the valley.

Zinal is a village with a long tradition as a mountaineering centre, and it has its own mountain guides' bureau even today. Those determined and active Victorian pioneers, Edward Whymper and A W Moore, both knew it well during the so-called Golden Age of Mountaineering which ended with Whymper's tragic first ascent of the Matterhorn in 1865, and a year before that momentous ascent he and Moore, with Christian Almer and Michel Croz as guides, made the first crossing of the Moming Pass between Zinal and Zermatt. On their way from Zinal to the glaciers their approach route took them below the Roc de la Vache and up to the Alp d'Ar Pitetta, which forms part of this walk.

As a base for a walking holiday Zinal has much to commend it. There are several hotels

and pensions, some with dormitories, offering a range of accommodation, and a camp site on the southern outskirts of the village for those who prefer to use their own, more portable, base. There are a few food stores and restaurants, and an indoor swimming pool for use on bad-weather days off from walking. The big mountains are never far away, but Zinal is almost too close to them to benefit from their full visual impact, for the prominent rock peak of Lo Besso manages to get in the way of some of the best, and it is only by pulling on your boots and taking to the network of footpaths that splay out from the village that the wonders of the region become properly appreciated. Roc de la Vache which rises just to the south of Zinal is one of the finest viewpoints in all the Alps that is easily accessible to walkers, rather than being the preserve of mountaineers, and it is this route to it, and beyond it, that is designed to draw out the full extent of panoramic grandeur available.

Like so many others contained in this book, this is a steep walk, but it has something of everything to maintain interest all the way; it has dashing streams and cascades, an ever-varied vegetation, gleaming tarns, a high col to cross, attractive and isolated alp huts, and some of the most exquisite high mountain scenery in all of Europe. There are no opportunities for refreshment along the way, so take a packed lunch and a flask of drink, choose a day of sunshine and clear skies and treat yourself to a day of magic.

The walk begins by the village church in Zinal with direction signs for Cabane Tracuit and Roc de la Vache. You should set out by following these along a road that heads out of the village for a short distance, winding through meadows and sparse woods. There are footpath alternatives in places, but it is not long before a signpost directs you away from the road and onto a narrow path climbing steeply among trees and shrubs that threaten at first to swamp the way, and then over rough pastures heading south-east. In a little under an hour you will come to a huddle of alp huts enjoying views to the Pigne de la Lé, the Bouquetins ridge and Grand Cornier on the opposite side of the valley. The path eases, makes a long loop along the hillside, then continues as a fine belvedere with views growing more dramatic to the south. Gazing back towards the hinted depths of the Rhone's valley far off, Val d'Anniviers begins to display its more modest charms; the mixed greenery of meadow and forest, the dark speckles of villages and alp hamlets, the long-running ridges that wall it.

The path leads towards a waterfall cascading from a cleft of rock, then climbs above it and comes to a junction of trails. The path for Roc de la Vache goes off to the right, while that to the left is bound for Cabane Tracuit. Roc de la Vache will be reached in little more than fifteen minutes from this point, so if you have time to spare it is worth taking the alternative path for a short diversion. It goes up to the little alp hut of Combautanna (2578m) on a shoulder of rolling pastureland in the Tracuit amphitheatre topped by Les Diablons and Tête de Milon, both around 3600 metres altitude. It's a bare, stony corrie above, enlivened by a fan of streams, but from the Combautanna hut you look out to the south-west for a wonderful view across Roc de la Vache to the Grand Cornier, snow and ice a-dazzle in the sunshine.

To return to the footpath junction you can either descend by the upward path, or break away into the bowl of pasture where a pool or two are to be found, and where streams amalgamate in a feathery patch of cotton grass and spongy turf. From here the mountains assume different dimensions.

From the path junction above the waterfall an easy amble of a quarter of an hour leads to the vantage point of Roc de la Vache (2581m), a grassy saddle on a rocky pedestal about two and a half hours after leaving Zinal. Suddenly the world is spread out before you in a glory of mountains, glaciers, snowfields and a deep, deep valley. Val de Zinal is some 900 metres below, a deep trench of greys and greens and silver streams. But it is not the valley itself that holds the eye, rather it is the glaciers that direct all one's attention towards the valley head and its great amphitheatre of magnificence. Out there is a multi-dimensional kaleidoscope of shapely peaks jabbing at the sky, ice walls like blue mirrors, snow slopes formed with perfection and grace, cornices trapped in waves along the ridges; a contrast of height and depth, light and shade with all

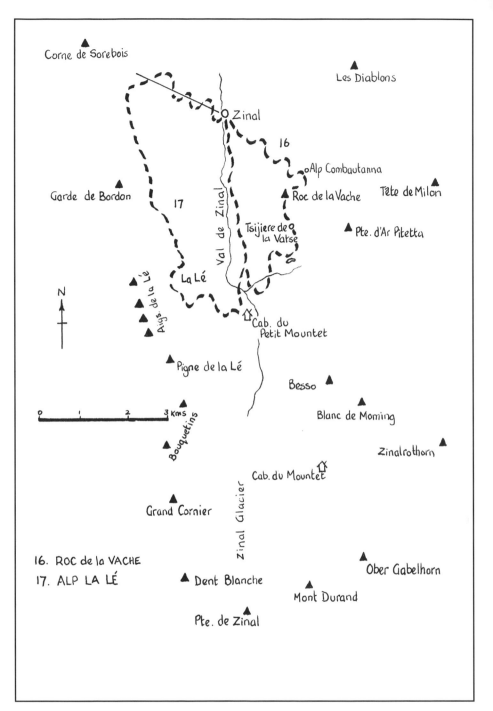

the colours ranging from brilliant white to darkest brown and down to green as the vista is scanned with a renewed sense of wonder.

The stupendous mass of the Moming Glacier is held back by the retaining wall of Lo Besso. The Zinalrothorn peeks shyly above a dazzling white crest, while Point Sud de Moming edges above its apron of ice. The Weisshorn (4505m), monarch of the valley and

the highest point on the ridge separating Val de Zinal from the Mattertal, is unseen from here by virtue of the rocks of Point d'Ar Pitetta, but on the descent southward so this beautiful shapely peak begins to appear and the cirque dominated by the Moming and Weisshorn glaciers spreads itself out for inspection to the left.

There is nothing difficult in the descent from Roc de la Vache, save for the problems associated with one's attention straying from the job in hand to gaze again and again at the glorious views, but when you come to the deserted hut of Tsijiere de la Vatse (2388m) it is worth pausing for a few moments to study the increasing scale of the glaciers and cream-curling cornices of the Moming ridge high above, and of the long shaft of the valley ploughed by the Zinal Glacier whose retreating mass appears in summer to be unwashed and grey with debris from the mountains. Grand Cornier and Dent Blanche battle to hold your concentration in preference to the nearer bowl of the Weisshorn.

Different again is the view from the collection of little tarns below the hut at the entrance to the Weisshorn's bowl, here green and grazed by sheep. This is the outer rim of Alp d'Ar Pitetta, as lovely a spot as you could possibly wish to visit.

When Whymper and Moore came this way in July 1864 they were looking for a chalet belonging to herdsmen and cheesemakers in order to spend a night under the protection of a roof before attempting the Moming Pass. This chalet turned out to be a rough hut which they found higher in the cirque in a position whose romance completely passed them by. Whymper described their lodging as: "a hovel, growing, as it were, out of the hill-side; roofed with rough slabs of slaty stone; without a door or window; surrounded by quagmires of ordure, and dirt of every description." This hut is marked as Cabane d'Ar Pitetta on the map and is found another five hundred metres higher, just below the Weisshorn Glacier. There is a path leading to it from the tarns, and another, but harder, route crossing the Crête de Milon to the east of Pointe d'Ar Pitetta above the cabane which shows the mountains in a dramatic view.

The diversion is worth tackling by those who are fit and energetic and have time to stray, but the tarns of Louchelet are in themselves so delectably set that it is tempting simply to laze by them and dream with the stunning mountain views all around.

To continue the walk take the path which bears right and drops through a region of alpenroses, juniper and larch—still with vistas of enchantment ahead—then swings down in steep twists among trees to cross a glacial stream near the valley bed. Shortly after this the torrent rushing from the Zinal Glacier is crossed and you then join a broad path coming from the Mountet hut, and this takes you down-valley all the way to Zinal.

It's a long walk down into the Zinal Valley, but with superb views of Dent Blanche all the way. (Kev Reynolds)

WALK 17: *Alp La Lé by Kev Reynolds*

Location: Val de Zinal / Val d'Anniviers, canton Valais, Switzerland,

How to get there: By train to Sierre in the Rhône valley, and by Postbus from there to Zinal. Most convenient international airport—Geneva. By road through Switzerland to Sierre, then south into Val d'Anniviers.

Valley base: Zinal.

Distance: 18 kilometres (12 miles).

Time required: 6–7 hours.

Height gain/loss: 865 metres.

Type of walk: Apart from the initial steep uphill to Sorebois, this is mostly an easy-graded walk, although traversing the Alp La Lé pasture bowl the path is not always easy to locate. It is an exposed walk and should not be attempted when storms are likely. Refreshments available at Cabane du Petit Mountet.

Transport option: Cable-car from Zinal to Sorebois, thereby saving about 1½–2 hours walk.

Map: Landeskarte der Schweiz 1:50,000 series, sheet no 5006 *Matterhorn—Mischabel.*

Guidebook: *The Valais—Switzerland* by Kev Reynolds (Cicerone Press).

A high route with views to the Weisshorn

One classic route has already been described from Zinal, that to the viewpoint of Roc de la Vache (Walk 16), but there are plenty of other possibilities in the same region that could quite happily be admitted to the category of a classic and should be considered by those staying in the area for a few days. There's the up-valley walk with a glacier crossing to the Cabane de Mountet, for example, with its superb full-frontal view of the "world of towering crag and eternal snow" highly recommended by G D Abraham. There's the easy, but no less lovely, down-valley walk from Ayer to St Luc and on to Chandolin, or up to Hotel Weisshorn (mentioned in the Chamonix to Zermatt walk), or the ascent of Bella Tola (3025m) from St Luc. And there's the high path that leads to Alp La Lé.

La Lé, formerly known as La Lex, or l'Allée to the pioneers, is a large basin of pastureland

On the crest of this vegetated moraine sits the Petit Mountet refuge. (Kev Reynolds)

The Weisshorn group, from Alp La Lé. *(Kev Reynolds)*

scooped from the western wall of mountains above the Val de Zinal, directly opposite the Weisshorn. The valley end of this basin is only about two hundred metres above the Zinal river, but in order to gain it from the village by the path described will entail a steep climb of nearly eight hundred metres. There then follows an undulating trail along the plunging mountainside with superb views to enjoy almost every step of the way.

This mountainside reaches its crest at just over the 3000 metre contour and has one or two passes in it that allow crossings to be made into the adjacent Val de Moiry to the west. One of these crossings is by the easy Col de Sorebois (again, on the Chamonix to Zermatt walk); another is by way of a steep gully leading to Col de la Lé directly above Alp La Lé. There's also a little glacier pass to the north of Pigne de la Lé, but these are not a walker's crossings, although the summit of the Pigne at the northern end of the Bouquetins ridge

should not be beyond the realms of possibility for seasoned scramblers, and it gives some wonderful views of the bigger mountains to the south.

But the object of this chapter is the walker's route to Alp La Lé and on to the Cabane du Petit Mountet, before returning to Zinal. It is a walk with no shortage of memorable viewpoints—which are often what makes a walk a true classic. There is an option of uplift by cableway to begin with, and this would save almost two hours of exercise and more than 750 metres of ascent, but the route is described for walkers all the way.

A narrow surfaced road goes down to the river near the village tennis courts in Zinal. A wooden bridge leads across the river and a track takes you on into the woods that clothe the lower slopes of hillside. There are various alternative paths, but the one to take is sign-posted to Sorebois. It goes beneath the Zinal-Sorebois cableway and climbs in a series of

tight zig-zags, first to the little alp of Le Chiesso snug above the forest, then over increasingly bare hillside to the upper station of the cable-car; an uphill walk of between one and a half and two hours.

Views are rather splendid from here, especially towards the south-east where Tête de Milon and the Weisshorn soar above the deep-cut valley. But it is impossible to ignore the forlorn sight of the hillsides surrounding the cable-car station that have been sacrificed to the winter downhill ski industry. Bare pistes shorn of all grass are reminiscent of a building site, and skeleton tows march in silver ranks towards the upper ridge. Whilst understanding the eagerness of Zinal's citizens to have a share in the lucrative winter tourist trade, one despairs at the apparent necessity for such bland desecration. What may just be acceptable under a deep coating of winter snow becomes at the least an eyesore in summer, but could also speed the erosion of acres of hillside, with all that that entails. None of this is what we have come here to see, but fortunately all this is quickly left behind as the traversing path soon escapes and heads south towards views of a more natural, unsullied landscape.

The path becomes narrow as it eases an undulating course along the steep mountainside. There are a few streams to cross where they spray down little gullies, alpine plants flowering in the damp nearby crevices; and there are rocky sections and grassy bluffs to wander over. And all the time the views are growing. On the far side of the valley the Tracuit basin is shown clearly at first, the stub of Roc de la Vache forming a thumb of grass-topped rock below Pointe d'Ar Pitetta. Then comes the Arpitetta cirque rimmed with glaciers, with the big wall of the Weisshorn's west face sweeping round to the Schalihorn and the vast turmoil of ice that hangs in a frozen cascade below Pointe Sud de Moming, partially blocked from here by the graceful pyramid of Lo Besso, seen at last in its true worth as a double-pronged summit. Way below the Zinal Glacier is a grey sleeping serpent in a wasteland bed of moraine.

The mountainside steepens below the Garde de Bordon where bands of rock create shallow terraces of scree and poor grass, but the path works a route along these without undue difficulty, gains some more height to come onto a grass-covered bluff, and then forks. The continuing, left-hand, path descends towards the little hut of Alp La Lé at 2184 metres, while the right-hand option explores the bowl of pastureland below the Aiguilles de la Lé.

The right-hand alternative is the longer, more interesting walk and is the one described here. It takes you on a delightful detour as you make a traverse of the alp, but it has to be said that the path is not always evident, although with care there should be no problem. An easy way out of the cirque is to make for the hut of Crevache (2466m) and descend the trail from there. This comes onto the main traversing path a little to the north of the La Lé hut.

Crossing the cirque there are streams to jump, scree runs and rough pastures. There are steep cliffs above and a steep drop below beyond the lip of the alp—and all the time those wonderful views across the valley to the Weisshorn, and towards the head of the Zinal Glacier where the Ober Gabelhorn reigns supreme in a company of unashamedly handsome peaks.

Wandering here one afternoon I looked up at the backing cliffs to see an avalanche of sheep thundering down towards me. They had

Undisciplined sheep of Alp La Lé. *(Kev Reynolds)*

somehow been grazing the crags, and as they descended at a gravity-induced gallop, so they funnelled into a long, single, bell-tinkling file, like one enormous tail of wool. The possibilities of a photograph became evident at once and I directed Alan Payne, who was with me, to hurry onto a skyline bluff in the hope that the sheep would follow, and I could then photograph him like a misplaced Pied Piper silhouetted with the string of sheep behind against a backdrop of the Weisshorn.

As he made for the bluff as requested I scurried to a decent vantage point, but when I turned to him with the camera ready, he was being head-butted at a rate of knots out of sight—savaged by the curling horns of the sheep of Alp La Lé!

Towards the southern end of the bowl of Alp La Lé a faint trail may be found which leads quite steeply in places down to the main hillside traversing path. Once having joined this bear right and follow it up-valley to the Cabane du Petit Mountet, an unpretentious little mountain hut built on the northern end of the moraine wall overlooking the Zinal Glacier. From it there are yet more lovely views. The Weisshorn, once again, shows itself to be the grand master of the valley and one of the finest peaks of the Pennine Alps. From the hut you can gaze almost directly at it, and into its cirque of Ar Pitetta opposite. But being closer to the head of the valley, and with no major mountain spurs in the way, the stupendous amphitheatre of ice-clad summits to the south is seen to full advantage, and it is this view that dominates.

The lofty pyramid of the Ober Gabelhorn (4063m) takes centre stage with the

Wellenkuppe and Trifthorn to its left, rising over a billowing mass of snow and ice that spills down onto the Glacier Durand. Mont Durand hunches its clean white shoulders to the right of the Ober Gabelhorn, with the Dent Blanche to the right of that. Given time and energy it is tempting to wander to the grassy Plan des Lettres (2465m) at the southern end of the moraine crest for an even closer view, but this will add more to your day than at first appears, since the way is not always straightforward and there are sections of ladder to negotiate where the crest of moraine has crumbled away. Better, perhaps, to relax outside the Petit Mountet with a welcome drink and absorb the vista before you. On another day, maybe, you will be drawn to the route which leads along the moraine and across the glacier to the Cabane du Mountet—another classic walk from Zinal.

The return to Zinal takes you down the short, steep slope of moraine heading north. There are two ways; one leads along a broad track, the other takes a more narrow (but more interesting) route on a path among shrubbery. The two combine near the white-walled hut marked as Le Vichiesso (1862m) on the map.

From here the way is clear. The track is well-trodden, for it is the main route to so many compelling mountains and it traces the one-time course of the Zinal Glacier, down to a gravelly flood-plain where streams converge and after heavy rain a wild foam of a torrent surges through the stony bed. A sturdy wooden bridge takes you across to the right bank and the continuing track leads over meadows and down at last to the surfaced road that goes directly into Zinal.

WALK 18: *Under The Matterhorn by Kev Reynolds*

Location: At the head of the Mattertal, Pennine Alps, southern Switzerland.

How to get there: By rail through Switzerland to Visp, and from there to Zermatt. Nearest convenient international airport—Geneva. By road to Visp in the Rhône valley, then south through the Vispertal and Mattertal. Cars should be parked in Täsch (no motor vehicles allowed in Zermatt) and the train taken from there to Zermatt.

Distance: 12 kilometres (7½ miles).

Time required: 4½ hours (One way. Return by the same route, about 3 hours, or with cable-car about 1½).

Height gain: 1654 metres.

Type of walk: Very steep and tiring, but on good paths virtually all the way. Excellent high mountain views.

Map: Landeskarte der Schweiz 1:50,000 series, sheet no 5006 *Matterhorn-Mischabel*.

Guidebook: *The Valais—Switzerland* by Kev Reynolds (Cicerone Press).

Other reading: *Scrambles Amongst the Alps* by Edward Whymper (latest edition published by Webb & Bower 1986—with superb colour photos by John Cleare).

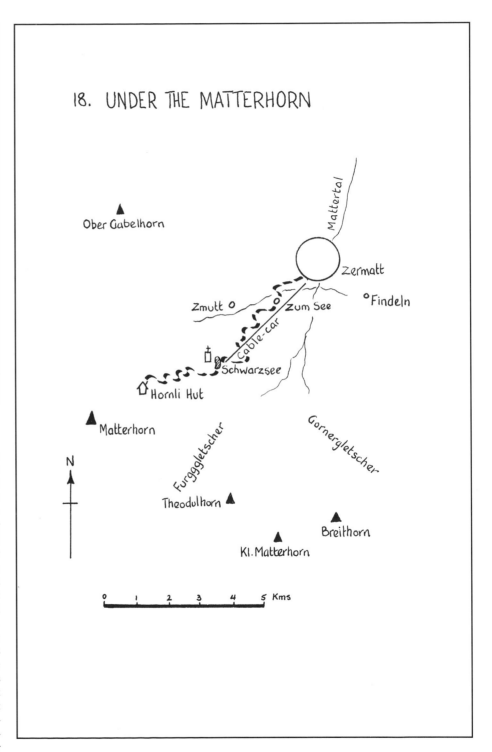

To the foot of the Matterhorn

No book about the Alps could possibly exclude the Matterhorn. It is, after all, the most instantly recognised mountain in the world. It is also one of the most spectacular and at the same time surely counts among the most beautiful of them all. Standing alone and rising above a high ridge of snow, this huge conical peak appears magnificent from whichever angle it is seen. An incomparable giant with its great ice-fashioned faces tapering to a needle-like summit (or so it would seem from below), the Matterhorn beckons from afar and dominates practically every view from Zermatt.

Zermatt is, of course, one of the great Alpine resorts alongside other such notables as Chamonix, Grindelwald and Cortina that have developed beyond simple mountaineering bases into centres of year-round appeal. And that year-round appeal is of such magnitude that it extends far beyond a selective sporting clientele to include as many or more general sight-seeing tourists as active climbers, walkers or skiers. The streets are crowded winter and summer, and its shops and boutiques offer the kind of luxuries that would not be out of place in any fashionable Paris boulevarde or West End salon. What Whymper and Croz would have thought about Zermatt's worldly development in the century and more since they first came here to climb the Matterhorn, is interesting to speculate!

But for all its growth and sophistication Zermatt still retains its mountain roots. The Matterhorn sees to that. For it is the Matterhorn, after all, that everyone comes to Zermatt to see. The development of one would not have been possible without the other, for the mountain on its own is guarantor of the resort's survival and continuing appeal.

Yet the Matterhorn is not the only mountain worth seeing here. Indeed, the superb ring of peaks at the head of the Mattertal includes the greatest collection of 4000 metre summits in all of Switzerland. The Matterhorn (4476m) is not even one of the highest. There's Monte Rosa, whose loftiest peak the Dufourspitze is shared with Italy and, at 4634 metres, is the highest point in the Alps outside the Mont Blanc massif. There's Dent d'Herens and Dent Blanche, Ober Gabelhorn and Zinalrothorn, with the Weisshorn to the north. There are huge concentrations of glacier and snowfield pouring from the Lyskamm, from the 'twins' of Castor and Pollux and the Breithorn that stands between them and the Matterhorn. (The Breithorn affords one of the easiest 4000 metre ascents in the Alps.) Each one has its own appeal, its own individual attraction, while together they form as magnificent a panorama as you could possibly wish to wave a camera at.

This walk, which goes up to the Hornli hut at the foot of the great Hornli Ridge of the Matterhorn, is just one of several superb walks available from Zermatt. Others include the easy trip to the magical hamlet of Findeln with its incomparable view of the Matterhorn, or to the Schönbiel hut overlooking a world of glacial majesty. There is also a steep route up to the Rothorn hut for dizzy views, or the ever-popular but crowded Gornergrat looking onto Monte Rosa.

The reason for offering this walk is two-fold. Firstly, it takes you close enough to the Matterhorn to reveal its true nature and to enable you to rub your nose against its rock (metaphorically speaking), and secondly, it leads to a wonderful vantage point from which to study the world of high mountains, expressed here by the neighbouring glaciers and towering peaks that have played such an integral part in the foundations of mountaineering. It is a steep, strenuous and somewhat tiring walk,

and it is unlikely that you will ever complete it without having plenty of company along the pathway (that is a price you pay for wandering in the shadow of the Matterhorn), but it fully repays the effort involved and rewards all who carry it through. For those who wish for an easier day there is cable-car access from Zermatt to the Schwarzsee Hotel, thereby saving about two and a half hours of effort; although what you save in effort is lost to experience.

Leaving Zermatt's crowded streets you wander south past the dark timbered chalets set on the outskirts of the resort which give an indication of what the village must have originally looked like, and continue along the footpath signposted to Zum See. From the very start the Matterhorn is the single focus of attention as it peers down from its unbelievably high pedestal with an air of aloof grandeur. At first the way leads along the true left bank of the Zmuttbach stream, but some way beyond the last of Zermatt's houses you cross this over a bridge and come to forested slopes forming a screen for the little hamlet of Zum See.

Zum See makes a remarkable contrast to Zermatt; a huddle of dark brown (almost black) timber buildings, most of which are set upon a white stone base, but with a few granaries resting on staddle stones, and with a pretty white-washed stone chapel to one side. A simple little place, so typical in style of the

Valais region, it caters for passing walkers with one of the buildings acting as a restaurant.

Once through Zum See the path suddenly rears up steeply in forest, making height in zig-zags and coming after some time to an isolated house set in a clearing and with views overlooking Zermatt, now beginning to look small some four hundred metres below. This is Hermetji (2053m), another tempting restaurant. Not far off the cable car which links Zermatt with the Schwarzsee Hotel goes whirring by.

There is no difficulty in finding the way; it just goes straight up the hillside! Once out of the forest rough grass slopes continue ahead with the Matterhorn now appearing somewhat stumpy through foreshortening, and after about two hours or so from Zermatt you top a rise and come to the Schwarzsee Hotel on a lip of hillside with a lovely view across the glaciers to Monte Rosa. All the world seems to gather here. Cable-car access sees to that.

In its deep bowl just to the west of the hotel is the little tarn of Schwarzsee with its photogenic chapel next to it; a scene that appears on numerous calendars and chocolate boxes. It's an idyllic spot whose simplicity and beauty is only tempered by the thronging tourists who gather there as part of Zermatt's pageantry.

Immediately behind the tarn the Matterhorn begins its rise with the Hornli Ridge twisting up between the mountain's north and east faces, the summit being almost two thousand metres above this point. If you peer up at the

Monte Rosa, seen from the Hornli path. (*Kev Reynolds*)

Schwarzsee, with its little white chapel, nestles below the Matterhorn. (Kev Reynolds)

mountain from here you can actually see the Hornli hut and Belvedere Hotel next to it on a shelving domed section of the ridge. The path which leads to it is at first broad and obvious, and passes above and to the left of the Schwarzsee.

There are grassy slopes initially, but these soon give way to a more barren and rocky terrain as you ascend in a series of steps, and in places the path has crumbled away to be replaced by a metal catwalk with ladders to help overcome obstacles such as steep crags and cliffs. Mostly, though, the pathway winds in an easy fashion up the lower ridge, sometimes over screes and windblown schist with views down onto the glaciers and the glacial troughs far beneath, grey and dreary when the snow-cover has gone. But as you gain height so distant views begin to spread themselves in a panorama of delight. Pausing on the pathway you should spare a minute or two to look back away from the Matterhorn towards the north where the Ober Gabelhorn and Dent Blanche rise in graceful shapes, and beyond them the stiletto point of the Zinalrothorn and the Weisshorn behind that. It is a glorious view, and one that is worth the effort to see.

Continuing, the route twists up the ridge and suddenly comes out above a rocky spur to the hut and hotel, standing side by side and looking out to the east. The views are splendid. From this rocky belvedere with the monstrous pyramid of the Matterhorn soaring above, you gaze across a sea of ice swilling down to the Gornergletscher, and off towards the huge shapely block of Monte Rosa and the snowy mass of the Weissgrat spreading northward to Strahlhorn and Rimpfischhorn. Nearer, but distorted in profile, Lyskamm and the Breithorn mostly hide the twins of Castor and Pollux. Also hidden is the ancient glacier pass of the Theodule by which the Italian resort of Breuil (or Cervinia as it is more often known today) is easily reached from Zermatt. It is a wonderful vista of high mountains, and if the weather is calm and warm it is good to take a table on the terrace outside the Belvedere Hotel and sit there with a drink or two and simply absorb the raw beauty of it all.

It is impossible to inhabit this spot without casting a thought to Edward Whymper and his colleagues who came here on 13 July 1865 and looked around for a site for their tent prior to making the first ascent of the Matterhorn. The story of Whymper's seven attempts to climb it, his final success and the tragedy that occurred on the descent, is one of the classics of mountaineering; a story known to non-climbers as to active mountaineers through the publication of *Scrambles Amongst the Alps*, a book

that has remained in print virtually ever since the first edition appeared in 1871.

At first light on the morning of 14 July Whymper, Michel Croz, Lord Francis Douglas, the Reverend Charles Hudson, Douglas Hadow and the two Peter Taugwalders (father and son) set off in anticipation of success, climbing the rocks that had been reconnoitred the previous day. They made good time, finding the route far easier than they'd dared hope or had been led to expect from study below, and at 1.40 pm stood upon the summit." The world was at our feet," wrote Whymper, "and the Matterhorn was conquered." It was a calm and clear day and the views were immense. Whymper enumerates in his book all the main summits in view, from the Disgrazia to Pelvous, from the Finsteraarhorn to Monte Viso and everything in between.

After an hour on the summit the party then began to tackle the descent, but shortly after three o'clock when they reached a difficult pitch, Hadow slipped and fell against Michel Croz, knocking him from his stance. The two fell, dragging Hudson down the slope and Lord Francis Douglas after them. Whymper and the two Taugwalders held tightly to the rocks and were saved from following the others when the rope between them broke.

Of the seven who had stood triumphant upon the Matterhorn's crown, only Whymper and the two Taugwalders returned safely to Zermatt. A storm subsequently broke over the world of mountaineering from which Whymper never really recovered. The winning of the Matterhorn had been a high-priced victory.

Now, of course, the Matterhorn is climbed by hundreds of mountaineers and non-mountaineers every summer. The guides who stay at either the Belevedere or Hornli receive a constant supply of clients, by far the majority wishing to repeat Whymper's route up the Hornli Ridge. It is not one of the finest of ascents in the Alps, but none would deny its historic appeal. The Matterhorn is, after all, the Matterhorn. But spend an hour or so at this spot and listen to the almost constant clatter of stones falling down the east face, or bouncing from the ledges of the Hornli, and you will realise then, perhaps with a degree of surprise, that this graceful peak is nothing really but a heap of loose rubble!

The little hamlet of Zum See outside Zermatt. (Kev Reynolds)

WALK 19: *Saas Fee Classics*
by Kev Reynolds

Location: Saastal, Pennine Alps, southern Switzerland.

How to get there: By train to Visp in the Rhône valley (or to Stalden in the Vispertal to the south), and Postbus from there to Saas Fee. Nearest convenient international airport—Geneva. By road through Switzerland to Visp, then south through the Vispertal and Saastal. Car parking compulsory on the outskirts of Saas Fee.

Valley base: Saas Fee.

Distance: 14 kilometres (9 miles).

Time required: 7–8 hours.

Height gain: 446 metres.

Height loss: 1221 metres.

Transport required: Cable-car Saas Fee to Felskinn.

Type of walk: One of the most varied day walks in this book with ice, snow, boulder fields, screes and soft turf under foot at times. There is an easy glacier to cross on a marked trail, streams to leap over and rough sections of path to negotiate. It is important to be well-shod and fit. A great deal of height has to be lost, but there are no exceptionally steep descents (or ascents) to tackle. Visually superb throughout. Take plenty of film for your camera. There are several opportunities for refreshment along the way, and two options for a quick descent to Saas via cableways from Plattjen and Hannig.

Map: Landeskarte der Schweiz 1:50,000 series, sheet no 5006 *Matterhorn—Mischabel.*

Guidebook: *The Valais—Switzerland* by Kev Reynolds (Cicerone Press).

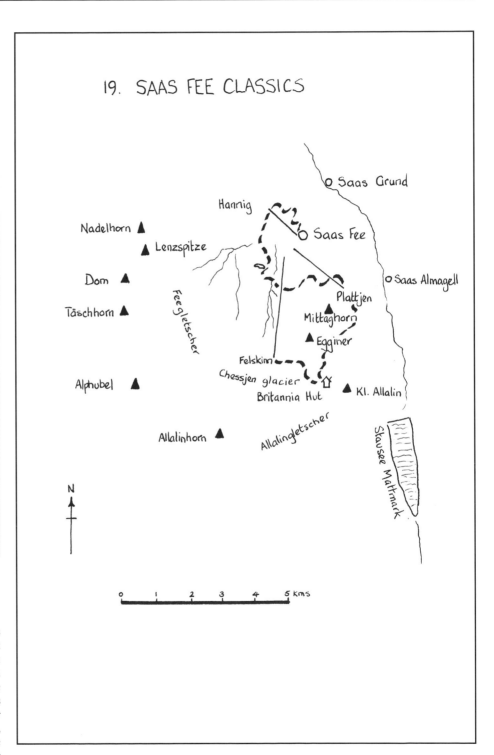

Around the glacier garden of Switzerland

Though not entirely unique in the Alps, Saas Fee's position is magical enough to warrant many of the superlatives that are heaped upon it in the tourist brochures. Occupying a high basin of meadowland below an exquisite amphitheatre of rock, snow and ice, this steadily growing village is indeed set in a glacier garden. Glaciers hang suspended above it, draped across the face of peak after peak like shining visors, dominating practically every view. As a resort of immense charm Saas Fee will have few equals anywhere that can boast such a remarkable assortment of high mountain views from practically every street and every doorway. These mountains are high, too. Among them, and towering over the dark timber chalets as centre-piece to the vast, almost vertical-looking Mischabel wall, is the Dom, at 4545 metres the highest mountain entirely within Swiss territory.

Saas Fee is conscientiously expanding into a major winter and summer resort, but in spite of that it still manages to retain both the size and scale of a village, restricted and dwarfed as it is by the great backdrop of mountain and glacier. It sits on a shelf above the Saastal in a cul-de-sac of splendour. Like Zermatt over the mountains to the west, no motor vehicles are allowed into the village itself, but two large car parks on the outskirts ensure that visitors do not have far to walk to their hotels or camp site.

As a mountaineering centre Saas has much to commend it. There are several three-and four thousand metre snow-peaks accessible from it that would make ideal introductory climbs for newcomers to the Alps, and there are some good high-level ridge-routes of a delicate nature for the more experienced alpinist, as well as those well-loved classic glacier passes, such as the Adler and Allalin, that provide access to a hidden heartland of snow and ice of impressive, if spartan beauty.

The ice-wall that greets you as you arrive in Saas Fee is topped by the snow dome of the Allalinhorn (4027m), with the saddle of Alphubeljoch to the right leading up to the flattened crest of Alphubel (4206m); then comes the sharp rock wall of the Mischabelhörner containing Täschhorn (4491m), Dom (4545m), Lenzspitz (4294m) and Nadelhorn (4327m). Across the amphitheatre the left-hand wall cannot compete with that of the Mischabel, but it manages nonetheless to provide balance and harmony.

Flowing north from both Allalinhorn and Alphubel is the generous sweep of the Feegletscher which, at its lower end, is neatly divided by a long band of consolidated moraine known as the Langflue, which has cable-car access of importance to Saas Fee's ski industry.

To my mind there is rather too much mechanisation here, with cableways swinging up to Hannig, Plattjen and to Felskinn as well as that to the Langflue, and an astonishingly bold, if unnecessary intrusion on the mountain world, the *Alpen Metro*, the world's highest subway. This amazing feat of engineering has been tunnelled through the rocks walling the Fee Glacier from the rocky island of Felskinn

The path below Hannig gives an opportunity to study the Allalinhorn on the ridge at the head of the great glacial cirque. *(Kev Reynolds)*

to serve a new revolving restaurant built on the Mittel Allalin. Unhappy though I am with such mechanical developments that can only devalue the natural mountain beauty, by swallowing one's prejudices and making use of the Felskinn cable-car, it is possible to link two of the region's classic walks and thereby create a fascinating full day's expedition.

On this walk there is a trouble-free section of glacier to cross along a marked trail leading to a mountain hut. Then comes a lofty belvedere of a path that edges along the east faces of the Egginer (3367m) and Mittaghorn (3143m) high above the valley, and around the shoulder of the latter to Plattjen where you join the so-called *Gemsweg*, or chamois path. This curves round the lower slopes of the glacial cirque above Saas Fee as far as Hannig on the hillside to the north-west of the village, before descending to it through fragrant woods and pastureland. It is a fine walk, full of variety and visual splendour, and although it will make a long day, there are two possible escape routes by cableway back to the village should you find it too demanding.

In order to make the most of the day it is advisable to start early by catching the Felskinn cable-car soon after breakfast. But before you do, check the condition of the glacial path either by enquiring at the tourist office or at the cable-car station. Under normal summer conditions the way will be trouble-free and clearly marked.

Swinging high above the glaciers in the cabin of the cableway the mountains seem to grow in stature as the village shrinks to a collection of dolls' houses, while from the Felskinn upper station you gaze over the tumbling layers of the Feegletscher where skiers twist, swoop and turn even in summer, to the superb expanse of the Mischabel wall and its trim peaked summits shafting northwards. It's an impressive view, but the upper rim of the cirque is lost from sight by crests of ice and the low crags of the Mittel Allalin distorting the true wave-like snow crown of the Allalinhorn, which is so evident from Saas, and it will be several hours before that view is regained.

The walker's trail to the Britannia hut across the Chessjen Glacier and through the obvious pass of Egginerjoch is made by snow-cat and is adequately marked. Even so, it is important not to stray from the track for the glacier is crevassed. Indeed, the route used will no doubt cross a few narrow crevasses that may be easily stepped over, or bridged with a wooden plank or two, but with care there should be no difficulty or danger.

Wandering with your back to the Dom and its lofty neighbours, the way leads between the red-brown rock tower of Egginer to the left, and the billowing icefields that form the lower slopes of the Hinter Allalin to the right. Soon the Britannia hut comes into view, and is reached in about forty minutes from Felskinn.

The Britannia hut was built with funds

A well-made path cuts round the mountainside way above the Saastal between the Britannia Hut and Plattjen.
(Kev Reynolds)

In the centre of the Mischabel wall is the Dom, highest mountain entirely in Switzerland. *(Kev Reynolds)*

raised by the ABMSAC (Association of British Members of the Swiss Alpine Club), and is extremely popular on account of its ease of access and the large number of glacier expeditions and modest summits available from it. It stands on a rocky saddle between the Chessjen and Hohlaub glaciers, immediately below the slabs of the Klein Allalin enjoying a wonderful panorama of icefield and rock; stark and almost monochrome, yet blissfully lovely all the same. None should move on from here before wandering up to the summit of the Klein Allalin (3069m), only ten minutes above the hut, for the views are magnificent overlooking the Strahlhorn, Rimpfischhorn and Allalinhorn with the glacier passes of the Allalin and Adler dividing them, while to the right of the Mittel Allalin directly ahead the Täschhorn and Dom show off their steep east faces. I know of few finer high mountain views that may be won with so little effort.

Continuing the walk, leave the hut and descend the lower part of the glacier to the north (there will be traces of path in the snow) and find a clear trail on the far side leading over stony terrain and past a couple of little ponds, then veering right to traverse the eastern slopes of first, Egginer, then the Mittaghorn. In places this path is exposed and craftily engineered where the rock slabs are steepest; in places it crosses boulder slopes guided by cairns. All the time you maintain

a high contour way above the valley, with the Weissmies rising as the main summit ahead to the north-east. Far ahead, way beyond the Weissmies, the snowy billows of the Bernese Alps confuse the horizon, whilst gazing back towards the head of the Saastal the milky waters of the dammed Mattmark lake are shown clearly below the Monte Moro Pass. The crossing of this ancient pass to Macugnaga in Italy is another Alpine classic, especially so since it takes you in full view of one of the finest and greatest mountain walls in the Alps, that of the unbelievably spectacular east face of Monte Rosa.

Eventually the path swings leftwards to cross the north-east shoulder of the Mittaghorn, and there ahead is a wonderful view of the Mischabel peaks seen in their full glory with Saas Fee still undetected and lost in its bowl unseen below. The trail leads on and in a few more minutes you are brought to the upper station of the Plattjen gondola lift and an opportunity for refreshment. It is from here that the *Gemsweg* begins, while those who feel they have walked far enough for one day can take the lift down to Saas Fee.

From the gondola lift-station the path descends to Berghaus Plattjen and a lower skitow/chair-lift where it then forks. The continuing chamois path heads west on an almost level contour with views becoming more and more immense as you go. Having left behind the

bare stony upper reaches of hillside it is good to be among tangles of alpenrose, juniper and bilberry, among larch and shrunken pine and wild flowers clustered amid rocks beside the path. The contrasts between these vegetated slopes and the ice-bound world only a few paces above, are quite astonishing, and one wonders just how recently was the route of this path buried beneath the glaciers?

Streams pour down the hillsides from the Feegletscher, and the path takes you over or through them. There are little rustic bridges in places, but elsewhere it is necessary to leap the icy torrents, sèracs looming above. Then you come to the Café Gletschergrotto, and soon after this pass close to the glacier snout and peer up to the frozen cascades hanging from the Täschhorn. Every section of the walk has its own visual speciality.

Now the *Gemsweg* winds among boulders and passes the north-eastern end of a trough of glacial debris before heading up a moraine bank. This effectively takes you onto the western hillside immediately below the Mischabelhörner, and with your back now to the great glacial cirque, views once more are dominated by the Weissmies and the long wall that stretches from it to include the Lagginhorn and Fletschhorn on the far side of the Saastal.

The path rises steadily with more streams to cross; then there is an alternative path breaking away and rising in a remorseless staircase of zig-zags to the Mischabel hut a thousand metres and more higher on the mountainside. Happily at this stage of the walk we do not need to adopt this path, but instead continue along the hillside heading roughly northward until at last the upper station of the Hannig gondola lift is reached. This swings up from Saas Fee and gives another opportunity to have an easy ride down. Refreshments are also available at the restaurant here, whose terrace enjoys a glorious vista of the ice-gemmed cirque embracing the pastures of Saas.

To wander down to the village and thereby make a satisfactory completion of this long and classic outing, it is necessary to continue beyond Hannig a short distance and then follow a track (signposted *Waldweg*) winding down the grassy slopes towards the woods, still with lovely views at almost every stride. Footpath alternatives then allow short-cuts to be made down to the village itself, which is reached in about an hour and a half from Hannig.

And by the time you stand in the main street of Saas Fee once more, you'll have gained through the day an intimate knowledge and a deep respect for the splendours of this glacier garden of Switzerland.

WALK 20: *Chamonix To Zermatt by Andrew Harper*

Location: France, Switzerland. Predominantly in the Pennine Alps of canton Valais.

How to get there: By train from Geneva; either through Chamonix to Argentière, or by link train from Martigny. Nearest airport—Geneva. Return by train from Zermatt to the Rhône valley, and main line train from there to Montreux and Geneva.

Distance: 160 kilometres (100 miles).

Time required: 8-10 days.

Total height gain: 7900 metres (26,000ft).

Total descent: 8900 metres (29,000ft).

Type of walk: Strenuous within reason.

Bad weather would drastically add to demands made on the walker. Snow lying could hinder progress and hamper route-finding. Waymarking is imprecise although paths are relatively easy to follow. Terrain is mostly exposed with limited opportunity for shelter.

Maps: Landeskarte der Schweiz 1:50,000 series. Sheets no 5003 *Mont Blanc—Grand Combin* and 5006 *Matterhorn—Mischabel*.

Guidebook: *Chamonix to Zermatt—the Walkers' Haute Route* by Kev Reynolds (Cicerone Press).

The walkers' 'Haute Route'

The accompanying chapters in this book will have their authors writing with keenness about their chosen routes. By broadcasting this enthusiasm we probably do ourselves a disservice in encouraging people to these areas, inevitably adding to the crowds we all tend to shy from. Seemingly, it is not in us to be introvert in such matters and so I am about to play my part in ensuring that you at least get to see the Matterhorn!

It is said that once an Englishman has seen the Matterhorn he remains in love with it for the rest of his life. The mountain is best seen

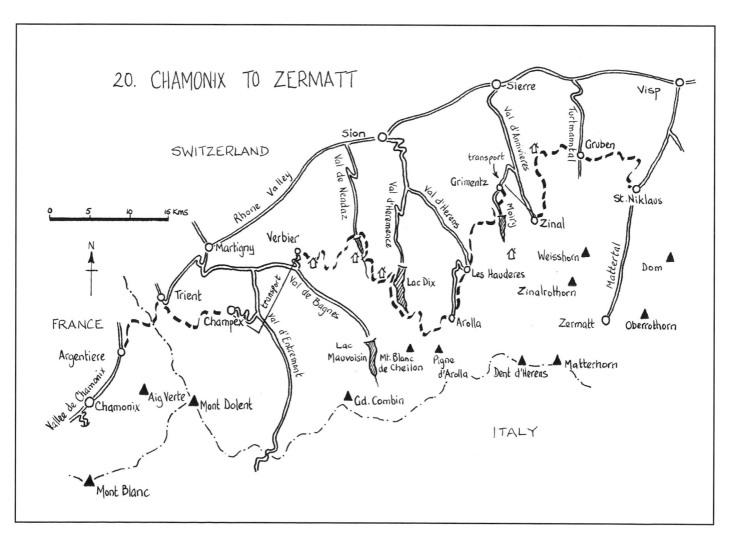

The commanding view of the Mattertal discovered when making the turn into the valley above St Niklaus, coming from the Augstbordpass. *(Andrew Harper FRPS)*

from the Swiss resort of Zermatt and anyone can get there by simply catching the narrow-gauge train from Visp in the Rhône valley and by experiencing one of the most attractive train rides in Europe. It takes well over an hour to cover the 36 kilometres, as the necessity of engaging with the line's rack system imposes a limitation on progress, simultaneously accommodating the difference in altitude which is a respectable 954 metres (3130ft).

A much more fulfilling manner of getting to Zermatt would be by the walkers' route that has traditionally linked Chamonix with Zermatt. Such an adventure will take significantly longer than the train journey, about ten walking days, to which must be added two or three days to enjoy the 'prize' at the end: exploring the glories that the Zermatt environs have to offer and, perhaps, following the path of Walk 18 in the shadow of the Matterhorn itself.

I set my sights on this route some twelve years ago and read as many as five accounts,

all of which dwelt on the problem created by the difficulty in crossing the Col de Cleuson and the permanent snow and ice stretch between it and the Col de Prafleuri; these two cols being located between Verbier and the Dixence dam. Accordingly, it remained one of the major Alpine routes that I had not undertaken.

My solution was to enrol for one of the UK-operated guided parties and chose Sherpa Expeditions, going to the region in July 1988. Nobody in the group had attempted the route before so the whole enterprise quickly became an adventure.

It was the first time for the leader, too, but as he had been given copious notes from his predecessor we felt we were in with a chance. In the event he steered our way through the 100-mile route with astonishing ease and never had to double-back to correct errors. The value for me was seeing how to negotiate the problematic quarter above Verbier. When it

came to it, we avoided the route these other reports had described and crossed the Prafleuri by approaching it from another direction.

Argentière to Verbier: 3 days

The commencement point is at Argentière at the upper, north-eastern, end of the Chamonix valley. The river here is the young Arve which runs down the length of the valley to gain in size to eventually join the Rhône at Geneva. The climb up to the Col de Balme gave ample opportunity for savouring the many wonderful views afforded by the Chamonix valley boundary walls and summits, which include Mont Blanc and the nearer-at-hand Aiguille Verte.

None of the others had visited the Chamonix valley before and with this short introduction there seemed to be a general resolve to return on another occasion to do the place justice.

There is belief that traders once used the

The path above Zinal leading to Hotel Weisshorn. *(Andrew Harper FRPS)*

route we were to embark upon, but what was it that they could have been trading that necessitated such a devious and tortuous route? The fable should be discounted, yet one can only be left wondering what its true beginnings were. Certainly it must vie for being one of the loveliest of all the set Alpine routes and there is a host of unbelievably exciting mountainous landscapes on which to concentrate the eye as the passage unfolds.

Never tiring of the Tour of Mont Blanc, the refuge at the Col de Balme is a familiar spot to me. Crossing the col here takes the walker from France into Switzerland, for it is astride the frontier. The gathering at lunchtime is multi-national and the chat is easily understood, whatever the language: enthusiastic tales about nice things observed and descriptions to others of the footpath conditions.

The continuing route follows the Tour of Mont Blanc path by descending to Trient, in the valley of the same name, where overnight accommodation is obtained, followed the next day by the crossing of the Fenêtre d'Arpette to reach Champex. The ascent necessary to reach this pass causes a groan or two in heatwave weather although most are surprised that the thing is negotiable at all as, when seen from a distance, it looks impregnable. Throughout the exposed climb, the mighty and exquisite Glacier du Trient helps take the mind off the exertions: it certainly is the dominant feature of this particular valley.

After the demanding ascent to the Fenêtre a new landscape is unfolded. Initially there is a tantalising steep descent into the Val d'Arpette which will be seen to be scree-ravaged at its upper end with lichen-covered boulders nearer at hand, down which the path continues to thread its way. Lower down, the valley is rich with attractive trees and the clearest of streams.

After Champex the route is interrupted by the Val d'Entremont and the Val de Bagnes.

Nowadays it is considered expedient to facilitate the crossing from Champex to Verbier by using public transport. The bus leaving Champex goes past its attractive lakeside before commencing the multi-twisted sweeps of the descending road to Orsières where a train connects with le Châble. This corner of the world is particularly attractive and the ever-changing views presented to us through the windows took all our attention.

The connecting bus needed to reach Verbier is phased with the train arrival, and by this stage in our interleaved journey no-one in the party had failed to become impressed with the efficiency of the Swiss passenger network. With this imposed laziness and in the heatwave weather, none of us took kindly to getting the rucksacks back to where they belonged as we walked from the bus terminus in Verbier to the cableway station at the higher end of the village.

Verbier to Arolla: 3 days

Now this narrative has reached Verbier, a word of explanation about the remaining journey should be given. The main mountains from here on are known as the Pennine Alps, the ridges of which stretch some fifty miles and also represent the frontier line with Italy. The route taken by the walker progresses over the passes associated with the northern-running ridges that reach down towards the valley of the Rhône, the bottom of which runs roughly west-east at the northern end of these slopes.

As each day unfolds, the real pleasure will be that of countless mountain scenes and backdrops. Practically every Alpine walk is invigorating—this one especially so—but if it's views you're after, this route has them in attractive abundance, although it would be a mistake to overlook the near-at-hand glories such as the flowers and the streams.

The cable-car is helpful in gaining height above Verbier, whereupon it is then a pleasant afternoon's stroll on a contouring path which heads towards the Cabane du Mont Fort. This popular refuge is nicely positioned for sunset and sunrise photography and from the terrace there is a grand vista of mountain scenery to admire and study. The massif of the Grand Combin is the idol of this corner of the Alps but the top of Mont Blanc can be seen behind the range above Champex and its sighting provides an accurate bearing on where we started.

There was a growing feeling that all the problems had sorted themselves out, just as though the days before had been some kind of rehearsal. The group was beginning to get to know itself, and so it should be simply a matter of dedication to progress the route that remained.

It was eerily quiet as we set off in the morning before the sun rose over the ridge: only the occasional marmot screech broke the calm. The path was excellent but we were to encounter our first significant snow patches before reaching the Col du Mont Gelé. There was also deep snow on the other side and we demonstrated degrees of caution as we precariously descended. As we reached the end of the snow the roughened ground displayed a whole gamut of miniature Alpine flowers which delighted us all. Birdwatchers in the party had their interests aroused with varieties hitherto unseen, and the penalty in carrying binoculars suddenly became justified. A swiftly-flowing river of tinkling clarity shared our remaining descent into a hanging valley where, at 11.30, we were ready for the services of the cafeteria and bar which we found there. We were at a place called Tortin in the Val de Nendaz

where the river is called la Printse.

Continuing ever downwards would have taken us too low, so we doubled round a corner into another contributing high valley and climbed to pass the reservoir at Cleuson to reach the Refuge St Laurent. Said quickly like that makes it hard to believe that the journey between the two refuges took the bulk of the day, and one or two found the pace rather daunting. On arrival at the refuge it was soon 'drinks all round', a delightful necessity to combat the humidity of the late afternoon as much as to celebrate a very invigorating and memorable day's walk.

The departure from the refuge took us initially up the most wonderful of valley floors—flowers in profusion with another of those crystal-clear and busy little streams. Further up, though, we had to ascend snowfields for over an hour and it was here as much as anywhere else on the holiday that we needed the consolation of each other.

Eventually reaching the Prafleuri pass, we were all enamoured by its excellent panorama. The air was absolutely still and with a cloudless sky we found it the ideal place to relax and absorb the benefits of our exertions. Shareholders in Kodak or Agfa would have drawn immense satisfaction from the rate at which everyone was using their film!

We were to make for a mountain refuge—Cabane de Prafleuri—at the opposite side of the rivulet-scarred and pond-strewn bottom of the valley into which we were shortly to descend. Once at lower level, getting over to the refuge was made surprisingly difficult by negotiating these water catchments, some of which were ice-covered to disguise their true depth!

An early setting sun and the ensuing chilly air had the foreseeable effect of driving sunbathers indoors, but those who had gone on a short skirmish from the refuge came in and told us that there were some ibex (also known as *bouquetin*) close by. These are the largest of the Alpine wild animals and they had been attracted to a salt-lick placed on the rocks nearby. They seemed quite tame although it was easy to sense that it wouldn't take much to frighten them off.

The morning brought our one half-day of inclement weather. We awoke to find snow falling through the surrounding mist and this had not eased by the time we prepared to leave the refuge. Gaiters were in evidence along with the odd scarf, and waterproof mittens appeared as from nowhere. The path down to the deserted buildings above the dam wall at Dixence was interspersed with the odd awkward snow chute and on one occasion we

roped-up for safety. This could well have been a case of 'one die, all die' but nobody dared to slip and so the point remains hypothetical.

We all seemed to thrive on this element of coming close to the unknown and by the time we turned the corner and could see the enormous length of the dam waters the weather palled to a miserable drizzle, even that not lasting the extent of the next hour.

The very top end of this enormous catchment has a frightening suspension bridge to cross the ravine which has the main flow of water passing at its foot. With 'best to look ahead; not down' advice we all got across, yet I can easily remember the strange quirky feeling which I experienced when half-way over the thing.

Lunch was a picnic affair, as on most days, and we sat at the far side of the footbridge alongside another forceful spume of water emanating from some other valley by one of the many special small-bore tunnels associated with the hydro-electric scheme. It was impossible to calculate its flow even on a bathfull-per-second basis as its bludgeoning waters spumed and pounded the rocks below prior to becoming an indiscernible addition to the voluminous reservoir.

After this rest, it was uphill all the way until reaching the foot of the Pas de Chèvres (2855m) with its vertical strip of fixed steel ladder. This method of overcoming the final few feet of the climb needed to reach the niche of the pass is well-known, and yet it could be quite unnerving to some people. The difficulty, I found, was not so much with general unease but with a feeling of annoyance with those who fixed it in position: it is too close to the wall and at places it is almost impossible to give the toes sufficient penetration over the rungs.

Once at the top one became aware of the beauty of the Val d'Arolla, down the centre of which flows its river, the Borgne d'Arolla. The dominant ice-clad mountain on the right is the Pigne d'Arolla and lower down one gets a splendid view of the symmetrically-shaped Mont Collon.

The valley we were leaving was not without its interest for the upper end of the Val des Dix is vast. An alternative approach to reach this col would be not to have crossed the suspension bridge but to have ventured up a path on the right just before it and have gone to the popular Cabane des Dix. This refuge is situated with high mountains attractively set around it, notably the ice-clad Mont Blanc de Cheilon. From the refuge there is a marked 'safe' crossing over the intervening Glacier de Cheilon which leads directly to a point at the foot of the iron ladder.

The village of Arolla seems little changed from what it must have been at the turn of the century, or perhaps even the one before that. It is a quaintly old-fashioned place with seemingly little development. Maybe this is because it is too inaccessible in winter to attract the money-spinning ski-ing clientele. Old it may be, but the coffee prices have certainly kept up with the times!

The venue for our overnight was significantly beyond the village and a long way down the valley road. It turned out to be beneficially tranquil and this was a good thing because the walk had been rather arduous and the general aim was to get a good night's undisturbed sleep to balance the books.

Arolla to Zermatt: 4 days

The tour organisers had arranged a half-day at this stage, so a relatively easy stroll down to Les Haudères and a subsequent short haul up to La Sage was all that was expected of us. Some parties conduct this part of the journey by using the infrequent bus service, but what could be better on a good day than to stroll as we did? True, the way down necessitates the use of the tarred roadway for half the distance, but there seems to be little traffic and the sure footing permits the scenery to be absorbed with unaccustomed freedom. At a point where the road embarks on its devious excursions to negotiate the valley drop (near a small white-painted chapel) a good path allows the walker a pastoral route of exceptional loveliness.

Most people broke the journey at Les Haudères, where the valley from here on down to the Rhône is known as the Val d'Hérens. The village has a lot of the old and traditional wooden buildings, the timbers of which appear to have been blackened by the effects of the elements.

The penalty for having rest days is that it is usually difficult to get the stride going again afterwards, but the pastures above the village were scaled in the morning without too much antagonism. We were lucky, too, in having fine weather for the steady climb. When we eventually got there the Col de Torrent (2919m) was, like the others, a place which tempted us to relax, but with lunch on our minds we started the descent more quickly than usual. We chose a spot alongside the blue-watered Lac des Autannes. It had a steep slope of melting snow slipping into one end that created a few ice-flows to give it an odd appearance.

Below this the path went close to a solitary dairy building and it didn't take long for the enterprising to advance on the place with a Swiss franc in one hand and an empty plastic mug in the other.

Turning a corner brought us above another of the hydro-electric dam catchments, but a smaller one this time: Lac de Moiry. Now in the Val de Moiry, our destination at the end of this particular day was to be Zinal. The 'accepted' way of progressing the journey should have been by continuing smartly up and over the intervening hillside, the Corne de Sorebois. But, with the heat of the day, most found this a daunting prospect and elected instead to walk down the valley continuing under the dam wall to reach Grimentz. This was an active little village and it was particularly nice to get into the provisions shops to indulge in chocolate and other luxuries. A connecting bus took us uneventfully to Zinal, which is in the larger Val d'Anniviers.

Having heard of it for years, Zinal was a bit of an anti-climax, as the place was much smaller than I had been led to believe. Our night's lodging was arranged at a very rustic hotel at the far end of the village. Thirteen bed-spaces for the fourteen of us cramped our accustomed style somewhat, although I am only too well aware that worse allocations than this can be the norm elsewhere. The food was good and the hospitality welcoming. As we had all slept soundly we reckoned to have had the best of the place and this fortified us for the traverse of the hillsides above Zinal which lead along to the Hotel Weisshorn.

Going along this path gave ever-widening views down to the valley where we had used the bus the evening before, with Grimentz made toy-like at this distance. This was a popular route for photography and there was a buzz of excitement when the sharp eyes among us saw the recognisable summit of the Matterhorn some way behind and beyond the upper reaches rimming Zinal.

The Weisshorn was a dilapidated place if ever there was one, narrowly being saved by its undeniably prestigious position with exceptionally good views. The food was plentiful and the staff went to the trouble of making a special cake for one of our number who celebrated his birthday in the environment of good companions and a superb mountain backdrop: possibly an unbeatable recipe.

Over a glen-like hanging valley behind and slightly above the Weisshorn premises, we commenced our ascent to the Meidpass (2790m), and then steeply down through dense trees at the lower levels, to get to our hotel alongside the river Turtmanna at Gruben, in the German-speaking part of the canton Valais. This narrow valley, the Turtmanntal, had all the ingredients for endearing itself to every one

of us. It seemed to have been lifted out of the middle of the last century and its essence was 'of the mountains'. Like any valley of note, it had its mountain blocking the upper end of the valley, the Tête de Millon, and it was the attractive sight of this with its accompanying glacier and the tip of the Weisshorn appearing behind it that gave us such visual enjoyment on the descent.

Out of the place with its comfortable dormitory-style under-the-roof bedding with the dawn was no problem now and, with just one more heave, we could expect to be in Zermatt by nightfall. The climb up to this final pass, the Augstbordpass, took the statutory time displayed on the signpost and with a snow-slope to skid down, we quickly faced up to the trek threading its way over to the corner where we turned to see the view over the Mattertal valley. To our left it was possible to see the distant surface of the Aletsch glacier in the Bernese Alps on the far side of the Rhône valley.

This had been a journey of wondrous and far-seeing views, but possibly the most stunning of all was the commanding sight of the length of the Mattertal which is encountered during the last day of the walk. From this vantage point the valley lays far below, bordered by its own high peaks and crests only to eventually terminate in the distance above Zermatt with the Breithorn, Kleine Matterhorn and the great snowfields. On the left the Mischabel range, featuring the Dom and Täschhorn. The brilliant tip of the Weisshorn can be seen further along the flank from where the path starts its tortuous descent down to the valley bottom at St Niklaus.

So, just a short wait for the train that would whisk us up the valley to the large and modernised Zermatt. Modernised, perhaps, but it still has its quota of old haylofts and cattle sheds which have survived the reconstruction activities. Most of these old wooden buildings are supported from the ground by pillars that have large circular stones intervening, supposedly to deter rats. Amazingly, even those in the middle of Zermatt are still used for housing cattle as a matter of practicality.

Zermatt's crowning glory is indisputably the majestic Matterhorn, a captivating feature which dominates the skyline. Nowadays the resort is geared mainly to cater for the influx of tourist visitors, although a significant number are obviously from the walking fraternity. What everyone has in common—whether in shoes or boots—is a love for the mountain environment. Let there be no doubt, though, that the pathways radiating from the village are just as attractive as ever, and these are left for the

On the way to the Meidpass. (Andrew Harper FRPS)

hillwaker to exploit with his leisurely pace and style whilst the cableways lift the impatient remainder to their various viewpoint terraces and cafeterias.

Tailpiece

So, another long walk to put in the memory bank and to relate at length to those willing to listen. Treading these hillsides was essentially a slow process, but who whould want it any other way? As a consequence the scenery unfolded gradually—to be savoured and absorbed at an almost ideal rate.

What of the wildlife? We had frequent encounters with the ubiquitous marmot, saw a number of the large-horned ibex, an occasional chamois and observed many varieties of birds.

The flowers were abundant and vivid. Sometimes a whole large area of hillside yawned at us in broad violet; sometimes it was yellow. Seeing my first edelweiss for years made me realise yet again what an uncompromising little treasure this is. There were flowers so small that one was made to wonder just how on earth they could eke out an existence in such hostile conditions. Little pads of moss with dozens of pink shoots pushing to its surface. Plenty to see on the wayside. Rock chippings of all sizes, colours, shapes.

Mont Collon above Arolla, the Dent Blanche and Ober Gabelhorn: all famous mountains but not seen by me before. The perspectives of these lovely shapes became an obsessive attraction as we crossed from one valley to another. It was just like a book of superb mountainous landscapes being unfolded as the days went by.

We had become almost intoxicated with the smells, sounds and sights associated with this fascinating region and were so engrossed in our activities that no-one seemed aware that this lovely trek was about to come to an end.

The standard waymark sign of a Bergweg – mountain path – in Switzerland. (Andrew Harper FRPS)

WALK 21: *The Grosser Aletschgletscher by Kev Reynolds*

Location: Goms, upper valley of the Rhône, southern Switzerland.
How to get there: By rail to Brig and on to Betten Fo. Cable-car from Betten Fo to Bettmeralp. International airports at Bern, Geneva and Zürich. By road through Switzerland and over the Grimsel or Furka Passes to Betten Fo in Obergoms.
Distance: 8 kilometres (5 miles).
Height gain/loss: 532 metres.
Time required: 3 hours.

Type of walk: Undemanding, although there is a short steep stretch leading to Hohbalm. Visually spectacular. Refreshments available at Hotel Bettmerhorn and by a short diversion to the upper Bettmerhorn gondola lift station.
Base: Bettmeralp.
Map: Landeskarte der Schweiz 1:50,000 series, sheet no 264 *Jungfrau*.
Guidebook: *The Valais—Switzerland* by Kev Reynolds (Cicerone Press)

Beside the largest glacier in the Alps

High above the upper valley of the Rhône beyond Brig where it becomes known as Goms, there runs a green shelf of hillside that is accessible from the valley only by steep track or cableway. On this shelf sits the little resort of Bettmeralp gazing south across the depths of the Rhône to the snow and ice mountains of the Pennine Alps. It has an idyllic situation for it faces the sun and is largely protected

The Grosser Aletschgletscher, largest in the Alps. *(Kev Reynolds)*

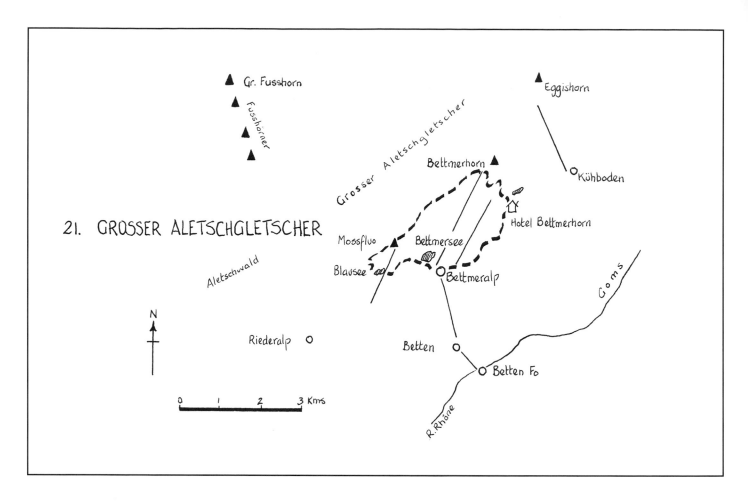

21. GROSSER ALETSCHGLETSCHER

from the cold northerlies by a natural wall that spreads behind it from north-east to south-west; a long ridge that provides shelter from the worst of the weather. (Statistics show that the village of Breiten on the lower slopes of the hillside enjoys on average 300 sunny days a year. Bettmeralp must have a similar record.) Behind its natural protective wall a complete scenic contrast to that enjoyed by the village itself waits to be discovered, for in a huge trench there comes sweeping the Grosser Aletschgletscher, longest of all the Alpine glaciers—twenty-five kilometres of ice-river spawned in a gigantic amphitheatre of mountains contained by the Aletschhorn, Mittaghorn, Gletscherhorn, Jungfrau, Mönch, Fiescherhorn and Grünhorn.

Although its upper band of spawning mountains are mostly hidden from view the glacier is in itself magnificent to look at, and this walk—the shortest in the book—allows just that in a half-day circuit that could be extended without difficulty to suit one's needs and aspirations. In fact there are numerous alternative walks along Bettmeralp's gentle green terrace, or over the ridge to the banks

of the glacier, that would easily fit the demands of a classic walk. There's the path that leads to the Marjelensee, for example—perhaps best begun from Kühboden farther along the hillside terrace—and then return all the way along the eastern moraine of the Aletschgletscher. There's the spectacular viewpoint of the Eggishorn (good enough to be afforded a special panorama in *Baedeker*), reached by cable-car or by very steep path from Kühboden, followed by a descending traverse of a mountain spur to Marjelensee—or back towards Bettmeralp before crossing the ridge for more glacier views. There's a walk that takes you to Riederalp and over to the delightful woodland of the Aletschwald by the glacier's snout, or another that goes across the glacier itself to peer into the inner sanctuary of the Oberaletschgletscher, or over the moraine and onto a path leading to the historic mountaineering village of Belalp.

The particular walk described here has much to commend it: little tarns, soft meadows, huge sunny views, low-growing shrubs and lichen-patterned rocks, glaciers and mountains and jagged walls of soaring rock. It is by no

means a hard walk, but there will be temptations to stray, so the outline time of three hours or so should be treated with some circumspection.

Bettmeralp sits on the edge of a walker's playground and despite its ungainly plethora of mechanical lifts (mainly of interest to winter skiers), makes an attractive holiday base. It is a spruce, modernised resort with plenty of hotel and apartment accommodation, while lodgings of a more modest kind may be had in nearby Kühboden where there's a Youth Hostel.

Leaving the village with its highly photogenic white-walled chapel standing on the lip of the hillside terrace below, a clear broad footpath heads north-eastwards aiming for Hotel Bettmerhorn. At first, it must be admitted, the overhead chair-lift rather spoils the outlook, but this will soon be forgotten once the ridge has been gained.

Before long the trail crosses a boulder-pocked pastureland and in about fifty minutes from Bettmeralp reaches the hotel and a junction of tracks. The continuing path goes to Kühboden, Marjelensee and the Eggishorn,

One of the classic views of the Alps: along the great swirl of the Aletschgletscher. (Kev Reynolds)

but we take the left-hand fork that sends a footpath uphill to the end of a narrow teardrop of a tarn where there's another path division. Once again it is the left-hand trail that should be taken, and this leads to the upper terminus of the chair-lift from Bettmeralp. A signpost here directs the continuing path up to Hohbalm, a rough saddle on the rock-strewn ridge at 2482 metres, and yet another junction of tracks. The right-hand path here goes up to the Bettmerhorn gondola lift station and makes a tempting diversion for the extensive views and opportunities for refreshment to be had there. (An extension of this way will take strong walkers over the Bettmerhorn towards the Eggishorn.) The main route, however, continues ahead and will eventually reach the Marjelensee after following above the glacier, and is to be recommended for a full day's outing. The left-hand path heads in the direction of Riederfurka and Aletschwald.

Before taking the left-hand path here it is

worth going ahead in order to make the most of a magnificent view onto the huge glacier spread out before you. Suddenly the brash mechanical intrusions have been left behind and forgotten, as everything ahead is as wild as nature intended. Only the narrow footpath picking its way among the boulders has been made by man. All else has evolved naturally over millions of years of ceaseless toil. It is a magical landscape. Not even the great Mer de Glace above Chamonix can compete with the Grosser Aletschgletscher as it winds round a long steady curve from unseen Konkordiaplatz, and the mountains that wall it to north and west are just breath-takingly beautiful. The big multi-buttressed Walliser Fiescherhörner up-glacier looks particularly impressive with its central band of ice creating the appearance of a gigantic cream slice, while directly opposite superb jagged arêtes adorn the Grosser Fusshorn and Geisshorn. Wherever you look there are snow peaks and rocky crests and ice-draped

faces clustering for attention.

This is one of the truly classical viewpoints of the Alps and it matters not a jot how often one has seen it depicted on calendars, in books or on chocolate boxes, the reality is something else. The panorama is unique and it is a privilege to wander there to see it, to feel the cool breezes washing from the ice and to sit among the rocks and listen to the soft murmuring voice of the mountains. Give yourself to the day and the view and forget the march of time.

Once the left-hand trail has been adopted you begin to discover that nature has laid out this one-time moraine as a flower garden. Early in the summer wayside rocks are flush with flowers. There are shrubs of alpenrose, of juniper and bilberry, giving their best at different times of the year. There are marmots scampering among the boulders, sometimes seen perched upon a rock as though acting as sentry. Then there'll be a high-pitched piping whistle and little stubby brown shapes will be seen romping off to their burrows. Small finches dart among the shrubs, or wait to pounce on crumbs left by a picnic party, and on warm summer days the occasional butterfly will drift up from hillside feeding grounds to bring a delicate contrast to the otherwise harsh, but beautiful landscape.

And all the time the great glacier grinds imperceptibly below, carving out a valley that one day—how many thousands of years hence?—will be lush with pastures and bright with flowers too.

It's an easy path now, along the undulating ridge crest, made difficult only by the temptation to gaze at the wonderful views. On the one side there is the Aletschgletscher and its grand vista of walling peaks, and on the other the far outline of the long chain of the Pennine Alps—particularly the Mischabel and Weisshorn.

Eventually you arrive at the upper station of the chair-lift from Blausee. This is shown as Mossfluh (2333m) on the map, with a bench seat erected here especially to enjoy a commanding view. Five minutes beyond this an alternative footpath breaks away from the main ridge path and slants down to the left. Unless you have time to continue all the way to Riederfurka and down to Riederalp (about as far again as the route from Hohbalm to Mossfluh), this is the path to take. It leads away from views of the glacier and takes you into a miniature series of intimate landscapes of hillocks and hollows bright with shrubs, and on to another trail junction.

The left-hand path will shortly bring you to the shores of the ever-popular Blausee, a small but attractive tarn in a splendid setting. It is unfortunate that a chair-lift intrudes on the scene, but it does enable countless numbers of tourists to enjoy it who might otherwise never be able to walk this far. It is as well, sometimes, to remember that not everyone who loves the hills has the physical ability to stride the paths outlined in books such as this. We who do should be thankful for the gift and try not to resent the mechanical means that allow others to enjoy just a brief sample of the glory that is available to us.

Passing beneath the cables of the chair-lift the continuing path heads down a grassy slope thick and fragrant with shrubs, to reach the larger Bettmersee—again an ever-popular spot for short-walk visitors and picnic parties. From here it is but a brief stroll down to the village of Bettmeralp where it is tempting to spread out the map to plan other walks for the next few days. Fortunately, there are plenty more to choose from.

The Füsshörner, seen across the glacier. (*Kev Reynolds*)

Walk 22: *Walking in The Gran Paradiso by Andrew Harper*

Location: France, Italy—in the Eastern Graians.
How to get there: From Chambéry, connection to Bourg St Maurice to reach Ste. Foy-Tarentaise in Val d'Isére for the start. At the end of the walk, bus from Champorcher to Hône in Val d'Aosta, then another bus through Verrès to town of Aosta. From here to Chamonix via Courmayeur and the Mont Blanc tunnel. Chamonix to Geneva for airport. Alternatively, bus from Hône to Milan or Turin.
Distance: 120 kilometres (75 miles).
Time required: 7–8 days.
Total height gain: 7000 metres (22,500ft).
Total descent: 6500 metres (21,250ft).
Start: Ste. Foy-Tarentaise.
Finish: Champorcher.
Type of walk: Mostly over rough mountainous country. Some sections steep, but all paths in good condition. Route-finding not problematical. Remnant snow would add to problems at significant places. Terrain is mostly exposed with limited opportunity for shelter.
Map: Instituto Geografico Centrale 1:50,000 series. Sheet no 3 *Il Parco Nazionale del Gran Paradiso.*

Through the Gran Paradiso National Park

An elderly acquaintance was clearing his attic and came across some touristy literature obtained in the early thirties. One of these was an illustrated promotional booklet featuring Switzerland, and one sentence in the editorial hit the mark with its observation that the Alps are, by some divine coincidence, *just the right size* in marrying up to our limitations and capacity to wander amongst them.

Most of the significant Alpine passes seem perfectly tailored to permit their ascent and descent during an average day. This has the effect of creating healthy appetites and the need for deep slumber, after which the rested muscles seem curiously anxious to repeat the exercise.

The area of the Gran Paradiso contains one of the major ranges on the Italian side of the Alps, the bulk of which is now a National Park. It is best seen by walking the route that

The path above Rhêmes. *(Andrew Harper FRPS)*

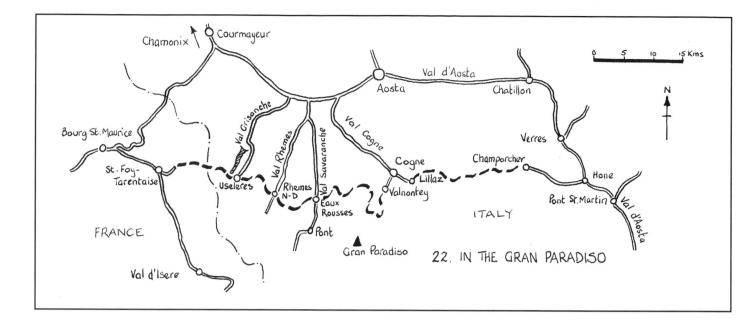

traverses it, from the French frontier in the west to the Aosta valley at its eastern end.

What has been said about the scale being related to man does apply to the route about to be described but, as parts of it are quite rugged, it will physically tax the most experienced. Offsetting these demands will be the reward of seeing some amazing Alpine scenery enhanced by the occasional encounter with some of the wild animals which are protected and thrive in its confines.

Ste. Foy-Tarentaise to Eaux Rousses: 4 days

Access to the area is by way of Chambéry and connecting transport to the resort of Bourg St Maurice which has its share of hotel accommodation, restaurants and shops. Bourg St Maurice is a railhead, and connecting buses link this Alpine town with the starting place, the village of Ste Foy-Tarentaise which is 9 kilometres along the busy road stretching towards the ski resort of Val d'Isère and the slightly-further-on Col d'Iseran.

The route leaves the outskirts of the village by taking a narrow lane signposted to le Miroir. In the twenty minutes taken to reach this little village, time-warp elements have been at play. Thankfully the busy highway has been left behind, with only the occasional passing Renault or Citroën edging its way to and from the holiday homes higher up the hillside. The occupants of the centuries-old premises seem to go about their tasks just as if they have abandoned all idea of joining the pace set by

modern society. Only the quarter-hour chimes of the church clock record the passage of time.

The wee cluster of houses is entrenched in the neck of a ravine and the continuing narrow road ascends alongside a tumbling river as it reaches higher to where there is a final group of homes. Some have curling smoke coming from their stacks—the whiff of smouldering wood adding its own charm as it catches the nostril. The way ahead is then by a very pleasant path which eventually rises above the treeline into a mountain-rimmed area which is husbanded by dedicated farmers who retreat to lower level overnight.

At the very head of the valley it is possible to stay at the privately-owned la Motte refuge. In 1989 the young couple custodians were particularly welcoming, the very mark of making the experience of stopping at such a place a pleasure rather than a drudge. Still in France, the refuge is nicely situated at the foot of an almost-two-hour climb up a spur leading to the Col du Mont, the position of which marks the frontier with Italy. There are very few way-marks, but the route is not difficult to follow as it is well-trodden, even eroded in places.

Just before reaching the col, the summit of Mont Blanc should appear over the ridgeline on the left. On Italian soil now, the legs will welcome changing gear into descent mode but after passing a gutted and derelict frontier building, going downhill becomes less of a pleasure as the gradient steepens.

The Val Grisanche is not significantly different from the landscape left behind on the French side. An opportunity comes to rest

awhile and freshen-up at a prominent water-fall, reached just before crossing the powerful stream coming down from another side valley. Just after the bridge the path widens to jeep-track dimensions; halfway along cheese and milk are available at a vachery.

Soon after, and on a brow, there is an assortment of deserted shepherds' buildings which would afford momentary shelter against the elements. The valley below has a long and narrow hydro-electric dam to mar its features, but the eyesore gets shielded from view as the path drops to cross the bridge over its top-end feed water at Uselères. In any case, the mind's attentions soon get switched to the discovery of a building at the roadhead that houses a bar and restaurant which shines nugget-like to the thirsty and hungry walker.

For those without a tent, good news comes with the introduction of a new and large refuge some two hours up the track ascending the facing hillside, the access to which is no more than fifty paces off the intended route. Its appointment is ideal, allowing the walker to loll outside in the rays of the setting sun whilst surveying the territory just undertaken, with the Col du Mont visible as a notch in the distance. The Refuge l'Epée is a good example of modern construction, having been built with practical forethought.

The refuge is backed by a sharp change in the altitude of two successive hanging valleys, a couple of zig-zags taking the path up to the bowl above. This final valley floor is quite wide, marshy in places and cut by the main down-going stream. The path is barely traceable as it veers over to the left, finally gaining height to the pass along the foot of boulder scree.

The last few steps up to Col Fenêtre are manageable over compacted black grit, but possibly made treacherous in icy conditions. The col itself is barely wide enough to get a secure stance whilst the views in both directions are inhaled. With the coming of this new vista, some high peaks of the Paradiso can be seen for the first time, tantalisingly incomplete due to the obtrusive escarpment on the right.

The visual prospect of the continuing path will send a shiver down any spine. Rather than delay, it is best to get on with the job but then only to give it the respect it deserves. There is no escaping its severity but, as with most things, it turns out to be less of a problem than feared. Lingering snow could easily have the effect of barring progress by this route and if there are such difficulties it is feasible to retreat and attempt one of the other two passes which cross into the Val di Rhêmes.

Getting below the steepest section the tension eases to allow a little self-congratulation. The path steepens again, but to nothing like the same extent, before reaching the valley bottom near the little village of Notre-Dame where remedial comforts in all categories are there for the asking. Well, *nearly* all.

Notre-Dame is nicely placed in the valley, which suddenly takes on a wider 'feel' on arrival there. The valley leads down to the larger Val d'Aosta, but in the other direction it is obviously hemmed-in by a rim of white-clad mountains, the glaciers that ooze from them shimmering brilliantly under an unrestrained sun.

In direct contrast to the bitter-sweet descent from the preceding pass, the approach to the next col is a really pleasant experience. Initially gaining height through an attractive wooded hillside, the path then surmounts a grassy promontory that is backed with hilly pasture, where the opportunity to bivouac might appeal. No other form of accommodation is available until getting to the next valley floor, so those without a tent would have to remain in Notre-Dame.

Curving to pass the deserted premises at Plan de la Feya, the going gets more rugged until it is possible to see the obvious pass high above that will take yet another hour to conquer. Arrival at Col di Entrelor will give additional glimpses of the high Paradiso summits. The view into Val Savaranche is wonderful, the two azure-blue lakes below showing the paths alongside looking like cotton threads.

The descent is nicely graded and the beauty of the lakes does not diminish at close hand where the rushing river gives the landscape just that added touch to indelibly etch it into the catalogue of memories logged throughout the holiday. To the north the Grand Combin picturesquely blocks the 'V' of the valley, giving a perfect balance to the scenery. The path contours the hillsides a little before passing a herdsman's farmhouse and the premises of the National Park wardens before sloping again to reach the valley bottom at the hamlet of Eaux Rousses.

There is a large hotel which offers a bar and restaurant facility. In addition, one of the shack houses takes in the odd wayfarer on a self-catering basis, permitting a unique insight into a lifestyle that the hotel could never offer and at a fraction of the price, too. The hotel will supply basic provisions and packed lunches, but for general shopping a pleasant 1½ hour diversion to Degioz further down the road is necessary.

Eaux Rousses to Champorcher: 3–4 days

The road passing through the village goes higher through the next village at Pont to eventually cross the road pass at Col de Nivolet. Pont is the starting point for the Rifugio Vittorio Emanuele, the traditional stopover and springboard for aspirants wishing to ascend the Gran Paradiso. By all accounts the Paradiso is one of the easiest summits to climb, but paths as such peter out long before its final approaches. The refuge has a reputation for being overcrowded.

From the Col di Entrelot the route leading to the Col Lauson can be seen in its entirety and its prospect is sufficiently daunting to make any ageing rambler contemplate retirement from the sport. The path starts at the wee bridge opposite the hotel, where the signpost indicates 'Col Lauson: 5h 10min'. Encouraged by the most magnificent of mornings (and leaving an hour or so before the sun could impose its effect) a slow and unrelenting pace proved the best way of tackling this giant. Getting above the treeline, the path reached the viewpoint at d'en Bas, where a picnic table provided the scene for a second breakfast. This was shared with a nudging goat whose company represented the only other visible lifeform that early in the morning.

Unfiltered sunshine met at this point caused that essential re-appraisal of clothing, and it was a fresh and revitalised man that left the spot in shorts with shirtsleeves rolled up, boosted with that special feeling of inner satisfaction that only the combination of perfect weather, perfect environment and perfect contentment can arouse.

The path levels to cross a stream-ravaged bowl before zig-zagging modestly to get above a brow. Hours passed without count but without any indication of fatigue. With minimal breaks, the technique of going at a very slow pace—almost a shuffle—was paying off in minimising the effort and conserving strength in progressing this route. Heartlifting were the encounters with three herds of ibex, some of which came almost close enough to touch. The scenery was fabulous, too.

Perseverance paid off and the pass was reached. It had taken exactly eight hours to get there. What had been envisaged as being a most brutal ascent turned out to be one of the most passive, being highly rewarding and full of interest. Subsequent mathematics showed the altitude difference as being 68 feet in excess of a vertical mile! By one of those strange coincidences, the villages on either side of the pass are identical in altitude at 1666 metres and the pass is head and shoulders above the others on the route at a very respectable 3296 metres (10,814ft). The ascent was conducted in the peace of mind of knowing that accommodation would be available at the Rifugi Vittorio Sella which is only halfway down the next valleyside and barely two hours from the col.

From the col the terrain changes immediately and dramatically, needing the back-up of the fixed handrails and chains to negotiate the upper twists, turns and drops, some of which are frighteningly exposed. Here again, compacted snow could seriously add to the problem. but even without it the feeling of heart-in-mouth is good for adrenalin flow. The path lessens its challenge to zig-zag safely down the scree slopes to reach firmer ground below.

Interest comes with the sighting of more groups of ibex and the smaller chamois, the *Babycham* advert and Disney's *Bambi* character brought to life. The refuge can be seen throughout most of the descent and booking in there represents the end of the active side of the day, the setting sun allowing a stretch on the adjacent spongy turf before the bell is struck to signify the availability of the evening meal.

The refuge is set on the edge of a cliff normally overlooking the village of Valnontey, situated at the bottom of the main valley which bears the same name. On the day in question, piercing morning sun revealed the valley below to be filled with thick cloud, its upper limit threatening to creep higher as wafts of mist licked the cliffs like a troubled sea off the Pembroke Coast.

Not anxious to exchange the warmth of a brilliant sun and clarity of vision for chilly misty

Rifugio Vittorio Sella. *(Andrew Harper FRPS)*

drizzle, most people at the refuge elected to spend the remaining hours of the morning above the upper extremities of the cloudline by setting off on the contouring path that goes at high level along the upper end of the main valley. This is a very interesting and remote part of the valley, with extensive views towards the icy upper ramparts of the main peaks. There were more sightings of those majestic animals along the stretch leading to the Herbetet buildings where the path changes direction to accompany the torrent of the Valnontey back along the ravaged valley floor and into the village of Valnontey.

Valnontey is at a roadhead and would seem to be a popular target for many an Italian family on a day's outing. There are a few good hotels and restaurants, all pleasantly styled and nicely grouped. An extensive camp site completes the amenities. The attitude of the place seemed particularly friendly; friendly, too, in

a practical way. Where else would it be possible to have a full luncheon produced as late as four p.m. where the restaurant had obviously been closed for at least an hour or more? The grimmer face of tourism has obviously not reached this pleasant spot.

Cogne is the main resort in the Gran Paradiso, a cross between being a small town and a large village. To reach it a path goes parallel to the busy roadway, eventually crossing flat meadows to get to its spread buildings. Cogne is served from the main Aosta valley by road and the amenities are adequate for the passing walker with many bars, restaurants, hotels and shops. The rarity of a Tourist Office will be of service to those in need of local information.

The exercise continues by walking through to the eastern extent of the village, where a path goes off to the right alongside the river Eyvia, thus producing a very pleasant walk for

an hour or so until reaching the village of Lillaz. Lillaz is mainly composed of the older style of building amongst which will be found the little store, the odd café and restaurant. There is a camp site there, too, which seems more suited to caravan placement than the lightweight tent.

Two valleys converge on the village, and the path continues by gaining height into the Vallon de Urtier up a series of steep zig-zags which head in the same direction as a service road. Once over a brow the path levels to pass through a fertile upper alp that is home to the odd holiday chalet and farm cottage.

The path converges on the river where it crosses to climb through woodland, twisting eventually to pass a National Park warden's cottage, then contouring the hillside where the river has divided one side of the valley from the other by an enormous gully it has eroded. That there are dairy farms at this altitude belies

Walkers on the path having crossed Col Fenêtre. (Andrew Harper FRPS)

belief. The cost of getting the milk to the valley would seem to be too great an overhead to allow a living to be made, let alone a profit. Once past the last of these buildings the path crosses a little section of marshland before reaching the foot of what is the final assault slope leading up to the col, the Finestra di Champorcher.

Most cols have their surprises. Sometimes it is an abrupt change in terrain and the Lauson was an example of this particular feature. More often it is the change of landscape that can catch one unawares and this is certainly the case with the Finestra. The view beyond is of an entirely different style to that behind: rounded hillocks, sculptured slopes. Green, rich and fertile valleys.

Dropping down the other side is a progressive affair, passing streams, ponds and lakes. The path is easy under the feet and with the end of the whole expedition in sight, the thought of a rewarding meal and celebratory drink on reaching the village of Champorcher

much later in the day becomes a driving force.

Reward comes earlier than expected when one twist in the path reveals a fully-active restaurant which is barely halfway down to the village. The menu on offer was bountiful, catering adequately for those of us who had worked up healthy appetites. The final paces down through the lush pastures were then accomplished with an aura of well-being and contentment due to the novelties, excitement, good views, wonderful air and healthy outcome that this satisfying holiday had produced.

Whilst the walking route finishes on entering the village of Champorcher, mention must be made of the fascinating bus journey linking it to the main Aosta valley. That anyone could contemplate the construction of such a tortuous roadway is one thing . . . to build it quite another.

Wayside Madonna; Cogne.
(Andrew Harper FRPS)

Walk 23: *Exploring Val Bondasca by Kev Reynolds*

Location: Val Bregaglia, canton Graubunden, south-eastern Switzerland.

How to get there: By train via Chur to St Moritz, then by Postbus to Promontogno. Nearest international airport—Zürich. By road through Switzerland to Chur, then over the Julier Pass to Silvaplana and via the Maloja Pass into Val Bregaglia.

Valley bases: Promontogno or Bondo. Camping at Vicosoprano.

Distance: 16 kilometres (10 miles).

Time required: 8–9 hours.

Height gain/loss: 1379 metres.

Type of walk: Strenuous, over much rough ground and with some very steep ascents, but visually very fine. This walk is not recommended for walkers unused to wild mountain terrain unless accompanied by experienced Alpine trekkers. In poor visibility the section between Sasc Furä and the Sciora hut could be difficult and dangerous.

Maps: Landeskarte der Schweiz 1:50,000 series, sheet no 278 *Monte Disgrazia*. Alpina Technica 1:35,000 *Bregaglia* (available from West Col).

Guidebooks: *Walks in the Engadine—Switzerland* by Kev Reynolds (Cicerone Press). *Bregaglia West* by Robin G Collomb (West Col Productions).

Sciora aiguilles; granite blades that block the valley. (Kev Reynolds)

From chestnut woods to glacial slabs

Val Bondasca is a glen of deep enchantment. It falls in a short, steep wedge to the Italian-flavoured Val Bregaglia in south-eastern Switzerland, where its waters mingle with those of the Mera to wash quickly down to the sun-splashed Lake Como.

At its head Bondasca thrusts sharp, splintered blades of granite out of a brief necklace of glacier and moraine. Up there the Sciora aiguilles gather one's attention with their dagger-like profiles, but then eyes stray to one side to the vast block of Piz Cengalo and its neighbourhood twin, Piz Badile, whose huge slab face was for several decades seen as one of the great Alpine test-pieces for rock-climbers, and along whose crest runs the Italian frontier. Together they form a good proportion of a most attractive and tempting grey granite cirque, wild and uncompromising, yet stagger-

ingly beautiful—whether seen from the green terrace pastures of Soglio off to the west, or from near-at-hand in the valley itself.

If the head of the valley is wild and savagely Alpine with its mixture of rock and ice, its entrance between the villages of Promontogno and Bondo is in marked contrast, for down there the soft breath of Tuscany ruffles the leaves in the chestnut trees. Down there great fronds of fern are drawn out to jungle-like exuberance by the dank, heavy warmth of the woods; flowers sparkle from the glade meadows and songbirds warble their morning arias. The bed of the valley is luxuriant and generous, its upper reaches stark and brazen.

It certainly is a valley of rich contrasts, and to wander into it is to experience not only the amazing range of belts of vegetation but to grow intimate with the mystery of the mountains.

There are two SAC huts in Val Bondasca. One, the Sasc Furä, sits on a vegetated lip high in the mouth of the little sub-glen of the Trubinasca cirque. The other, the Sciora Hütte (or Capanna Sciora as it is also known), is perched on a crust of boulder and scree at the head of the valley, immediately below the

Punta Innominata and Sciora di Fuori. Both are magical huts in magical positions, and this walk makes a point of visiting them both.

In *Classic Walks in Europe* (edited by Walt Unsworth, OIP 1987) I contributed a chapter on The Bregaglia Circuit which includes part of this loop of Val Bondasca. That circuit is a superb multi-day trek, while this section of it is a long and stiffish walk with a height gain of thirteen hundred metres, and is definitely not recommended for the first day of a holiday! It's also pretty rough under-foot for much of the way, with a high col to cross and moraine, screes, glacial slabs and the last icy remnants of a glacier or two to negotiate. Novice mountain walkers should only attempt it in the company of experienced Alpine trekkers.

That having been said, it is a most rewarding and enjoyable loop, with some glorious mountain scenery practically every step of the way.

It begins in Promontogno, a thick stone-walled village separated from neighbouring Bondo by the Bondasca torrent and a charming little tree-lined cobbled lane. There is pension and modest hotel accommodaton to be

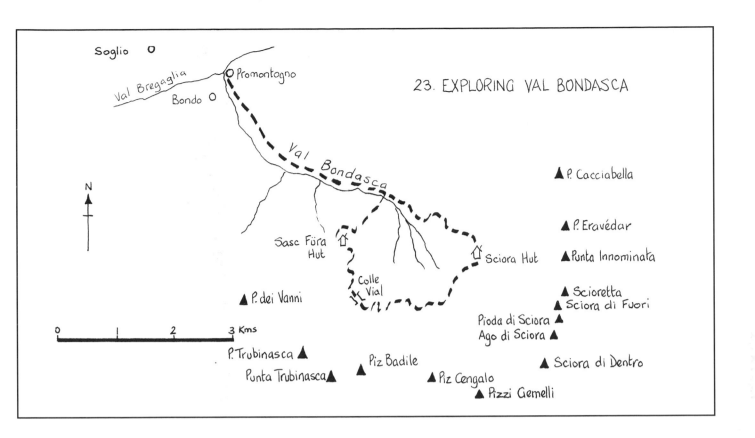

had here, and a Youth Hostel of even more modest proportions on the edge of the village. Of a summer's evening swifts race screeching between the houses and villagers gather to play a game or two of *boccia* under lights strung among the chestnut trees. It's a gentle place, nestling in a fold of archaic tranquility.

A narrow but motorable track winds out of Bondo to climb a short distance into Val Bondasca, but for walkers based in the Bregaglia this is of little importance except for those who would rather deprive themselves of an hour or so's exercise, and cars should be securely parked in one of the villages. A footpath climbs up among trees immediately before the hump-backed bridge that takes the Promontogno-Bondo lane across the river, and soon joins the track, which you follow up-valley for a while with growing views towards the south-east where the Scioras rise almost unreal in their sense of drama. A footpath continues from the track, and shortly after the trail divides and you break away to the right and drop down to cross the river. High above to the right can be seen a scoop of mountainside which indicates the Trubinasca glen; scooped out as if by a gigantic thumb. Piz Trubinasca and Badile

make a pair of majestic gateposts, but it seems incredible from below that a pathway could possibly reach them.

Across the bridge a faint path winds over a tussocky meadow and among tangles of wild raspberry before beginning its very steep ascent of the hillside. It is steep, too. One of the steepest sections of path in this collection of walks. It hauls its way among waist-and even shoulder-high vegetation, up tree-trunks and rocky slabs, then in the shade of woodlands where squirrels leap from branch to branch overhead, crossing gullies with streams leaking down them, then levelling to traverse a little to the right before turning the edge of a promontory and slanting up to the Capanna Sasc Furä (1904m). Just before you reach it there's a neat timber hut to one side of the path, making a foreground of interest to a lively view of the Scioras, but then a moment later a great flood of relief washes over you as the Sasc Furä appears ahead. It's wonderful to be there at last, to collapse with a cool drink and to enjoy the sudden outcast of views.

Immediately behind the hut the great north ridge of Piz Badile (3308m) soars in an incredible sweep of firm granite. Follow with your

eyes its summit ridge westwards, to Cima Santa Anna, then to Punta Trubinasca and Piz Trubinasca with its flat top and vast north wall—a splendid sweep of mountain. Then gaze westwards beyond the sudden plunging hillside, out to the north side of the Bregaglia where the village of Soglio appears far off like a clutch of dolls' houses in a blaze of greenery.

The continuing route takes you over the rocky spur descending from the foot of Badile's north ridge, but first you must climb almost three hundred metres of this spur, following a vague line of pathway aided by some paint flashes and the occasional cairn. At first, immediately behind the hut, there are smooth slabs to negotiate, then weaving among rough granite boulders and scanty shrubs on the right-hand side of the spur. After half an hour or so you begin to move towards the crest, working a way up to the little notch of a pass, Colle Vial, at about 2,200 metres.

Standing on the pass one's immediate impression of the descent down the eastern side is sobering. It drops steeply, broken only by a series of ledges, to the rocks and moraine of the Cengalo Glacier. To the north-east, beyond the snouts of little glaciers, the Sciora

Telephoto shot of Piz Badile in Val Bondasca, taken from the woods above Soglio. *(Kev Reynolds)*

hut can just be seen as a speck of red upon a moraine wall. A vague trail leads to it.

With caution your guide, descend the series of gritty ledges, here and there cushioned with strips of turf, and with droplets of water falling on you from the wall above. Down from this wall you have a boulder-field to cross, again aided by paint flashes and a line of cairns, then up onto a moraine cone where vegetation has already begun to clothe the mountain debris.

Next come several glacial slabs worn smooth by the polishing effect of the shrinking icefields that once covered them, and now washed by the very streams that are born in those icy wombs above. Take care as you cross these slabs, for they can be very slippery and they are also in a direct line of fire from stones expelled by those very same glaciers.

There are more boulder wildernesses; more crusted moraines; more streams, often ice-sheathed until mid-morning. Then a short stretch of glacier, dirtied by stones and grit during the summer, before the path resumes and gives an easier finish to the hut approach.

From the Sciora hut those fine aiguilles immediately behind are seriously foreshortened. They still make dramatic fence-posts, it is true, but you're almost too close to capture their essential grace and perfection of form. However, one of the best things about the hut is its commanding view overlooking the cauldron of the valley, and of the beautiful pure light that floods into the Bregaglia from Italy. It's a view that encompasses all the contrasts for which the Bondasca is noted; the soaring heights and cascading depths, the raw cliffs, the cluttered moraine and scree and the deep velvet of shadowed woods and forests far below.

In his classic *Walking in the Alps*, J Hubert Walker wrote with great enthusiasm about this wonderland when seen from below: "He must be very dull of soul indeed who could not see without a catch of his breath the sudden upward surge of the Bondasca peaks of Badile and Cengalo, as he turns into that glen . . ." But equally could that be said of the view from the Sciora hut. It is a different view from that below, of course, but no less memorable, and as evening slides into the valleys and day leaves the peaks last of all, those who have opted to stay overnight here would do well to don an extra pullover and lean on the balcony of the hut to capture the splendour of the changing fortunes of light slipping from the mountains.

The way down to Promontogno is straightforward enough and is ever-interesting and varied. The path is clear and as you descend so you trade moraine for rocks and boulders,

Almost as soon as you enter Val Bondasca the Sciora aiguilles entice you on
(Kev Reynolds)

and rocks and boulders for grassy patches and rough alps, then wild raspberries again and tall ferns and trees with little streams here and there. At last you come to the track which leads unnerringly down to Bondo, and from Bondo along the cobbled lane to Promontogno whose gentle mercies are a far cry from the world of granite aiguilles and dying glaciers at the head of the Val Bondasca.

But that, after all, is one of the pleasures of wandering in the Alps.

Walk 24: *Fuorcla Surlej Crossing by Kev Reynolds*

Location: Upper Engadine, south-eastern Switzerland.

How to get there: By train via Chur to St Moritz. Nearest international airport—Zürich. By road through Switzerland to Chur, then over either the Julier or Albula Passes.

Valley bases: St Moritz, Silvaplana, Sils Maria, Pontresina.

Distance: 18 kilometres (11 miles) basic route; via Coaz hut 20 kms; add 5-6 kilometres for return walk, Pontresina to St Moritz.

Height gain: 933 metres.

Height loss: 950 metres.

Time required: 5–6 hours.

Type of walk: Tough, but not over-strenuous as the paths are of mostly good quality. Fine scenery and with several diversions to tempt. Refreshments available at three different sites en route.

Transport options: Cable-car from Surlej to Corvatsch middle station below Fuorcla Surlej.

Map: Landeskarte der Schweiz 1:50,000 series, sheet no 268 *Julier Pass*.

Guidebooks: *Walks in the Engadine—Switzerland* by Kev Reynolds (Cicerone Press). *Footloose in the Swiss Alps* by William Reifsnyder (Sierra Club).

From the Engadine to Val Roseg, with views to Piz Bernina

This crossing of the neat little saddle of Fuorcla Surlej (2755m), slung between the dome of Piz Rosatsch above St Moritz and the ski mountain of Piz Corvatsch, makes a very popular walk and one that is tackled every summer by numerous visitors to the Engadine. And little wonder, for there is much of it to enjoy.

First there are the wooded hillsides of the Engadine that lead to a small tarn with an isolated restaurant on its shore. There is the continuing path that gives fine views of the lakes of Champfer, Silvaplana and Sils, the barren hanging valley that rises to the Fuorcla Surlej itself from whose noted viewpoint, depicted on so many calendars, you gaze directly onto the ice-crusted face of Piz Bernina. There is an ever-interesting descent into Val Roseg and an easy stroll along the gently sloping valley,

Walkers on the path from the Coaz Hut. Piz Roseg rises in a cone of snow and ice as a backdrop. (Kev Reynolds)

24. FUORCLA SURLEJ CROSSING

Map labels: St. Moritz, Pontresina, Val Bernina, Champfer, Hahnensee, P. Rosatsch, Silvaplana, Surlej, P. Surlej, Val Roseg, Sils ~ Baselgia, Munt Arlas, ~Maria, Fuorcla Surlej, Engadine, Piz Corvatsch, Tschierva Hut, P. Morteratsch, N, Maloja, Coaz Hut, Piz Bernina, P. Scerscen, Piz Roseg, P. Gluschaint, 0 1 2 3 4 5 Kms

---

among woods and past lonely alps, to Pontresina.

Weather permitting it is a superb day's outing, but you'll seldom be fortunate enough to have it all to yourself. It's far too well-known for that, and with a cable-car giving easy access to a little below the pass the high point will almost certainly be thronged with trippers. Be that as it may, no-one should allow prospects of sharing the mountains and their paths with others to dissuade them from tackling this walk. Set out early and enjoy the day at a leisurely pace, for there are opportunities to stray.

Fuorcla Surlej has been noted for its view-point for a very long time; long before the cable-car was strung from the little hamlet of Surlej, opposite Silvaplana, it was known as a place from which to capture the splendour of sunrise. There is a berghaus/hotel here (there's been an inn of one sort or another on the pass for a hundred years or more) that caters for those who fancy spending a night in such an exalted location, and it is well worth consider-ing this possibility. To watch night draw onto the mountains and then be lit by the stars (better still time your stay to coincide with a full moon), is an experience to treasure, while sunrise itself, shafting over a profile of misted peaks to stain those nearby, is a gift of full magic; an incomparable vision of loveliness.

St Moritz is where this walk begins, although it could as easily start from Silvaplana or Sils Maria. Sils Maria, up-valley of St Moritz, allows a more steady approach to the pass and uses a terrace path high above the Engadine among shrubs and with long views. Silvaplana's is the shortest approach, but loses out on account of the regular companionship of the Surlej-Corvatsch cableway buzzing overhead, while St Moritz makes an obvious base and gives a very pleasant start with a good path all the way. The town is also easily reached from Pontresina at the end of the day—either by Postbus, train or by continuing footpath.

St Moritz is a two-part resort on the shores of the Lej da San Murezzan (a Romansch name, since this is the 'home' language of the valley). St Moritz Dorf, the main part of the town, rises on natural hillside tiers above the lake and is where some of the fanciest hotels and the up-market shops and boutiques are to be found. This is also home of the Cresta Run and Bob Run in winter. St Moritz Bad, on the other hand, is the spa section of town which lies to the south and west of the lake. Apart from its large hotels and soaring, out-of-place apartment blocks there is also a Youth Hostel, while the resort's simple campsite is situated nearby on the edge of woods. It is here, in St Moritz Bad near the *Heilbad*, that the walk begins with a signpost directing a footpath to Hahnensee and Fuorcla Surlej.

It climbs steadily among larch woods that are beautiful in October when the hillsides are painted with a golden brush, heading south along the lower slopes of the Rosatsch massif, whose several minor summits make handy des-tinations for other walks, and whose southern top, Munt Arlas, overlooks the Fuorcla Surlej. The path makes height without too much effort and in a little over an hour brings you to the tree-and rock-circled tarn of Hahnen-see, a lovely spot on a bright summer's day, with its restaurant tempting with early refresh-ment. As with many other features in the Engadine this tarn bears two names. The map gives its Romansch title, Lej dals Chöds. A few paces beyond it there are glorious views down

A few paces from the little tarn of Hahnensee a grand viewpoint overlooks the lake-filled Upper Engadine. (Kev Reynolds)

to the lakes of the Upper Engadine, and beyond them to the dip of the Maloja Pass where the valley falls into the Bregaglia. Piz de la Margna stands regal and aloof at a vantage point above Maloja where it gazes down the valley, and from some angles it is possible to see the tops of Piz Badile and Cengalo peeping over one of la Margna's shoulders. (These two peaks are seen close-to on the Bondasca walk—Walk 23.)

From the tarn the path climbs on over a minor ridge and soon begins to work its way round to the south-east among screes in order to enter the hanging valley scooped out of the hillside where the massifs of Rosatsch and Corvatsch merge. This is a barren, stony landscape, Corvatsch rising across it with a cluster of spires that assume proportions out of all sense of reality, the cableway catching the sunlight and its middle station standing on the slopes opposite with broad tracks running from it. This hanging valley is a major feature of

winter skiing in the Engadine, but is a somewhat drab place when the snow has gone.

The path climbs without difficulty through the hanging valley and rises at its head to the saddle of Fuorcla Surlej, whose hotel has been in sight for some time.

There is another small tarn here, trapped in this broad, rocky pass to cast reflections. It helps add colour to the magnificent views which scan across the sudden depths of Val Roseg to the nearby clutch of stunning ice-draped peaks topped by Piz Bernina (most easterly of all 4000 metre peaks of the Alps). Piz Scerscen and Piz Roseg are its close neighbours, and together with Bernina send their great hanging glaciers into an amalgamated ice-stream that flows down to Val Roseg. The view also includes Piz Morteratsch and Boval, and looks to the head of the valley where Piz Glüschaint and the Sella peaks display their snowfields and glaciers as a gleaming wonderland. It is a blissful viewpoint indeed.

The descent to Val Roseg is by way of an easy path swinging down the eastern slopes of Munt Arlas, at first bare and rocky but then turning to grass and a few shrubs and low-growing trees, and then passing a lonely alp (Surovel) with a grandstand view overlooking the valley and across to Bernina and its attendant peaks growing ever-higher as the path takes you down. Eventually the trail leads to the bed of the valley beside Hotel Roseg where day trippers come from Pontresina and where welcome refreshments are available. It is then an easy, gentle, down-valley stroll to Pontresina.

There is an alternative descent from just below Fuorcla Surlej, and this leads to the Swiss Alpine Club's Coaz hut, perched above the Roseg Glacier in a dramatic setting. It is not a difficult path, a little longer, perhaps, to reach Pontresina, but worth considering nonetheless. It begins about a hundred metres beyond the pass at a junction of trails. The left-

Lonely alp perched way above the Val Roseg. *(Kev Reynolds)*

hand path is the route that leads via Alp Sur-ovel to Hotel Roseg, the right-hand option goes to the Coaz hut. It crosses slopes of scree, then contours the hillside with a few ups and downs before cutting off to the hut. From its base climbers set out to tackle a variety of routes, including several glacier passes at the head of the valley. It's a great place from which to study the work of glaciers, as well as to capture some astounding views of Bernina and Roseg opposite.

The path down-valley to Hotel Roseg and the main Val Roseg track is obvious enough and a real joy to walk on a bright summer's day. Marmots are often to be heard or seen, while flitting among the few clumps of trees are little alpine finches. To the right, the bed of the valley is a mass of grit, stone and old moraines with milky torrents swirling through. On the far side the Tshierva hut sits on the moraine bank of the Tschierva Glacier beneath Piz Morteratsch and makes yet another diver-

sion worthy of consideration. To take advantage of both the Coaz and Tschierva huts it is advisable to break the walk by spending the night in one of them. Both will repay with a memorable experience, caught as they are on the very edge of the glaciers.

To reach the Tschierva hut go past Hotel Roseg and along the track to the bridge over the river, and then turn right. The path goes all the way to the hut with constant snowy views to the Sella peaks at the valley head.

Over the bridge the main valley track swings left and heads down through the rich and verdant lower reaches of Val Roseg, passing an alp or two, and winding in and out of spacious woodlands. The track is busy at times with horse-drawn carriages and, in winter, horse-drawn sleighs, their light jingling of bells harmonising with the rumble of the stream. No motor vehicles are allowed in the valley, except for the delivery of goods to the hotel.

As an alternative to walking along the broad,

dusty track, a footpath cuts off from it to follow close alongside the river, in woodland nearly all the way, and comes out onto the track again at the mouth of the valley not far from Pontresina station. Trains go from here to St Moritz, while the Postbus may be taken from the village itself. There is also a very pleasant woodland and pasture walk that will take you back to St Moritz round the northern ankles of Piz Rosatsch and by way of Lej Staz in about an hour and a half. By which time you'll have earned a good meal and a comfortable bed.

Walk 25: *Through The Swiss National Park by Kev Reynolds*

Where Nature reigns supreme

Location: Lower Engadine, south-east Switzerland.

How to get there: By train via Chur and Samedan. Trains (and Postbuses) run from Samedan to S-chanf, and from Scuol for the return journey. Nearest international airport—Zürich. By road through Switzerland to Chur, and then over either the Albula or Flüela Passes.

Valley bases: S-chanf, Zernez, Scuol and Scharl.

Distance: 41 kilometres (25 miles).

Time required: 3 days.

Total height gain: 2737 metres (8980ft).

Height loss: 2790 metres (9154ft).

Type of walk: Moderately strenuous over mixed ground. Paths mostly clear but some sections faint on the ground. Route finding could be problematic under adverse weather conditions. Please note restrictions in operation before entering the National Park, and observe the Park's code.

Map: Landeskarte der Schweiz 1:50,000 series, sheet no 259 *Ofenpass*.

Guidebook: *Walks in the Engadine— Switzerland* by Kev Reynolds (Cicerone Press).

Useful address: Swiss National Park Information Office, National Parkhaus, CH 7530 Zernez, Switzerland.

Where Nature reigns supreme

Surprising though it may seem, Switzerland has only one National Park, and that is to be found on the southern flanks of the Lower Engadine in the south-eastern corner of the country.

Were access to magnificent scenery the sole criterion under consideration, a large proportion of Switzerland would qualify for National Park status. But the *Schweizerische Bund Für Naturschutz* (the Swiss Society for the Protection of Nature) has a concept that is probably unique in Europe, so far as National Parks are concerned, that in itself reduces the possibilities of other regions being considered, and at the same time imposes restrictions on expansion of the Park's boundaries. For this is a natural reserve, an Alpine sanctuary protected from human interference where animals, birds and plants can develop freely, unfettered by man's demands. It spreads over a number of mountains and valleys that have largely escaped agricultural, industrial and commercial exploitation, thereby creating an environment of virtually untouched wilderness. Within the Swiss National Park there are no buildings catering for visitors, other than the Blockhaus Cluozza—a rustic mountain inn snug among the larches high above the Ova da Cluozza, three hours walk from Zernez—and an hotel at Il Fuorn on the Ofen Pass road that bisects it; both are run by the National Park authorities.

There are no farms, no villages, no Alpine Club huts, no camp sites. There are no domestic cattle, sheep or goats grazing the meadows, no tractors bumping along broad tracks. No broad tracks at all. In fact there are only a few footpaths, and wanderers should not stray from them. Man's presence is put into perspective; there is no place here for the moulding of nature to his own personal needs or desires.

In the Swiss National Park nature reigns supreme and man has a very low profile, his impact kept firmly in check.

Walking through the Park is a revelation. Crossing remote passes, dropping into—and climbing out of—wild inner glens gives a chance to take stock, not only of the mountain environment, but of life itself, and especially of man's headlong and often myopic race to a total domination of all he surveys.

It's good to sit on a breezy col and sniff the ibex; or to rest on the edge of a natural meadowland to watch marmots at play, unconcerned at your presence—or to spy early on a summer's morning at the deer and chamois grazing dew-damp grass almost near enough to touch.

This is not a vast open zoo, however. There are no restrictions on the animals that live here. The only restrictions are on we humans who can hopefully sense the great privilege of being as we experience this remarkable, unique area.

The walk will take about three days, with en-route accommodation in the Blockhaus Cluozza and at Il Fuorn, and a last night spent on the Park's outskirts in the lovely little hamlet of S-charl. Camping and bivouacking are forbidden within the Park, so make sure of a bed in advance of setting out by making a reservation first. This can be arranged at the National Park House in Zernez, on the edge of the Park beside the Ofen Pass road. A visit in advance of the walk is highly recommended in any case, for there you will gain a good background of information that will be of immense value during the traverse.

S-chanf to Blockhaus Cluozza: 1 day

The mountains that wall the Lower Engadine may not have the raw savagery or the abundant snow and ice that so characterise some other regions of the Alps, but what this corner of Switzerland does have is a soft charm, a warmth and colour all its own. It is a region of tenderness, with dense velvet-textured forests, sunny glades, tempting alps and delightful villages. S-chanf lines the old Engadine road above the left bank of the Inn and gazes across the valley to the modest mountains of the National Park. The village is linked with such places as St Moritz (up-valley) and Zernez (down-valley) by rail and by Postbus, and is the most convenient starting point for this south-north traverse of the Park.

From S-chanf a road crosses the river and leads to the entrance of the Val Trupchun, the most southerly of the valleys of the National Park. There is a car park here and a broad track continues into the valley, which is followed as far as the Varüsch hut (*Chamanna Varüsch* in the Romansch language of the region), set among meadows not far from the Park's entrance. As an alternative to staying in the Engadine proper prior to setting out on this walk, it would be worth spending the night here.

Continue ahead through Val Trupchun and within about fifteen minutes of leaving the hut you will enter the National Park where there is a large board with a list of the Park regulations posted for all to see. To British eyes these regulations may seem at first somewhat restrictive, as indeed they are. But with a moment's consideration they should be accepted for what they are, for what they achieve, and as the walk progresses you will come to appreciate just how remarkable a truly natural landscape is. Without such regulations it is extremely dubious whether such a landscape would be able to survive.

The route continues along the northern bank of the stream, then crosses to the southern side and comes to a junction of paths at Alp Purchér. The right-hand path goes deeper into Val Trupchun to reach the lovely open meadowlands of Alp Trupchun, a good place to watch a variety of animals in their natural surroundings. The path which will lead to Val Cluozza, however, returns to the northern side of the stream to meet another junction of paths at the entrance to Val Müschauns.

The climb to Fuorcla Val Sassa at the head of the valley now begins, and at first the way takes you along the bed of the Ova da Müschauns stream, but then climbs out, heading up-valley among sparse woods and patches of gentians, the trail faint at times but with paint flashes as a guide. High above Piz Quat

tervals assumes contrasting shapes as the way zig-zags to and fro to gain height.

Having crossed a grassy bluff a sterile basin is traversed, then gritty screes cause a spell of discomfort before you finally come out onto the pass of Fuorcla Val Sassa (2857m), a bare and breezy saddle slung between Piz Serra and Piz Quattervals. Quattervals (the peak of the four valleys) is the highest in the National Park at 3154 metres, while Serra, to the south, is right on the frontier between Switzerland and Italy.

There's a broad vista to be had from here that includes the snowpeaks of the Bernina range far off in the south, as well as a splendid overview of the deep shafted valleys of the Park stretching before you. Val Sassa below gives a wild appearance, and the descent takes you down into it, over more scree and patches

of snow. Difficulties with route-finding may be experienced in poor visibility here, but soon cairns are found to guide you down to the confluence of the Val Cluozza and the forest path that leads directly to the dark-timbered inn of Blockhaus Cluozza, with its bedrooms and dormitory accommodation.

Blockhaus Cluozza to S-charl: 2 days

A night spent here will be a memorable experience. It has a natural friendly atmosphere, this old inn, half-hidden from the world among the larches and with views over the valley to meadows where deer and chamois graze. Red squirrels scamper in the branches hanging over the blockhaus, and it is not uncommon to watch through the windows as

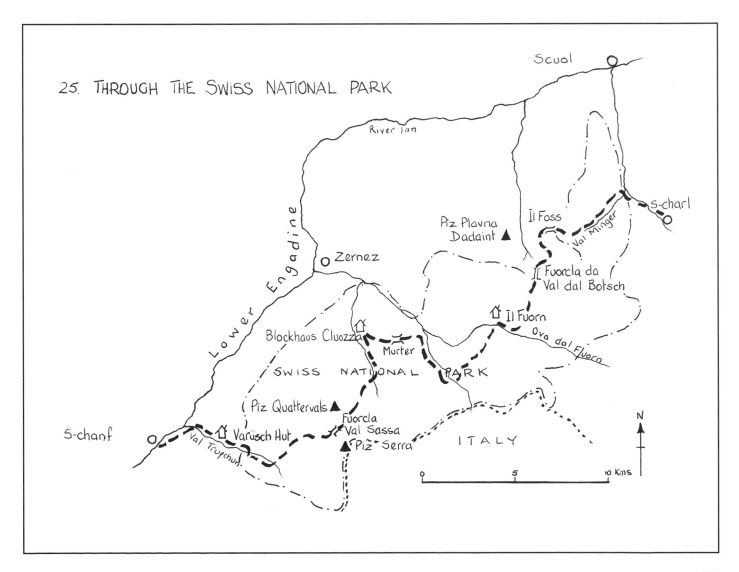

The densely forested Val Cluozza, where nature reigns supreme.
(Kev Reynolds)

red or roe deer wander past on their way down to the river.

On the way to Il Fuorn next morning another pass has to be crossed, but there's not so much height to be gained as on the previous day going over Fuorcla Val Sassa, and it is a much more straightforward ascent and descent to look forward to. At first there is forest shade as the path retraces part of yesterday's route and then breaks away heading east, but this gives way after an hour or so to flower-bright pastures extra fragrant as the bright morning sun dries overnight dew. The path zig-zags in an endless succession of switchbacks to reach the wide grassy saddle of Murter (2545m); a good spot to rest for a while, to enjoy the views and to scan the hillsides and ridges for sight of chamois.

On the eastern side of the saddle the path loses height over more flowery meadows above Val dal Spöl, then lower down enters forests of larch that are especially fine late in the year

when their needles turn to burnished gold. Once in the valley proper you are brought close to the road which cuts right through the Park, linking the Engadine with Val Müstair by way of the easy Ofen Pass. But instead of going to the road here, you bear right at a junction of trails, climb for a short distance, then make a traverse of the hillside: a gentle, pleasant course wandering through bird-lively woods above the river, climbing and falling and skirting mountain spurs until at last the way takes you down to a sturdy bridge, Punt Periv, and takes you across the boisterous river Spöl.

If, having once crossed the river here, you bear right and continue alongside it, a path will take you to Punt dal Gall and the long and narrow Lago di Lavigno in Italy. But our route leaves the river, swings left and climbs the slopes of God la Schera, eventually gaining the road at Il Fuorn where the National Park Hotel has matratzenlager accommodation as well as standard bedrooms.

Despite the proximity of the road the meadows near the hotel are often grazed by herds of red deer in the evening and early morning, which is another good reason for spending a night here and rising with the sun.

A fairly strenuous day's walking concludes the traverse of the National Park. There are two passes to cross (Fuorcla da Val dal Botsch and Il Foss) and some superb remote country to wander through. First you head up-valley on a path along the south side of Ova dal Fuorn, then cross the river to enter Val dal Botsch which slices the mountain wall to the north. Initially the way leads through forest with little height to be gained, but then a stream is followed and as you progress through the rising valley with good views to the pass ahead, there are opportunities for sighting chamois on the open slopes. Shorty before reaching the pass grassy hillsides are traded for rocks, then you come onto the pass itself and feel justifiably inclined to relax there.

S-charl, with Val Sesvenna, makes a fine base from which to explore parts of the Swiss National Park.
(Kev Reynolds)

Fuorcla da Val dal Botsch (2678m) throws open a window onto a new set of valley systems. There are glacial cirques, distant beckoning corries, long shafted glens, dolomitic spires and, far away to the south over a tangle of intermediary ridges, the Bernina snowcaps once more. It's all such fine country, so easy to love and to feel privileged in its presence.

Il Foss, the next pass to tackle, lies a little east of north on the far side of a one-time glacial cirque at the head of Val Plavna which flows down to the Lower Engadine near Tarasp. Val Plavna is outside the Park's limits, in fact the boundary here runs round the head of the cirque, so as you descend from the first pass and climb to the second, so you stray outside it for a while (about an hour and a quarter should be sufficient to cross to Il Foss).

Il Foss (2317m) is a green and pleasant pass with a superb view behind you to the graceful lump of Piz Plavna Dadaint (3166m) with its craggy fingers of rock gesticulating from its

south ridge. Turning your back on this you begin the final descent, leading down now into the charming Val Mingèr (one of the best of the whole walk) with its clear streams, its meadows bright with flowers, its sparse woods of Arolla pine and its scattered rocks gleaming white or patterned with artistic daubs of lichen. Chamois, deer and marmots may be seen as you amble down towards the Val S-charl, but shortly before reaching this main valley, look off to the right to a curious sandstone outcrop dividing Val Mingèr from a minor side valley. The rocks have been fashioned by agents of erosion—frost, wind and water—over thousands of years to make, among others, the face of a witch and a raven's head.

Once down in Val S-charl you leave the environs of the National Park. There is a minor road here leading left, down to the Engadine at Scuol (12 kilometres away and served from here by Postbus), or to the right

a short distance to the quiet summer-only hamlet of S-charl that, in itself, makes a very fine centre for a walking holiday, with various standards of accommodation available.

Comfortable of an evening in S-charl, with the aches of the day's walking settling to that gentle, best-of-all sensations of weariness, with a meal before you served in a pine-panelled room that looks out at mountains dusky in the setting sun, it's good to take stock of the lessons of the past few days and realise that there are times when it is right to give the world of nature a more elevated priority. When man the dominator becomes man the observer. It's a way of redressing the balance; if only for a brief but profound period in time.

Wandering through the Swiss National Park one can learn that lesson, and be thankful.

Walk 26: *Through the Central Rätikon by Cecil Davies*

Location: Vorarlberg, Western Austria.
How to get there: By air or by train to Zürich, and train from there to Bludenz. Buses run from Bludenz south via Brand to the Lünerseebahn.
Distance: 21 kilometres (13 miles) [Prelude 1—6 kms; Prelude 2–8 kms; Ascent of Sulzfluh–6 kms extra].
Time required: 3 days.
Height gain: 2542 metres (8340ft) [Ascent of Sulzfluh—610m extra].
Start: Douglass hut (Lünersee).
Finish: Gargellen.
Valley base: Bludenz.
Type of walk: Unglaciated. No difficulties in good weather. (Prelude 2, ascent of Schesaplana, is more serious).
Maps: Kompass Wanderkarte 1:50,000 sheet 32 *Rätikon-Bludenz Montafon.* Freytag & Berndt Wanderkarte 1:100,000 No 37 1:50,000 No 371.
Guidebooks: *Mountain Walking in Austria* by Cecil Davies (Cicerone Press). *Walking Austria's Alps from Hut to Hut* by Jonathon Hurdle (Cordee). *Alpenvereinsführer: Rätikon* by Flaig (Rudolf Rother, Munich) (In German).

Douglass Hut to Gargellen: 3 days

Marvellous diversity is the hallmark of the Rätikon, a mountain group whose history is as varied as its rocks and plant life. The very name stems from Roman times, though it has not been firmly applied and limited to this group for much more than a century, while Rhaeto-Romanic names like Schesaplana, Zimba and Sarotla, standing cheek-by-jowl with thoroughly German ones such as Schwarzhorn and Drei Schwestern, are an indication of the multiplicity of its earlier inhabitants, who also included Celts and Illyrians. But it was the enthusiasm of a Briton, John Sholto Douglass, that led the newly founded (1869) Vorarlberg Section of the German Alpine Club (DAV) to build on the shores of the Lünersee, over 1940 metres (6365ft) above sea level, the first ever Alpine hut of the DAV in 1872.

The original Douglass hut was swept away by an avalanche in the winter of 1876/7, and its successor was drowned when the level of

the Lünersee was raised by thirty metres as part of a hydro-electric scheme. The third Douglass hut (1979m) stands near the new dam on the natural rock lip of the great water-filled basin, relic of the Ice Age, with stupendous views on the one side of the turquoise lake (the 'jewel of the Rätikon'), in its magnificent setting of high pasture and snow-streaked rock, and on the other of the Brandner Tal far below leading away north, but invisible from here, to Bludenz, *the* Rätikon town with many mountaineering associations: here, for example, on 23 August 1873, the German and Austrian Alpine Clubs united—a union which lasted until 1937.

There is a good public road and a bus service from Bludenz via the mountain village of Brand to the huge car park (1565m) at the valley station of the Lünerseebahn, a cable-car which will lift you and your rucksack in 3½ minutes up the 414 metres to the hut. If this seems too soft an option, or it is after 5.00 pm (no cable-car!) the Böser Tritt path from the Schattenlagant hut (1483m—the penultimate bus stop) will take you up in about 1½ hours. The Böser Tritt ('bad step') is a small and harmless rock step just below the final zig-zags. The hut, in its own splendid situation, is quite cosy when the day-trippers have gone down: the cable-car can transport 450 people per hour!

If time permits, two rewarding one-day preludes to the proposed three-day walk offer themselves.

Prelude 1: Round the Lünersee

The first prelude, the circuit of the Lünersee, is a mere doddle, but useful for orientation and pleasant in itself. Walk east from the hut, impressively across the dam, then uphill keeping right. A gain in height of a mere hundred metres is rewarded by a quite stunning view of the lake, the precipitous Seekopf (2698m) and the hut perched on its narrow ledge between air and water. A little further, if you go up to Point 2155 (on the map) you get a fine view of Zimba (2643m), a bold pinnacle of a mountain whose name may be derived from the 'Red Ring' around its summit block. Keeping right again, carry on round the lake

to the Lünersee Alm where milk can usually be obtained. The continuation around the lake is perfectly straightforward, the whole circuit taking only 1½-2 hours. But before completing this, take the path south from the alm, keep right at a fork and continue up to the Cavell (Gafall) Joch (2238m) on the Austro-Swiss frontier, whence a broad, grassy saddle leads west to the Lünereck with a national frontier stone and comprehensive views of the Central Rätikon from the Schesaplana in the west-north-west, along the tops and steep southern cliffs of the Kirchlispitzen and Drusenfluh, to the Sulzfluh in the east-south-east. Return to the lake and round to the hut.

Prelude 2: The Schesaplana (2965m)

The other prelude is the ascent of the Schesaplana, the most westerly high mountain in Austria and the highest in the Rätikon, a rather more serious piece of mountaineering than the main walk itself. It is a snow mountain, and though not glaciated on this side, is not to be underestimated, especially when iced or misty.

Set off west from the hut for about fifteen minutes, then take a path right, which leads to the Totalpsee (or Zirmenseeli) at 2318 metres—often frozen and hidden under snow even in summer. The Totalp hut is a little above to the left and may easily be by-passed on the way up. The gradually rising route on snow bears right and becomes steeper, the steepest section being a narrow neck of snow below the final summit basin. This basin is traversed high up from right to left, then easy walking to the summit. Return the same way with opportunities for refreshment at the Totalp hut.
Note: The German guidebook expressly warns inexperienced or ill-equipped tourists not to attempt this mountain.

The Walk: Day 1—Douglass Hut to Lindauer Hut

The normal route (red-white-red waymarks) from the Douglass hut to the Lindauer hut starts round the lake in an anti-clockwise direction, avoiding gain and loss of height. At the Lünersee Alm turn south as if to the Cavell

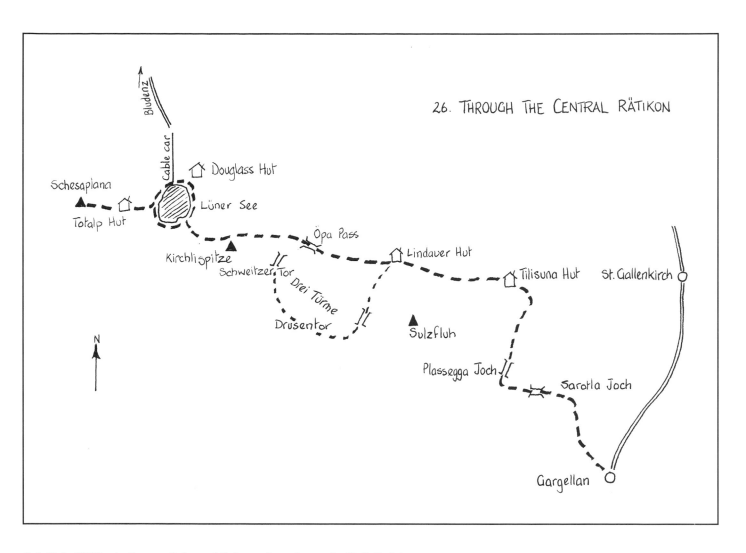

Bludenz

Cable car

Schesaplana

Douglass Hut

Totalp Hut

Lüner See

Kirchlispitze

Öpa Pass

Schweitzer Tor

Lindauer Hut

Drei Türme

Tilisuna Hut

St. Gallenkirch

Drusentor

Sulzfluh

Plassegga Joch

Sarotla Joch

Gargellan

N

Sulzfluh (2818m), Drusenfluh and Schesaplana beyond. (Cecil Davies)

Kirchlispitzen, Drusenfluh and Sulzfluh from Lünereck. *(Cecil Davies)*

(Gafall) Joch, but soon keep left and cross a stream. A little above and to the left is a sturdily built customs house (Zollwacht Haus). Rounding a nose, continue up the little valley keeping the stream on your right and beyond it the steep walls of the seven-peaked Kirchlispitzen. (Here on the high pastures live plenty of marmots.) In probably under two hours from the Douglass hut you reach the first col, the Verajöchl (2330m) for a well-earned pause.

Before you is the mighty Drusenfluh (2828m), the most massive of all the Rätikon mountains and a Mecca for rock-climbers of all standards, seen from here as a vast pyramid towering nearly seven hundred metres above the intervening pass, the Schweizer Tor (2137m), to which you now soon drop down. Immense vertical crags form the Cyclopean posts of this 'Swiss Gate', much favoured by smugglers—witness another customs hut!

It is possible to lengthen by some two hours the route described, by passing through the Schweizer Tor into Switzerland, dropping south-east (not south-west) on to a contouring path which leads across pastures into a great basin of rock-debris, and then up to the

Drusentor (2343m) at the other end of the Drusenfluh—a picturesque and dramatic col, from which a good path leads past yet another customs hut, down over scree to moraines and then to the Lindauer hut.

The standard route, however, the Schweizertorweg, continues east on the Austrian side to another col, the Ofapass (2291m) immediately north of the Drusenfluh summit. Glance back from here to the Verajöchle and beyond it to the Schesaplana group before starting the long descent (almost 550 metres) down the stony Sporentobel, shelterless on a hot afternoon. From here the splendid lines of the Drusenfluh lead the eye up to the right until the fairy-tale 'Three Towers' suddenly come into view, and the green pastures and woodlands below draw you down to the Obere-Spora-Alm, and beyond its well-kept wooden buildings to the deservedly much photographed Lindauer hut (1744m) on the edge of the woods called the Porzelangawald—a lovely friendly hut in an exceptionally beautiful setting, complete with a celebrated Alpine Garden and with the operatically theatrical Drei Türme ('Three Towers') as backdrop.

Two of these towers (not the 'little' one) are accessible to experienced scramblers with a day to spare. Take the path to the Drusentor, but do not attempt to go off to the right too soon—follow the waymarks.

Day 2: to Tilisuna Hut and Sulzfluh

To enjoy fully the pleasures of this day's walk make an early start so as to ascend the Bilkengrat before the sun gets on it. You begin south-east (not on the north-east path down the Gauertal) through the Porzelangawald, losing height gently. At the far side of the woods, close underneath the northern precipices of the Sulzfluh, do not take the left fork, but continue east to where the path divides, near Point 1684 on the map. (To the right is a direct route to the summit of the Sulzfluh, but only for experienced mountaineers with light packs.) Go left and mount interestingly on to the vegetated spine of the Bilkengrat. In doing so you cross a significant tectonic dividing-line from the limestone of the Sulzfluh on to volcanic and metamorphic rocks—granite, gneiss, and crystalline in the lower part of the Bilkengrat. Ascend steeply in tight zig-zags, glad you made an early start, until the path finally bears left off the ridge to the Schwarze Scharte ('Black Col' 2336m) where the geological and scenic interest culminates in the sombre richness of greenish-black serpentine. You can look back from here away past the dominating Drusen-fluh as far as the Schesaplana. Eastward the scenery has a totally new character: immediately below, set in rich green pastures, is the Tilisuna Lake (2103m), while beyond the Ill Valley stretches the whole range of the Fer-wall summits.

An easy descent leads to the Tilisuna hut (2208m), where you book in and leave your heavy baggage so as to enjoy a rucksack-free ascent of the Sulzfluh—at first over grass and then by a cairned route over limestone pavements. It is one of the easiest and most rewarding of all high Alpine walks, with stunning views all the time, especially of the proud Weissplatte (2630m) to the east, and from the summit a grand perspective past the Drusen-fluh to the Schesaplana, and a deep view into Switzerland to the south. The first recorded ascent was made by two priests from Prätigau. They reached the summit and visited the mountain's caves in 1782 and 1783.

The whole trip can be abbreviated by going straight down from the Tilisuna hut to Tschagguns. A chair-lift saves seven hundred metres of descent.

Day 3: to Gargellen

On this final morning follow the Plasseggen-weg over delightful pastures south-east, up to, but not over, the Gruben Pass, not omitting to look back at the hut and its lake. Continue south, still on pastures, climbing steadily up the head of the Gampadelstal to the Plasseggen Joch (2354m) on the Swiss frontier. Notice an old pill-box on the Austrian side of the frontier, but aimed *towards* Austria, presumably to stop refugees from the Nazis—echoes of *The Sound of Music*. Cross into Switzerland and follow a good traverse path south-eastward under the Sarotla Spitze to the Sarotla Joch (2389m). Here you take your leave of Switzerland, cross back into Austria and wander pleasantly down the 900 metres of height past the Röbi Alm to Gargellen.

From Gargellen the Postbus runs to Schruns, 13 kilometres down the valley, and from there trains go to Bludenz.

The Tilisuna Hut *(Cecil Davies)*

Walk 27: *High Above the Virgental by Cecil Davies*

Location: East Tyrol, Austria.
How to get there: From the north, by road through the Felberg-Tauern Tunnel to Matrei, then west to Hinterbichl and Streden. From the south via Lienz—which has rail links with Innsbruck. Buses run from Matrei to Hinterbichl. International airports at Salzburg and Munich.
Distance: 25 kilometres (16 miles) [Visit to Defregger House, 7 kms extra. Variation via Sajat hut: 1.5 kms extra].
Height gain: 2577 metres (8455ft)—basic route.
Time required: 4 days.
Start: Obermauern.
Finish: Hinterbichl.
Valley base: Matrei or Virgen.
Map: Alpenvereinskarte 1:25,000 No 36 *Venedigergruppe.*
Guidebooks: *Mountain Walking in Austria* by Cecil Davies (Cicerone Press). *Walking Austria's Alps from Hut to Hut* by Jonathon Hurdle (Cordee). *Kleiner Führer Glockner—Granatspitz—und Venediger Gruppe* by Hubert Peterka & Willi End (Rudolf Rother). (In German.)

Hut to hut beside the Venediger

The little town of Matrei in the East Tyrol lies at the junction of the Tauerntal and the Virgental. The former, thanks to the Felberg-Tauern Tunnel, now gives access to the area from the north. The latter, a cul-de-sac to the west, remains one of the most unspoiled of inhabited valleys in Austria. Unscarred as yet by bulldozed piste, uncluttered still by the pylons and cables of downhill skiing, and with its crags and peaks formed of rock too friable to interest the modern rock-climber, the Virgental has been unobtrusively 'developed' in the interests of the mountain walker.

A bus runs from Matrei past the villages of Virgen, Obermauern and Prägraten to Hinterbichl, while a car can continue for about two kilometres further to Streden, where there's a paying car park, after which the walker enjoys the beauty of the Umbal Valley with its famous waterfalls, constantly under threat from hydro-electric schemes.

To the south the Virgental is bounded by the Lasörling group, where the Bergersee hut is reflected in the Bergersee, and Lasörling (3098m) rewards a long hard day with a magnificent viewpoint. But it is on its northern boundary that the Virgental comes into its glory, for here lies the massive and magnificent Venediger group. The Grosser Venediger (3674m; 12,053ft) is itself one of the easiest of the highest mountains of the Eastern Alps, while the Venediger-Höhenweg, which involves some climbing of Grade I+ and roped glacier crossing, embraces the eastern and southern flanks of the massif from the St Pöltener hut, windily perched on the ancient Felber Tauern Pass, to the Essener-Rostocker hut at the head of the Maurer Tal.

The walk described here has been called 'the heart of the southern section of the Venediger-Höhenweg'. It avoids glaciers and the difficulties of climbing on unsound rock, while at the same time presenting the walker with the beauties and excitements of this celebrated route high above the Virgental.

Day 1: Obermauern to the Bonn-Matreier Hut

If you have time take a few minutes at Obermauern to look at the church. There is a gigantic St Christopher painted on the exterior and a small relief of the Magi set into the wall. The interior is practically covered with murals, mostly showing the story of Jesus in comic strip style. But if the weather promises to be warm, do not delay too long.

Leave the village almost due north and follow the hut signpost, bearing sharp left quite soon (path 922 on the map) and then very steeply up the meadows of a large spur—the Eselsrücken (the 'Donkey's Back')—always full of the sound of grasshoppers: you will climb 680 metres in about 1.5 kilometres. Here, a few metres off your direct route, is a refreshment house, the Nilljoch hut, where a longer, but less steep, path from Prägraten joins your route. From here you get excellent views of the whole length of the Virgental, east and west, as well as of the steep and wooded slopes of the Lasörling group across the valley.

You now enter the Nilltal, a grassy sun-trap where the path, now less steep, keeps to the left of the stream, the Nill Bach. After about 1.5 kilometres you will notice a little shed, the

valley station of the hut's goods cable-way, now superseded by helicopter deliveries. In the 1960s the hut warden, a shepherd, used to ride up on this at the end of the day, together with any rucksacks left in the shed by walkers. Don't leave your bag there now. The shepherd-warden was succeeded in the job by his son—not a man to risk his neck by riding the goods-box.

Soon the path turns sharp left, climbs steeply and then swings clockwise in a huge arc, rising steadily round the valley head. Before this you will have glimpsed the hut and now, with a final pull up, reach it at 2750 metres. If you feel tired just remember that from Obermauern you have climbed some 1450 metres (4760ft)—well over the height of Ben Nevis.

The hut, built in 1932 and enlarged fairly recently, is run jointly by the Matrei Section of the Austrian Alpine Club (ÖAV) and the Bonn Section of the German Alpine Club (DAV)—a unique arrangement made long before anyone could imagine that Bonn would become a capital city! It stands proudly and theatrically on a fine spur, as on a stage, with neighbouring rock spurs as wings and a backdrop of picturesquely jagged peaks of which the easiest is the Sailkopf (Säulkopf) (3209m), Grade I—though in some years this can involve up to 300 metres of cramponing, even in summer.

Near the hut is a rock-chapel where visiting mountaineer-priests sometimes say Mass.

The path from this hut to the Badener hut includes the worst section of unsound rock on the whole Höhenweg. Do not attempt it unless you have a strong party with rope. A notice near the hut urges you to seek the warden's advice.

Day 2: To the Eissee Hut

An easy day, but rewarding. Leave the hut, to whose setting morning mists often contribute a Wagnerian atmosphere, and retrace yesterday's steps across the head of the Nill Tall to a fork in the path near Point 2624. Take the right-hand, upper, path (No 623), which traverses the desolate Sandboden, to a nick high on the 'Donkey's Back' and so to a further rocky col on very steep grass slopes above the Wun Alm—always with an inspir-

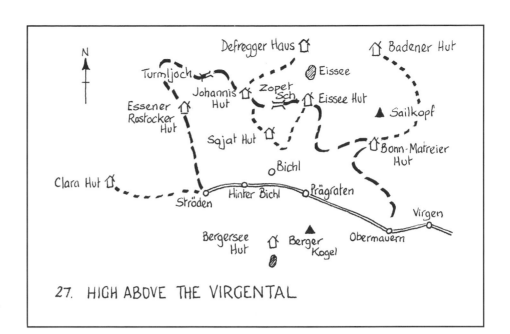

27. HIGH ABOVE THE VIRGENTAL

Rock summits above Bonn-Matreier Hut. (Cecil Davies)

ing mountain panorama to the south across the valley. Do not be deceived by these apparently benign green banks: they are dangerous. Farmers scything them have always worn crampons, and as recently as 1974 Girstmair Anda slipped to his death descending from the half-built Sajat hut when a sudden thunderstorm transformed a summer pasture into a steep and slippery slide. Keep to the path.

Above Prägraten the path swings to the north round the south-west spur of the Wunwand to continue up the eastern side of the Timmel Tal. The character of the walk suddenly changes. Far below, some 600 metres below on the left, the Timmel Bach foams down its deeply cut valley. Before you the valley head rises abruptly in a series of forbidding cliffs above which peeps a glimpse of the glaciated heart of the Venediger group. And there—a mere speck in the centre of the picture—is the Eissee hut. On rougher ground, crossing just below the rocky tips of the huge western spurs of the Hoher Eichhan (3371m) and the Grosser Hexen Kopf (3313m) you walk directly to this privately owned hut, which has, however, all the atmosphere and qualities of an Alpenverein hut as well as an incomparable view down the Timmel Tal towards the Lasörling group.

If you have arrived early you can walk up by the headwaters of the Timmel Bach to the Eissee that gives the hut its name.

Day 3: To the Johannis Hut over the Zopetscharte

Continue west from the hut, soon turning north as if for the Eissee or for the continuation of the *Höhenweg* via the Wallhorntörl and the glacier route (*crevasses*) to the Defregger House, but instead cross the stream at Point 2555 and climb some two hundred metres in zig-zags, followed by a rising traverse southwest. Then follow the waymarks carefully and beware of the loose and friable rock (fixed ropes). Stonefall is also a danger.

The Zopetscharte (2958m; 9705ft) is in more senses than one the high point of this walk, with the pyramidal Zopetspitze to the north, the Tulp Spitze to the south, dramatic views of the Eichham and Hexenkopf on the east and a whole new vista of peaks and glaciers to the west.

The descent is easy: a good path down a stony corrie passes below a big spur and continues in zig-zags, rough and steep in places, to the Johannis hut (2121m)—one of the oldest (1857) purpose-built mountaineering huts on the south of the Eastern Alps, and one which retains its old-world atmosphere. From it you can visit the Defregger House (2962m) the

The Gross Nilalpe and Sailspitze. *(Cecil Davies)*

114

Türmljoch (2790m) *(Cecil Davies)*

highest hut in the Venediger group, and base for the shortest route to the Grosser Venediger's summit.

Alternative Route

Should bad weather or snow conditions preclude you from using the Zopetscharte take the path from the Eissee hut straight down the Timmel Tal to the Wallhorn Alm (2128m), and then take the Prägratener Höhenweg to the Sajat hut (2600m): good overnighting here. Then go over the Sajatscharte at about 2800 metres. It is loose in parts, but on the far side a fine path, blasted out in places and with some fixed ropes, joins the path from the Zopetscharte just before the spur already mentioned.

Day 4: To the Essener-Rostocker Hut

Leave the hut as if for the Defregger House, but after a few metres turn left and cross the Dörfer Bach by a natural bridge over a dramatic gorge. Do not then fork right up the wild

and inhospitable Dörfertal, but continue upwards until you can turn the northern end of a rocky barrier, the Aderkamm. From here you ascend without problems some four hundred metres to the Turmljoch (2790m) whose situation and views are, if anything, finer than those of the slightly higher Zopetscharte. The Türml, or 'Little Tower' is both shapely and massive; glaciers dominate the views to the east and north-east, while in the other direction are ranged the major peaks of the western part of the Venediger massif.

The descent on the Schweriner Weg begins with steep zig-zags. The twin huts are soon perceived far below, but the route has to go round-about into the upper valley of the Maurer Bach, a stony wilderness below the glaciated Maurer Törl (3108m), so that you eventually approach the huts from the north. Their joint effect is undeniably hideous. The original Rostock hut, provided in 1912, is stone-built and in harmony with its surroundings. The grey-clad hut of the Essen Section

joined to it is ugly, urban and unsympathetically utilitarian both outside and in. The original Essen hut in the South Tyrol was lost to Italy in 1919. The next, in the Umbal Tal, built in 1928, was destroyed by an avalanche nine years later. Another, called the Philipp Reuter hut, was built higher up in 1939, but this too was destroyed by avalanche in 1958: a tiny unwardened substitute hut was built in 1978. In 1964 this third Essen hut was started in agreement with the Rostock Section, which was unable to provide funds to enlarge its own hut.

Having refreshed yourself here take the good path that goes down the Maurer Tal past many fine waterfalls. The austerity of the upper Maurer Tal gradually gives way to greenery, and eventually a charming brookside path reaches the Streden car park, from which point a less charming road leads to the bus terminus at Hinterbichl.

WALK 28: *Round The Gosaukamm by Cecil Davies*

Location: Northern Austria (south-east of Salzburg).

How to get there: By road from Salzburg, either through the Salzkammergut to Goisern below the Potschenhöhe, then west to Gosau, or from the west via the Gschütt Pass. Nearest airports—Salzburg and Munich.

Distance: 15 kilometres (9½ miles). [Without use of cable-car: 2 kms extra. Ascent of Gr. Donnerkogel: 2.5 kms extra].

Height gain: 672 metres (2205ft). Without using cable-car 582m extra. [Gr. Donnerkogel—479m extra.]

Start: Vorderer Gosausee dam.

Time required: 4 days.

Type of walk: Moderately energetic on mostly good paths, with opportunities for diversions, including the ascent of the Grosser Donnerkogel (2054m). Superb mountain views.

Valley base: Gosau or Gosauschmied.

Map: Alpenvereinskarte 1:10,000 No 14a *Gosaukamm*.

Guidebooks: *Mountain Walking in Austria* by Cecil Davies (Cicerone Press). *Walking Austria's Alps from Hut to Hut* by Jonathon Hurdle (Cordee). *Salute the Mountains* by Walter Pause (Harrap—1962). *Kleine Führer durch das Dachsteingebirge* by Willi End (Rudolf Rother). (In German.)

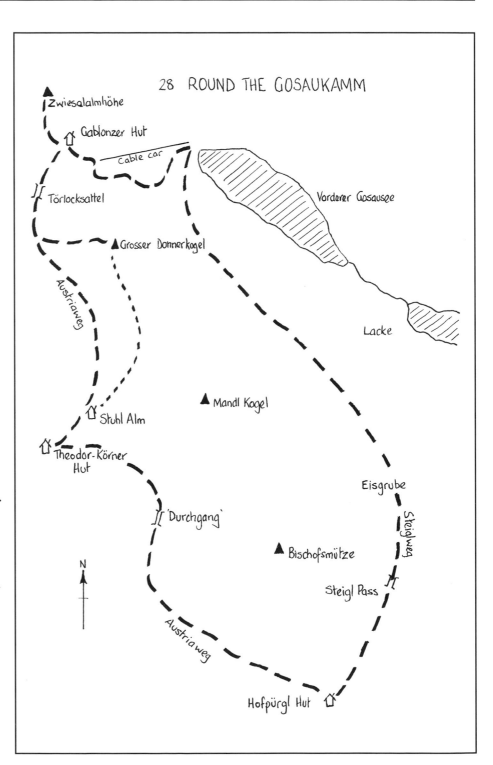

4 Days in the Dachstein Massif

Taken as a whole the Dachstein group is the most splendid, interesting and varied of the northern limestone Alps. Viewed from the south, from the Rossbrand above Radstadt or from the finer vantage-points on the summits of the Schladminger Tauern, it presents itself as an uncompromising wall of rock rising abruptly out of gentle Alpine meadows. Approached from the north, through Austria's lakeland, the Salzkammergut, it hides its magnificence even from the magically beautiful town of Halstatt, cradled, as it were, in the arms of the vast crescent of peaks and glaciers. It was here in the Echerntal in 1845 that the great Austrian writer, Adalbert Stifter, when walking with Friedrich Simony, the principal explorer of the Dachstein massif, conceived his moving story *Bergkristall* in which two children, sent on an errand from one village to the next, lose their way and have to take shelter in an ice-cave under one of the Dachstein's glaciers.

The north-western arm, or horn, of the crescent, unlike the massive bulk of the Hoher Dachstein, consists of towers, pillars, pinnacles and delicately gigantic needles which have earned it the supplementary title, the 'Salzburg Dolomites'. This is the Gosaukamm, six kilometres long, with many summits rising well above 2000 metres. On its north-east side the Gosau Valley runs parallel with it. From the dam at the foot of the Vorderer Gosausee, the starting point of the walk, pause to look up the valley at one of the most celebrated, most painted and most photographed views in the Alps. At the valley head lies the cirque of mountains, including the Hoher Dachstein (2993m) itself, which frames the Great Gosau Glacier; to the right the jagged ridge of the Gosaukamm, all rock above and well wooded below, forms an incredible three-dimensional wing for nature's romantic stage-setting, while the foreground is the blue surface of the lake: the walk round it is pleasant in itself. Our walk, however, will take you round the northern end of the Gosaukamm, southwards along its western flank, round the southern end, over a dramatic pass and northwards along its eastern flank, high above the lake, until you drop down again to the dam.

Day 1: To the Gablonzer Hut

It would not take a full day to walk to the Gablonzer hut, and indeed it can be ignored altogether and the Theodor-Körner hut easily reached in three or four hours by those obsessed with haste. But this walk is one to enjoy at a leisurely pace.

Path 620 leaves the south-western end of the dam at 940 metres, and climbs with many curves and zig-zags to the Gablonzer hut (1522m)—nearly two thousand feet in British reckoning, so the guidebook time of 1½ hours may be rather optimistic for the average walker with a load. Be careful to take the 620, the right-hand path; the left-hand path (612) is the one by which you will eventually return. Alternatively there is an excellent cable-car which will lift you in a few minutes to within three hundred metres of the hut.

Except for November and from mid-May to mid-June, this hut is open all the year round and is doubtless much busier in the skiing season than it is in summer. If the weather is clear and you have time to spare it is worth walking north for about a quarter of an hour to the Zwieselalmhöhe (1585m), a deservedly famous viewpoint.

Gosaukamm Pinnacles from the Steiglweg. (Cecil Davies)

Day 2: To the Theodor-Körner Hut

Take path 611 uphill past the Breiningalm, soon following a rising traverse under the Törleck (radio station) to the Oberer Törlecksattel (1594m), continuing in the same direction (south-west) on a falling traverse to the Unterer Törlecksattel (1575m): about 25 minutes from the hut. Here the path divides, the right-hand fork, 611, the *Austriaweg*, leading directly to the next hut, the left-hand fork (628) to the summit of the Grosser Donnerkogel (Great Thunder Peak—2054m). Unless you have good reason (e.g. bad weather) do not omit this summit: it is the only one in the Gosaukamm without fixed ropes which is accessible to non-climbers.

The path climbs steadily up slopes covered with dwarf pine (*Latschen*) and with some rock steps. If you intend to return the same way, as will be suggested here, it is sensible to dump rucksacks before the steepest sections are reached. There are no difficulties, in fact it is not unlike the easy way down from an English limestone crag, but the limestone mud can be slippery after rain. After crossing a spur the route winds up another latschen-covered slope, the Hengstfeld (Stallion Field—there are no horses here however), gradually bearing left. At 2000 metres a path branches to the right, marked *Only for the experienced* as it involves exposure and fixed ropes. Keeping at about 2000 metres it reaches the Steinriesenkogel (2013m), crosses a rocky spur of the Strichkogel (2035m)—which can be climbed—and descends via the Kleine Weitscharte through the Tiefenkar to the Stuhlalm and Theodor-Körner hut.

Manndlkogel from the top of the 'Durchgang' (Cecil Davies)

But beyond the junction your route continues almost due north to the summit. After the comparatively uneventful ascent it is a breathtaking spot. The lake, over 1100 metres below, seems to lie at your feet under the stupendous cliffs. To the south-east the wildly romantic view of the 'Sea of Peaks' (*Gipfelmeer*—the German guidebook's poetic flight), rugged and deeply fissured, stretches away for four kilometres to the Bischofsmütze (2459m) towering above it all.

Return to the junction with path 611, the *Austriaweg*, at the Unterer Törlecksattel. This gently undulating trail leads below the great limestone buttresses and spurs for about three kilometres, through woods, natural rockgardens and finally across Alpine meadows to the Stuhlalm and, a little beyond it, to the idyllic Theodor-Körner hut nestling among the

trees at 1454 metres by the Schattleitenkopf (1465m). It is a small, *gemütlich* hut, built in 1923, with rustically primitive sanitary arrangements. It is run by the Viennese Academic Section of the Austrian Alpine Club and its atmosphere certainly takes one back to the period when most mountaineers seemed to be drawn from the ranks of academics, clergymen and the like. If it is full, accommodation may be found at the Stuhlalm.

Day 3: The Hofpürgl Hut through the Durchgang

Return about two hundred metres towards the Stuhlalm, then fork right, soon passing a hunting lodge. At the hut the mountain scenery was dominated by the Angerstein, a square-cut wedge of a mountain presiding sternly over the Stuhlalm. Now you are walking directly

towards the north-western aspect of the Bischofsmütze. The *Austriaweg* traverses in a wide arc below the buttresses of the Manndlkogel (2278m) until it swings round more sharply and steeply to the foot of the Durchgang ('through-way'), a steep but easy gully that climbs about 100 metres to a small, yet significant pass through a rock spur.

Here you begin a completely new section of the walk. Having turned away from the south-west face of the Gosaukamm you now face extensive views to the south, where the Rossbrand (1770m) hides the Enns Valley, beyond which the high mountains of the Radstädter and Schladminger Tauern form the skyline about thirty kilometres away. You cross the so-called Krautgarten ('herb garden') and continue almost due south for about a kilometre, to Point 1633 on the map. The

118

route turns east and traverses in a huge S-bend, rising slightly, below the southern outliers of the Bischofsmütze. Soon the Hofpürgl hut comes into view backed by the Torstein (2947m), a vast beast *couchant* hiding the barely higher Hoher Dachstein.

This large and popular hut, easily reached from the car park at the Aualm only about 340 metres lower, is also the base for climbing the Bischofsmütze, whose split twin summits suggest the bishop's mitre that gives it its name. This is not a walker's summit, as even the easiest route demands rock-climbing ability. It is, however, the symbol of the Gosaukamm and pictures of the hut with the mountain behind it are much-used by Austrian travel agencies.

Day 4: The Steiglpass and the Steiglweg

In drama and diversity the last day forms a true climax to this walk. Go due north from the hut up into a wild, bare, stony corrie to a fine rock ledge, safeguarded by a fixed rope, that crosses an enormous slabby rock face, up to the Steiglpass (2015m). (To the east is the Steiglkogel (2205m), three quarters of an hour from the pass: exposed, with fixed ropes.) Admire the Bischofsmütze to the west, then take a last look at the hut and the southern panorama before beginning the descent of the Steiglweg, initially a stony trough between rock walls. Soon you see ahead the prominent Gabelkogel, and you then enter the romantically rugged Eisgrube (the 'Ice Hollow') just below it. Beyond the Eisgrube the path's character changes yet again and traverses lightly wooded slopes below a multitude of towers and pinnacles, and above a lower wall of cliffs which drop into the deep valley where the unromantically-named Lacke ('puddle') varies in size according to the season.

A memorial chapel on the site of a former alm celebrates with beauty and sadness all who have lost their lives climbing here, and especially the first woman to climb the Daumling (literally, the 'Little Thumb'—2322m), who was then killed as she abseiled from it.

You are still over six hundred metres above the Gosausee, whose length, some two kilometres, you have yet to walk as you drop—at first gradually and then more steeply down path 612 to the dam.

Before rushing either to a restaurant or your car, stop once more to drink in the famous view, and this time especially to gaze up at the Grosser Donnerkogel upon which you have stood above that huge precipice on its remote and tiny summit.

The Grosser Donnerkogel, from the dam. *(Cecil Davies)*

WALK 29: *Dolomite Alta Via 1 by Martin Collins*

Location: South Tyrol, Northern Italy.
How to get there: By road over the Brenner Pass. By train via the Brenner Pass; change at Fortezza (Franzenfeste) for the Brunico-Dobbiaco line and alight at either Monguelfo (Welsberg) or Villabassa (Niederdorf). Postbus services operate from the stations to Lago di Braies.
Distance: 120 kilometres (75 miles).
Time required: 7-10 days.
Start: Lago di Braies.
Finish: Belluno.
Type of walk: Exhilarating and varied with superlative views over the spires and turrets of the Dolomites. Considerable exposure will be encountered, so a good head for heights is essential.
Maps: *Geografica Carta Touristica* 1:25,000 sheets 1 and 3.
Guidebook: *Alta Via—High Level Walks in the Dolomites* by Martin Collins (Cicerone Press).

A classic traverse of the Dolomites

Whether you approach the central Dolomites from the north—over the Brenner Pass and along Val Pusteria—or from the torrid Venetian Plain in the south, the eye at first refuses to believe all that dizzy-angled rock. To those of us accustomed to the eroded stumps of British hills which lie on the landscape like slumbering dinosaurs, Dolomite mountain architecture seems to have come straight from the brothers Grimm.

It is hardly surprising that the evolution of steep wall ascents and artificial climbing techniques in Europe is linked inextricably with the Dolomites, yet who would guess this region is also a walker's dream? In fact several high-level trails have become established, switchbacking along ancient mule tracks, military roads and cunningly built footpaths through the heart of the major Dolomite massifs.

Each *Alta Via* (as they are known) carries an overall number. Waymarking often includes locally numbered footpaths, but red and white paint flashes and signs generally leave you in little doubt about which way to go. Alte Vie 1 and 2 represent the finest treks and are justifiably regarded as showpieces. They run north to south, roughly parallel to each other from the South Tyrol to the edge of the Venetian Plain and, although the going may occasionally be strenuous, scenery along the way is Wagnerian in splendour.

At times it is hard to imagine hill walking more unlike that in Britain. Rough progress over stones and scree alternates with boulder fields or dusty tracks. In a few vertiginous places you clip onto anchored metal cables or ladders using a sling and karabiner for protection. Elsewhere, paths zig-zag up to locations high enough for snow to linger well into the summer. On the whole, paths are well maintained, but landslip and snow-filled gullies on north-facing slopes provide unpredictable hazards; here and there, extremely steep scree calls for surefootedness.

Above all, it is the usually settled weather and extravagantly dramatic land forms which distinguish the Dolomites from other mountainous areas of Europe. As you might expect, such attributes draw in climbers too. Many peaks and rock faces remain the preserve of the 'hard men' preoccupied with extreme routes on vertical and overhanging rocks, but walkers with a head for heights may enter the edges of this domain by tackling *via ferrata* routes.

Throughout the Dolomites, sections of metal ladder, rungs and cables are attached to steep rock, linking stretches of easier ground and providing access to mountainsides otherwise only reachable by conventional roped climbing techniques. Some *vie ferrate* are hugely popular—it is not uncommon for queues to form—but they are not for those who suffer from vertigo. Others are serious and exposed enough to deter all but experienced climbers. (For more information see *Via Ferrata—Scrambles in the Dolomites*, published by Cicerone Press.)

Alte Vie were conceived as high mountain treks, so pass few settlements of any size. However, a number of road cols transect your line of travel, and descent to these usually yields a hut (*rifugio*), an hotel or two and the inevitable ice-cream-and-souvenir razzamatazz laid on to separate car-borne tourists from their cash. For shops, banks, doctors and other services it is necessary to leave the walks altogether and detour to the nearest valley town.

As elsewhere in the European Alps, huts are heavily patronised during the summer season (mainly July and August). Italian huts are often well appointed, but book in advance or arrive early; most open from late June to late September. If, like me, you prefer a bit of peace and independence, you'll have to carry a tent and ignore the sniggers of our continental friends who view bulky rucksacks with incredulous amusement! However, backpacking is not all plain sailing, to mix metaphors. Water can be hard to find on the limestone uplands, and by no means all huts allow camping in their vicinity.

Dolomite weather is normally fairer than that in the Alps further west and north, though summer thunderstorms can play havoc with your plans: exposed rock ridges bedecked with ironmongery are not ideal places from which to admire electrical storms. Walking at around 2000-2500 metres (6500-8200 ft) for most of the time, you should really go prepared for every kind of weather, even if it does not materialise. I recall a mid-August trek on one *Alta Via* during which we were sun-blasted and thirsty one day and wrapped up against snow flurries the next. In the far south, damp winds rising from the plain cause more precipitation, but elsewhere humidity tends to stay low and visibility can be superb. September is a favoured month to undertake these walks—snow will have all but disappeared, temperatures have moderated and there is less risk of unsettled spells.

Before setting off for the Dolomites, it is worth attuning legs and lungs to carrying a loaded rucksack uphill: without some preparation walking through a landscape of unyielding verticality will seem like purgatory. Stout footwear is essential to protect your feet from terrain which rarely resorts to the luxury of grass.

Both *Alte Vie* 1 and 2 begin in the South Tyrol, until World War I part of the Austro-Hungarian Empire. Annexed to Italy under the Treaty of Versailles, yet still predominantly German-speaking, it is a region of *lederhosen* and cooked sausage, of feathered hats and apple strudel, where the Austrian way of life prevails. During the Great War, Austrian and Italian Alpine troops were engaged in bloody combat here, leaving behind numerous traces of battle in the mountains: tunnels, trenches, gun positions, even boot soles and barbed wire.

Lago di Braies to the Lagazuoi Hut: 2 days

As an introduction to Dolomite wandering, AV1 cannot be bettered. Popular and well walked, it was the first such route to be inaugurated and remains the best known. Its physical demands are met in easy instalments and it is not quite as long, high or remote as its sister route AV2.

Walking begins at Lago di Braies, a tree-ringed lake of great beauty cradled beneath the vast north face of Croda del Becco. The Italians enjoy their countryside—hence a large hotel, restaurant, souvenir shops and boating on the lake!—but do so in a civilised way. From the lake's far end a forest path leads you up, through a ravine and out above the tree line to marvellous views back over the snow capped Tyrol. A rising traverse over scree, and zig-zags up a rocky valley under the striated cliffs of Monte Muro, bring you to your first col—Porta Sora'l Forn (2388m). First of many superlative viewpoints, it takes in the distant wedge of Monte Pelmo and, shining to the south-west, the glaciated Marmolada, highest summit in the Dolomites.

If it is too early to stop at the Biella hut, visible below, an old military road continues to a sequence of huts between one and four hours away. Already this is wilder country, yet the huts are well used, linked to civilisation as they are by 4-wheel drive vehicles which (at a price) lurch sightseers up dusty hairpins to the limpid waters of Lago di Limo, a popular day-trip destination.

High peaks crowd in. Soon after passing Malga Fanes Grande, a mountain farm, a rough variant leaves south-east up Vallon Bianco to the ridge between Monte Castello and Monte Cavallo, still littered with remains of World War I fortifications. AV1 heads across the rugged eastern flanks of Val di Fanes towards a skyline notch and Forcella del Lago (2486m).

The descent south involves launching yourself into thin air down what passes for a path over precipitous rock and scree—one of those places (mercifully few on AV1 and 2) which are far more hazardous to negotiate than rock climbs with their ritualised protection. The col can be by-passed, however, and the two paths link up at the next tarn.

Lago di Lagazuoi heralds easier going, followed by a stiff pull up to the Lagazuoi hut at 2752 metres, unforgettably poised above the Falzarego road col to which it is joined by cable-car.

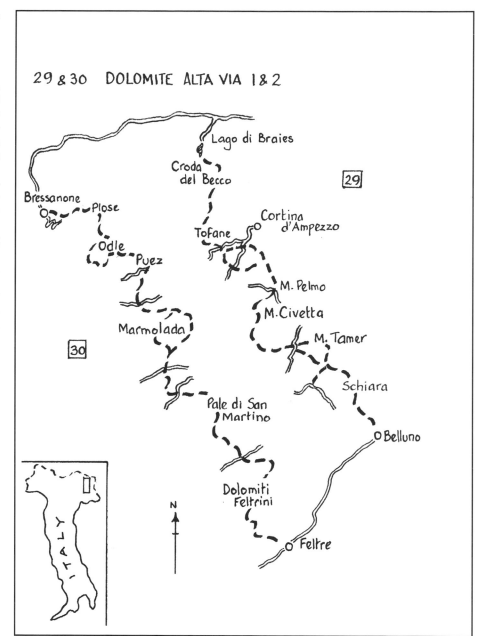

29 & 30 DOLOMITE ALTA VIA 1 & 2

Lagazuoi Hut to Passo Duran: 3-4 days

Labyrinthine wartime passages honeycomb the rock of Piccolo Lagazuoi and are open to the public, but you will need a torch. Farther on lie more relics—not just shell cases and split trenches by the path, but a sensational gallery in the bowels of Monte Castelletto, a spur of the mighty Tofane massif. Zig-zagging up inside the mountain past hewn-out sleeping quarters, ammunition stores, gun positions and latrines, exploration is airy!

Down at the motor road, the fleshpots of Cortina d'Ampezzo beckon, but it is a long way off route to walk. You could bus or hitch and, if time is of no consequence, the town is well worth a visit. Ahead, AV1 rises to grassy alps and the Scoiattoli hut under Cinque Torri's extraordinary cluster of rock towers frequented by climbers.

Walking over bare, inclined rock, you follow a well loved route up to the Nuvolao. At 2575 metres (8448ft), and equipped with a good hut, this peak is one of AV1's premier viewpoints.

Panoramas from the narrow rocky crest are of a very special order in clear air: behind you to the north stand the Tofane, Monte Lagazuoi and the now dwarfed Cinque Torri; to the south, myriad towers and ridges lead the eye irresistably to the imposing bulk of Monte Pelmo.

An abrupt drop aided by cable, a long scree-filled gully and you are down on meadow at Passo Giau, contouring round hillsides as green as the South Downs. Minor cols lead on (a variant loops east via Lago Federà) and within three hours you have reached the Citta di Fiume hut. Between pine trees, Monte Pelmo's beetling north face—1000 metres of rock and scree—stamps an intimidating presence.

Several kilometres of dirt road link Pelmo with Monte Civetta. Another variant strikes off east to the Venezia hut for those desiring a closer acquaintance with Monte Pelmo's massive southern recess, like some gargantuan armchair and known as the Caregón. John Ball, one of few British mountaineers to open up routes in the Dolomites, first climbed Pelmo in 1857.

High car parking at Casere di Pioda (1816m) encourages the world and his wife (with apologies to feminists!) to labour up the steep path to the Coldai hut for a meal, a beer and a peep at Lago Coldai, the only softness in a world of stones and pale rock.

Monte Civetta's legendary west face is unique in the Alps: 7 kilometres ($4\frac{1}{2}$ miles) of overhanging slabs, pinnacles, buttresses and towers hang 1200 metres (4000ft) above the trail. Civetta itself (3220m) was first climbed by the Victorian pioneer, Francis Fox Tuckett, in 1867; two compatriots—Raynor and Phillmore—finally scaling the sheer north wall in 1895.

Undulating along rugged mountain levels and besieged by stupendous scenery, you eventually lose height down flowery Val Civetta and drop through pine forest to the Vazzoler hut. AV1 descends still further to round the head of Valle di Cantoni then rises over scree and rock to steep little Forcella Col dell'Orso. In a wide curve under the Moiazza's impressive south face, you pass (or stay at) the Carestiato hut, separated from verdant Passo Duran by a good track down through forest.

Passo Duran to Belluno: 3 days

This final leg traverses remote country. Being less well supplied with huts and further from roads than the route thus far, it is wise to take stock of the weather, provisions and blisters! The start is easy enough through pine woods

On the trail below the Monte Lagazuoi Hut. *(Martin Collins)*

and over boulder fields, scree and meltwater ravines flanking Monte Tamer, but beyond the Pramperet hut things get less cosy. (Yet another variant swings east from Passo Duran following old hunting and forestry trails on the other side of the Tamer massif.)

From high on the ridge between Cima di Citta and Monte Talvena at around 2500 metres stretches a primitive wasteland of denuded limestone, a desolate moonscape through which most will travel quickly and be glad to descend—temporarily at least—to less hostile surroundings. Zig-zagging tortuously down the best part of 900 metres, you arrive at Pian de Fontana's bivouac hut, converted from old barns.

A sting in the tail, if ever there was one, now confronts you. Not far ahead, a path dives down an attractive wooded valley to La Muda hamlet and buses for Belluno. If you dislike *via ferrata* scrambling, take it. Without rock climbing experience, or an expert companion and possibly a rope, the traverse of Monte Schiara would be alarming to most hill walkers. This

escape route would also be useful at the onset of bad weather.

But what of Monte Schiara? An uncompromising 700 metre slog delivers you, breathless, to an airy perch on Forcella del Marmol. Paint flashes direct you up to the metal Sandro Bocco shelter (a good starting point for climbs to the Schiara's summit along the east ridge), whereafter descent begins in earnest.

The way down is not walking, but 600 metres (1970ft) of ledges, corners, buttresses and exposed traverses equipped with various artificial aid on the Via Ferrata del Marmol. Below the Porton, a huge overhanging cave, easier slopes drop to the 7th Alpini hut set against an amphitheatre of rock walls bearing all manner of climbing and *via ferrata* routes.

All that is left is to walk out beside the tumbling Ardo torrent to the roadhead at Case Bortot and a few hilly kilometres of suburban lanes to Belluno on the River Piave. With its Venetian and Renaissance buildings, its monuments, piazzas and blissfully shady gardens, it is as good a place as any to lick your wounds.

Monte Pelmo (centre) peeps over intervening rocky heights – a view ahead from the summit of the Nuvolao (2575m) (Martin Collins)

WALK 30: *Dolomite Alta Via 2 by Martin Collins*

Location: South Tyrol, Northern Italy.
How to get there: By road over the Brenner Pass. By train via the Brenner Pass to Bressanone.
Distance: 150 kilometres (93 miles).
Time required: 12—15 days.
Type of walk: Airy and exposed, but safeguarded with artificial protection. A long and strenuous route through superb mountain scenery.
Start: Bressanone.
Finish: Feltre.
Maps: Geografica *Carta Touristica* 1:25,000 sheets 5, 6 and 10.
Guidebook: *Alta Via—High Level Walks in the Dolomites* by Martin Collins (Cicerone Press).

An airy walk among spectacular mountains

On the whole AV2 is a rather more rugged proposition than AV1. As well as climbing and dropping more, the trail stays consistently higher, reaching the greatest altitude on either walk at 2932 metres (9616ft). It is also about thirty kilometres longer and its final stage is surprisingly remote. Notwithstanding this, it is an equally magnificent trek—some would say an even better one—passing as it does the Marmolada, highest mountain in the Dolomites.

A feature unique to AV2 is the crossing of three limestone tablelands—rock plateaux high above the valleys and fringed with jagged peaks. Just as on AV1, where exposure or steepness exceed normal safe walking limits, artificial protection is usually provided in the form of cables, rungs, hoops and ladders—not, incidentally, always needed but reassuring in wet, icy or windy conditions and when carrying a heavy pack. Great care is required on very steep slopes just below some cols and in snow-filled gullies which sometimes pose problems. Generally, though, paths are clear and well waymarked.

Apart from a long tape sling and a couple of karabiners for use on aided sections of path, mountain walking gear such as you would take on an expedition over British hills in summer will be perfectly adequate (but include an ice-axe early in the season). One exception on AV2 concerns a mountaineering variant which traverses a small glacier to reach a col on the north-west shoulder of the Marmolada: as well as the necessary skills, you would need ice-axe, crampons and rope, glacier cream and goggles for this particular route option.

Bressanone to Passo Gardena: 3–4 days

It all begins at the elegant and historic town of Bressanone. Once part of the Roman province of Rhoetia, it has for centuries been a cultural and spiritual centre here at the southern edge of the Austrian Tyrol. Though tariffs and currency are Italian, the Germanic tongue predominates.

Eyes will be drawn involuntarily to the white Plose hut (the official start) on the Telegraph summit almost 2000 metres above: indeed, until this green and rounded barrier is surmounted, the spectacular peaks of the Putia and Odle massifs are obscured from view.

You need such incentives, for the climb to the Plose hut is a brutal introduction to the trek by any yardstick—a real baptism of fire—and will take you between five and six hours. Neither the cable-car to Val Croce nor the onward chair-lift operate regularly outside the skiing season, but if you can procure a lift, 21 kilometres of good road followed by a rough but motorable track will get you most of the way up. For purists on foot, surroundings change from cultivated valley side around pretty San Andrea hamlet, through pine forest and out across rugged summit slopes.

Immediately, views ahead are sensational, particularly of Sasso Putia and the Odle massif's rock spires. Ski pistes do nothing to help clarify the way, but you lose height, pass an hotel and follow a delightful wooded path over shallow Passo Rodella into the Puez Geisler Nature Park.

Your first real col—Forcella della Putia—gives a hint of what is to come. Steep and stony, the ascent crosses loose scree and snowy gullies with the shrill cry of marmots echoing from enclosing cliffs. Views from the top are worth pausing to admire.

Contouring past rocky outcrops, you soon reach the Genova hut and begin a rising traverse over steeper hillside, confronted now by the impressive bulk of Punte del Puez. Contented cows graze the alp below and chalets sell dairy produce. A variant drops west, skirting rather than penetrating the Odle massif and giving access by gondola-lift to the town of Santa Cristina, but AV2 presses resolutely on, growing more exposed and entering zigzags up very steep scree to Forcella della Roa.

An hour or so's rough walking ahead, you cross another col, veering left over a fan of shattered mountainside to reach the rock-strewn Alpe del Puez, an undulating natural platform high above Vallunga. The Puez hut lies at the heart of a vast limestone wilderness scattered with snow patches—a primitive and desolately beautiful landscape whose ancient origins in coral seas are betrayed by many fossil remains. Gradients are gentle, but in mist it is easy to become disorientated.

At Passo di Crespeina (2528m), beyond the vivid green waters of Lago di Crespeina, the plateau rim is approached and there are stirring views ahead to the great square buttresses and snowfields of the Sella massif. To reach Passo Gardena—internationally renowned for its skiing—you thread down through a forest of limestone spires (*campaniles*), eroded into jagged pinnacles. The road pass is a busy place, on bus routes if you need them and sporting several hotels and restaurants.

Passo Gardena to Passo di San Pellegrino: 3—4 days

The Sella massif's perpendicular walls seem unlikely to yield to mere walkers, yet an airy zig-zag path mounts scree and old snowdrifts up the Stygian recess of Val Setus. Narrowing and steepening to a rocky scramble, it delivers you to a broad shelf and the Pissadù hut. A very popular *via ferrata*—the Tridentina—scales cliffs farther east, but at peak holiday times becomes dangerously congested.

Once again you are in awe-inspiring surroundings. Flanking Cima Pissadù and continuing through wild Alpine scenery for the next two to three hours—rough going in places—will bring you to the Boè hut at 2873 metres. This is a wonderful situation, but if weather and time permit I would recommend a traverse of Piz Boè, south-east from the hut up a scrambly ridge. The second, higher, summit is

Monte de Soura (left) and the Puez plateau from Passo di Crespeina. (Martin Collins)

crowned by a hut at 3152 metres (10,341ft) and AV2 can be rejoined down the south-west ridge. Panoramas from the Sella plateau, not to mention Piz Boè, are quite unforgettable in clear visibility.

Over intermittent, shallow-angled snowfields, the main route follows poles and cairns above the miniature Grand Canyon of Val Lasties. Although the entire landscape here seems devoid of life, summer sunshine does foster tiny Alpine plants, lichens, insects and some bird species, and as August gives way to September the snow shrinks and warmth is held by acres of bare rock for a few fleeting weeks.

At Forcella Pordoi, AV2 dives down a scree-filled gully and descends to Passo Pordoi. If you need it, a cable-car will whisk you down far quicker from Sass Pordoi (2952m), a shortish climb away to the west. I was glad of this escape route once when thunderclouds amassed with alarming speed and obliterated the tops in violent storms not long after we had reached the road col. Cable-cars, however, equal crowds, so it may be with relief that you turn your back on Passo Pordoi and take to the Vial del Pan, an ancient grain smuggling route.

It is broad and well walked, offering unsurpassed views over the deep Avisio valley to the ice- and snow-clad Marmolada and its neighbour, the Gran Vernel. Without difficulties, the path leads on to the western end of lovely (though artificial) Lago di Fedaia and the Castiglioni hut. Blocked by the Marmolada massif, forward progress is forced east in a wide arc, though a more direct line is open to those able to negotiate Forcella della Marmolada, joining AV2 at the Fuchiade hut.

From the Castiglioni hut you are faced with almost 600 metres of descent (complicated by new road building) to Malga Ciapela. A three-stage cable-car ride to the Punta Rocca hut on the Marmolada, though not cheap, is well worth taking if weather conditions are right.

John Ball, first President of the Alpine Club who pioneered many new routes in the Dolomites, reached Punta Rocca in 1860, but it was the lower of two summits by 31 metres. Four years later, Paul Grohmann from Austria, accompanied by Italian guides, climbed to Punta Penia itself at 3340 metres (10,958ft). During World War I, Austrian and Italian troops engaged in bitter hand-to-hand combat on the mountain, the Austrians even excavating some eight kilometres of galleries within the glacier to escape enemy fire. Deaths were not caused by fighting alone: storm and avalanche took their own terrible toll.

Rough tracks—cross-country ski routes in winter—and bouldery alps eventually take you to Passo di Forca Rossa and round to meadows and a motorable track at the Fuchiade hut in the Cigole valley. Holiday chalets abound and Italian families brave the dirt road from the San Pellegrino pass to picnic and collect wild flowers, the latter an unfortunate habit.

Above Alpe Medagles' dairy herds the rock walls and screes of Punta del Puez are crossed by Alta Via 2 at Forcella della Roa (top right). (Martin Collins)

Passo di San Pellegrino to Passo Cereda: 3–4 days

Ski development and tourism exert a heavy price on the Alpine environment, no more so than at San Pellegrino, but it is soon left behind by walkers on AV2. Ahead stretches a grassy upland littered with granite boulders above Lago di Cavia—the Altipiano degli Zingari. As you drop to Passo di Valles, there are tantalising glimpses of the next major landmark, the Pale di San Martino.

Badly eroded slopes lead up to Forcella di Venegia and a possible variant to the town of San Martino di Castozza should bad weather threaten or you wish to avoid the steep and somewhat hazardous Sentiero delle Farangole. Meanwhile, on these grassy, almost British hillsides, can be found heather and ling as well as the Arctic poppy. Monte Mulaz and Cima di Val Grande, with its little hanging glacier, dominate the near horizon.

From here onwards the going gets tough. The trail negotiates complex, broken ground and minor passes beneath unworldly rock architecture, and in three to four hours reaches the Mulaz hut. The ensuing few hours of walking call for a steady head and secure movement: aid is provided here and there, but the terrain is often loose and steep, culminating in an evil ascent to Passo delle Farangole, at 2932 metres (9619ft) the highest point on AV 1 and 2. My own experiences and recent reports from other walkers confirm that this is perhaps AV2's *mauvais pas*. Beyond, the land drops away to Valle delle Comelle and you are crossing rough scree below soaring precipices. Difficulties relent along the Comelle valley and up to the tableland of the Pale di San Martino and the Pedrotti hut.

If you are hankering after *haute couture*, expensive perfume and other luxuries, or just the reassuring crush of fellow humans after days of mountain wilderness, the Rosetta cable-car and a lower chair-lift will take you down to the smart town of San Martino di Castrozza. Alternatively, you could detour up slanting rock slabs to the summit crucifix on Cima della Rosetta (30 minutes or so) and gaze down on the toytown buildings over 1200 metres vertically below.

Even the Puez plateau encountered earlier in the trek is dwarfed by this rolling expanse of dissected grey limestone edge with peaks, conspicuously Croda della Pala on the western rim. Paths are mere scratchings across a hard crust of snow-patched land, but are well signed.

Steep, stony zig-zags and craggy ledges precede the snowy approaches to Passo del Ball and the Pradidali hut. Huts accessible only on foot invariably possess greater character and this one is a dark womb of varnished timber serving such Italian delicacies as marmalade omelettes, minestrone soup and espresso coffee. Terraces of broken rock up to Passo delle Lede (2640m) are replaced by relentlessly steep ground the other side. In less than an hour you have reached the Carlo Minazio bivouac shelter and are losing altitude through pine woods to the rough road in Val Canali.

Climbing begins again in forest, past the Treviso hut, on above the tree line and up

On the descent from the Puez plateau to Val Gardena. *(Martin Collins)*

bare, bouldery slopes to Forcella d'Oltro, almost a twin col divided by a point of rock in a slender ridge that provides magnificent views east and west. Beneath crags and rock faces and over some awkward gullies, the trail eventually drops to flowery meadows and a good track leading to Passo Cereda, for walkers a disappointingly agricultural road col lacking the usual amenities.

Passo Cereda to Feltre: about 3 days

Some believe this stage was devised simply to terminate AV2 at a sizeable town, though the Feltrini Dolomites through which you pass do contrast with the ranges further north. Logistically, it is a more committing stage, containing just two huts and a bivouac shelter and offering escape from high ground at only three locations. Obviously, discretion is the better part of valour and only those sure of a favourable weather forecast and who are well prepared should set out. Surface water is scarce and will often have to be carried along with

provisions. If in doubt, better to call it a day at Passo Cereda than risk getting into difficulties.

This is wild, lonely country at the Dolomites' southern extremity—more vegetated than you would expect, the result of overall lower altitude and higher rainfall. Leaving Mattiuzzi village, the trail climbs past the scene of a 1972 landslip and over an old smugglers' pass to a comfortable bivouac shelter. Threading beneath mountain walls and past large caves, you arrive at the Bruno Boz hut, for many a sensible place to spend the night.

Monte Zoccare Alto's summit ridge is pierced by World War I tunnels, and AV2 itself follows artificially cut ledges and steps here, and onto rugged Sasso Scarnia (2226m). Busa de Giazz, a massive cave twenty minutes off route and usually choked with snow and ice, once supplied the brewery at Pedavena and the town of Feltre with ice. You are in a protected Nature Reserve, one of three in the Feltrini Dolomites forming, with others further north, the possible nucleus of a future

Dolomites National Park. There is great scientific interest and walkers are asked not to stray off the trail or damage this remarkable environment, untouched so far by human settlement.

Down at the flat and verdant Passo di Pietana, a mule track takes you south to the final significant col on AV2—Passo le Vette Grande (1994m; 6542ft) and for the first time the prospect ahead is a lowland one over the River Piave and the green Pre-Alps beyond. From the Giorgio dal Piaz hut, an old military road twists down through woods to the suburb of Pedavena, whence it is just three kilometres to the centre of Feltre.

The town is unpretentious, very Italian and considerably less tourist-orientated than Belluno, its counterpart on AV1. Despite a chequered history in which the old walled quarter, dominated by its castle, has been destroyed and rebuilt, there is much of interest still to see.

APPENDIX

Useful Addresses:

Austrian National Tourist Office
30 St George Street
London W1R 0AL

French Government Tourist Office
178 Piccadilly
London W1V 0AL

Italian State Tourist Office
1 Princes Street
London W1R 8AY

Swiss National Tourist Office
Swiss Centre
New Coventry Street
London W1V 8EE

Map & Guidebook Suppliers

Edward Stanford Ltd
12-14 Long Acre
London WC2E 9LP

McCarta Ltd
122 Kings Cross Road
London WC1X 9DS

Guidebook Publisher

Cicerone Press
2 Police Square
Milnthorpe
Cumbria LA7 7PY

Contributors

Kev Reynolds has been walking in the Alps for more than twenty-five years. He has lived and worked in both Austria and Switzerland, and led groups of walkers in the mountains there. He is the author of a series of guidebooks to the Swiss Alps, as well as numerous other books, including *Classic Walks in the Pyrenees*, *Classic Walks in Southern England* and *The Mountains of Europe*, all published by The Oxford Illustrated Press.

He is a full-time writer, photographer and lecturer, member of the Alpine Club and a passionate advocate of the outdoors and its protection from man's exploitation. His work frequently appears in a number of magazines, while his lectures on mountain and countryside topics take him all over Britain. Kev Reynolds is married and lives in Kent with his wife and two daughters.

Martin Collins is a full-time writer who has contributed to other books in the Classic Walks series, and is author of *Classic Walks through History*. He has also written a number of walking guides to Alpine areas as well as Britain. *Walking the French Alps: GR5, Chamonix-Mont Blanc*, and *Alta Via: High Level Walks in the Dolomites* have all proved very popular with British mountain walkers. He is married and lives in North Wales.

Cecil Davies first visited Austria in 1964 and has returned almost every year since. He is a member of the Austrian Alpine Club, a former actor, schoolmaster and university teacher and author of *Mountain Walking in Austria*, an authoritative guidebook which covers seventeen different mountain groups. He has also translated from the German, *Via Ferrata: Scrambles in the Dolomites*.

Brian Evans is an illustrator by training, a printer and partner in the well-known Cicerone Press guidebook publishing company and a very experienced Alpine walker, climber and skier. He has written several guidebooks, including two volumes of *Scrambles in the Lake District*. He collaborated with Kev Reynolds on a guide to *The Jura* in which he described some magnificent ski traverses. His latest work covers the Vercors, the region he describes in this book.

Andrew Harper is best known as the author of *The Tour of Mont Blanc* and *Tour of the Oisans: GR54*. He also contributed to Walt Unsworth's *Classic Walks in Europe* and writes occasionally for the outdoor press. An experienced photographer and a Fellow of the Royal Photographic Society, Andrew formerly worked for the BBC.